# Industrial Archaeology

Industrial archaeology is defined as the study of the tangible evidence of social, economic and technological development of the period since industrialisation, generally the last 250 years. Marilyn Palmer and Peter Neaverson argue that industrial archaeology must be firmly placed within the context of mainstream archaeology, and be set within a methodological framework.

*Industrial Archaeology* introduces the origins and development of the discipline in its international context. The first two chapters consider industrial landscapes and buildings as the visible symbols of the processes of production in both space and time. Landscapes are analysed – such as the linear landscapes created by rivers, canals and railways – as well as buildings, in terms of function, typology and context, both topographical and cultural. The authors evaluate the techniques of field survey and documentary research, finally considering the problems and potential of the cultural resource management of the industrial heritage.

The authors argue that conventional archaeological techniques and concepts need to be modified because of the nature of physical evidence and the availability of documentary sources. The analysis of sites and structures needs to extend beyond the functional to the cultural; only then will the complex nature of industrialisation be revealed in a more meaningful way than that derived from documents alone.

**Marilyn Palmer** is Reader in Industrial Archaeology and History at Leicester University. **Peter Neaverson** is Honorary Research Fellow at Leicester University. The authors have for many years jointly edited the *Industrial Archaeology Review* as well as writing many articles and books, including *Industry and the Landscape: 1700–1900* (Routledge).

# Industrial Archaeology

## Principles and practice

Marilyn Palmer and Peter Neaverson

London and New York

First published 1998
by Routledge
11 New Fetter Lane, London EC4P 4EE

Simultaneously published in the USA and Canada
by Routledge
29 West 35th Street, New York, NY 10001

Reprinted 2000

*Routledge is an imprint of the Taylor & Francis Group*

Typeset in Garamond by Keystroke, Jacaranda Lodge, Wolverhampton
Printed and bound in Great Britain by T.J. International Ltd, Padstow, Cornwall

*British Library Cataloguing in Publication Data*
A catalogue record for this book is available from the British Library

*Library of Congress Cataloging in Publication Data*
Palmer, Marilyn.
    Industrial archaeology : principles and practice / Marilyn Palmer
and Peter Neaverson.
        p.    cm.
    Includes bibliographical references and index.
    1. Industrial archaeology.  I. Neaverson, Peter.  II. Title.
    T37.P35    1998
    609—dc21                                          97–25430
                                                        CIP

ISBN 0–415–16626–8 (hbk)
ISBN 0–415–16769–8 (pbk)

# Contents

# Plates

# Figures

# Preface

Despite its existence as a discipline since the 1960s, industrial archaeology continues to have a bad press among professional archaeologists. Many still regard it as the province of the enthusiastic volunteer anxious to preserve locally important steam pumping engines, railways or canals, and having no place in the serious study of archaeology. But the last decade has seen an increasing recognition of the international significance of the survivals of Britain's industrial past, and major research programmes have been undertaken by the national bodies concerned with the recording and conservation of both the archaeological and the built heritage. Similar programmes are taking place elsewhere in the world, often under the aegis of historical archaeologists with whom industrial archaeologists have much in common.

There is, consequently, a need for people with some understanding of industrial archaeology in the professional field, but few university courses in archaeology yet include its study in any major way. This is partly because archaeology is largely concerned with elucidating developments in human society from physical evidence, whereas industrial archaeologists have in the past generally contented themselves with a functional analysis of sites and structures, failing to put them in any wider topographical, social or cultural context. Given the availability of documentary evidence, they have felt that the social background is the province of the economic historian, not the industrial archaeologist. Yet the majority of sites in the industrial period provide structural evidence for the social upheaval and redefinition of the class system which accompanied the process of industrialisation, and the cultural context is as important as functional analysis in the understanding of any industrial site or landscape.

This book sets out to place industrial archaeology within the mainstream of archaeology and to set the discipline within a methodological framework. It is also a practical book, discussing the ways in which conventional archaeological techniques need to be modified because of the nature of the physical evidence and the availability of documentary, oral and pictorial sources. Attention is also paid to the theory and practice of the cultural resource management of the buildings, landscapes and artefacts resulting from past industrialisation, since conservation has always played a major role in industrial archaeology. Above all, it seeks to encourage those involved in industrial archaeology to remember that the industrial monument is but one part of a network of linkages relating to the methods and means of past production, and that its location, form and development are the result of individual human decisions. It is the task of the industrial archaeologist to use all the sources available to him or her in elucidating these past linkages and decisions.

# Acknowledgements

The authors' understanding of industrial archaeology has been greatly enhanced through their positions since 1984 as editors of *Industrial Archaeology Review*, on behalf of the Association for Industrial Archaeology, which has brought them into contact with contributors from all parts of Britain and beyond. They have also benefited from discussions and fieldwork undertaken with their students, both from further education and from undergraduate and postgraduate courses. Their research has been greatly assisted through the services of Leicester University Library, the Library of the Ironbridge Gorge Museum Trust and many local archive repositories. They are grateful to many friends who have commented on parts of the text, including Garry Campion, Dr Neil Christie, Steve Dobson, Keith Falconer, Richard Storey and Dr Kathryn Thompson. Help with illustrations has been received from Victoria Beauchamp, Garry Campion, David Cranstone, Philip Craxford, David Crossley, R. S. Fitzgerald, Mark Fletcher, Andrew Lowe, Gary Marshall, Philip Newman, John Powell, Shelley Richards and Matthew Watson, and from Cornwall Archaeological Unit, the Royal Institution of Cornwall, the Historic American Engineering Record, the National Library of Wales and the Royal Commission on the Historical Monuments of England. Particular thanks are due to Deborah Miles of the School of Archaeological Studies, University of Leicester, for transforming rough sketches into the presentable figures with which this book is illustrated. The authors are grateful that the University of Leicester is one in which industrial archaeology is recognised as an academic study and taught at both undergraduate and postgraduate level. They acknowledge financial assistance from the university for attendance at conferences and research visits overseas, together with a period of sabbatical leave to complete this book.

# Abbreviations

| | |
|---|---|
| AIA | Association for Industrial Archaeology |
| CAD | Computer-Aided Design |
| CBA | Council for British Archaeology |
| DNH | Department of National Heritage |
| DOE | Department of the Environment |
| EDM | Electronic Distance Measurement |
| HABS | Historic American Buildings Survey |
| HAER | Historic American Engineering Record |
| HMSO | Her Majesty's Stationery Office |
| *IAR* | *Industrial Archaeology Review* |
| *IG* | *Inventaire Générale des monuments et des richesses de la France* |
| IRIS | Index Record for Industrial Sites |
| MPP | Monuments Protection Programme |
| NMR | National Monuments Records |
| NRIM | National Record of Industrial Monuments |
| OS | Ordnance Survey |
| PIE | Projectbureau Industrieel Erfgoed |
| *P-MA* | *Post-Medieval Archaeology* |
| PRO | Public Record Office |
| PUF | Presses Universitaires de la France |
| RCAHMS | Royal Commission on the Ancient and Historical Monuments of Scotland |
| RCAHMW | Royal Commission on the Ancient and Historical Monuments of Wales |
| RCHM | Royal Commission on Historical Manuscripts |
| RCHME | Royal Commission on the Historical Monuments of England |
| SAS | School of Archaeological Studies, Leicester University |
| SMR | Sites and Monuments Records |
| SPAB | Society for the Protection of Ancient Buildings |
| TICCIH | The International Committee for the Conservation of the Industrial Heritage |
| UNESCO | United Nations Educational, Scientific and Cultural Organization |
| WEA | Workers' Educational Association |

*Chapter One*

# The scope of industrial archaeology

The serious study of industrial archaeology is a phenomenon of the second half of the twentieth century, but even in that comparatively short period it has come to mean different things to different groups of people. Practitioners from backgrounds as diverse as public and private museums, railway preservation societies or canal restoration groups, and academics from a variety of disciplines as well as professional archaeologists and architects concerned with the recording of historic buildings would all class themselves as 'industrial archaeologists'. Such a diversity of interests has resulted in a continuing debate concerning the scope of the subject but the general consensus now favours a definition of industrial archaeology as the systematic study of structures and artefacts as a means of enlarging our understanding of the industrial past. On the basis of this definition, the subject is now achieving a respectable professional standing not only in Britain but throughout the world. It has not yet, however, achieved a comparable academic standing, the result being that many of its practitioners have received no formal training in the specialist techniques required. The purpose of this book is to discuss these techniques in their wider archaeological context so that industrial archaeology can take its place in normal undergraduate courses to satisfy the demand for trained personnel to enter this new and exciting field.

## THE ORIGINS OF INDUSTRIAL ARCHAEOLOGY

There have been various attempts to demonstrate that the term 'industrial archaeology' has its origins in the late nineteenth century, but it did not pass into popular usage until the mid-1950s in Britain. It arose out of a concern to record and even preserve some of the monuments of the British industrial revolution at a time of wholesale urban redevelopment. Its earliest champion was Michael Rix, whose work with Workers' Educational Association (WEA) classes at the University of Birmingham highlighted the rapid transformation of the major iron and steel district of the Black Country. In an article entitled 'Industrial archaeology' in *The Amateur Historian*, he wrote:

> Great Britain as the birthplace of the Industrial Revolution is full of monuments left by this remarkable series of events. Any other country would have set up machinery for the scheduling and preservation of these memorials that symbolise the movement which is changing the face of the globe, but we are so oblivious of our national heritage that apart from a few museum pieces, the majority of these landmarks are neglected or unwittingly destroyed.
>
> (Rix 1955: 225)

Unlike previous industrial historians, Rix placed the emphasis firmly upon what could be learnt from the physical remains of industrialisation. His use of the term 'archaeology' inspired the Council for British Archaeology (CBA) in 1959 to set up a Research Committee on Industrial Archaeology and to call a public meeting, at which it was resolved that recommendations be made to national government urging the formation of a national policy for the recording and protection of early industrial remains. Before any formal action was taken, a significant monument from the earliest days of locomotive railways, the Euston arch, designed by Philip Hardwick as a triumphal entrance for the London terminus of the railway to Birmingham, was demolished. This caused a public outcry, and in 1963 the Industrial Monuments Survey was established jointly by the CBA and the Ministry of Public Buildings and Works. Rex Wailes became the first Survey Officer and a basic index record was begun, known as the National Record of Industrial Monuments (NRIM). From 1965 this passed under the direction of R. A. Buchanan in the Centre for the Study of the History of Technology at what was later to become Bath University. The data collected was not, however, transferred to the county Sites and Monuments Records, which were themselves in their infancy, and this transfer is only now beginning to take place in the 1990s.

The Royal Commission on the Historical Monuments of England (RCHME) had included some industrial buildings such as malthouses and watermills in its county inventories, but was then working to a cut-off date of 1700. In Scotland, on the other hand, nineteenth-century industrial buildings had been included in the county inventories prepared in the 1950s by the Royal Commission on the Ancient and Historical Monuments of Scotland (RCAHMS) at the instigation of the then secretary to the commission, Angus Graham. This emphasis on compiling lists of industrial sites was also reflected in the earlier publications on industrial archaeology, many of which took the form of regional gazetteers, but little attempt was made to prioritise these sites on a national basis. From the late 1960s, however, a number of industrial monuments were added to the schedules, largely as a result of recommendations from the CBA's Advisory Panel which considered lists of sites prepared by the Survey Officer and others on either a thematic or a regional basis. The scope of the thematic surveys depended on the interests of the volunteers prepared to undertake them, and included lighthouses, water-raising by animal power and existing steam plant in water supply, sewage and drainage pumping stations. While creating a valuable record, the scope of these thematic surveys was obviously highly selective and did not enable the majority of sites to be placed in their context. The Industrial Monuments Survey, then the responsibility of Keith Falconer, followed the NRIM to the University of Bath in 1977 and both were transferred to RCHME in 1981. From a national point of view, then, the CBA was the first archaeological organisation to espouse this new aspect of archaeology but did not altogether maintain its interest, whereas the Royal Commissions were slightly later in the field but have been responsible for maintaining and developing the records created in those early years.

The Newcomen Society, which was formed in 1920 to pursue the study of the history of engineering and technology, encouraged the new discipline to the extent of supporting the *Journal of Industrial Archaeology*, first published in 1964. A series of annual conferences, mainly at the University of Bath, resulted in 1973 in the foundation of the Association for Industrial Archaeology (AIA) with L. T. C. Rolt as its first president. The aims of this organisation were to encourage improved standards of recording, research, conservation and publication as well as to assist and support regional and specialist survey and research groups and bodies involved in the preservation of industrial monuments. The AIA in 1976 launched *Industrial Archaeology Review*, first published by Oxford University Press but becoming the AIA's house journal in 1984 and now the only surviving national journal in the discipline. The aims of the AIA reflect the dichotomy within industrial archaeology between research and preservation, which has perhaps hindered its acceptance as an academic discipline. Recently, however, the Association has played a much greater role in influencing national trends in industrial archaeology, notably through its publication of a policy document entitled 'Industrial archaeology: working for the future' (Palmer 1991) which stated the objectives of industrial archaeology in the 1990s and offered recommendations for their implementation.

At the local level, the cause of industrial archaeology was taken up by a variety of people who all brought their own particular skills and expertise to bear on the subject. It flourished in university adult education and WEA courses, while numerous preservation groups were established to maintain monuments, particularly those containing prime movers such as waterwheels and steam engines. The cultural resource management of industrial sites in Great Britain will be discussed in Chapter Seven, although some mention is made of the international dimension of the conservation movement in this chapter. The landscape, however, is not a static environment; it is constantly evolving and to conserve more than a selection of the physical evidence of the industrial past is neither possible nor desirable. Preservation is only part of industrial archaeology, and its main thrust should be towards the recording of artefacts and structures and illuminating the context of people at work in the past. This balance has not always been achieved, but the over-emphasis on monuments is now disappearing and industrial archaeology can now take its place as a fully fledged branch of archaeological studies if it will at the same time accept the need for a research agenda with a theoretical content.

## INDUSTRIAL ARCHAEOLOGY AND ARCHAEOLOGICAL THEORY

Industrial archaeology became an accepted area of study in the 1960s at the same time as archaeology itself was adopting a more theoretical stance. Yet, as E. G. Grant has said:

> Industrial archaeology has neglected almost all theory in some kind of mistaken belief that it could approach the material remains of industrial society with no particular methodological or explanatory framework.
>
> (Grant 1987: 118)

It is undoubtedly true that much of the work carried out in industrial archaeology has been of a descriptive rather than an analytical nature, concentrating on the physical remains of past industries as entities in themselves rather than as expressions of human endeavour. Or, as Matthew Johnson has put it: 'most work in this area has concentrated on the archaeological elucidation of the development of the technologies involved rather than the social and cultural parameters' (Johnson 1996: 12). This is partly because much of the work undertaken in industrial archaeology, as in post-medieval archaeology, has been small-scale site work which has not been susceptible to the generalisations beloved of processual archaeologists. Explanations have often been limited to site-specific ones framed in an historical mode, in the belief that if all the details leading up to the establishment of a site or structure are known, this is in itself sufficient explanation. Industrial archaeology has hitherto lacked a broader research agenda and has rarely tried to contribute to wider historical debates, e.g. on the origins and effects of industrialisation.

If the 'new archaeology' did nothing else, it taught archaeologists to approach both fieldwork and the analysis of data with a series of often complex questions in mind. But the data of industrial archaeology is generally limited to the physical remains of sites and structures plus map, documentary and photographic evidence; what is nearly always lacking is normal artefactual material for analysis. There are large numbers of industrial museums which all display artefacts, often in their social context, but no real attempt has been made to build up reference collections of pottery, glass, metal artefacts, slags, etc. Few British archaeologists working on sites of the industrial period have treated artefacts in the same way as, for example, historical archaeologists in America or Australia (Deetz 1977; Glassie 1975). The stratigraphy of artefacts on industrial sites has rarely been noted, and the assemblages have been discarded rather than preserved. If we accept that material culture is meaningfully constituted, we therefore lack the raw data from which to extract those meanings. Even the documentary sources so successfully used by Lorna Weatherill to determine consumer behaviour in early modern Britain (Weatherill 1988) are more fragmentary for the industrial period, which makes it even more important to take note of artefacts. An example of how consumer attitudes can be inferred even from contemporary articles of material culture is the comparative work carried out by Shanks and Tilley on the design of contemporary beer cans in Britain and Sweden, which can be shown to indicate the differing attitudes of the two countries towards the consumption of alcohol (Shanks and Tilley 1987). Despite the problems of retaining the often vast assemblages derived from sites of the recent past, some attempt should be made both to build up reference collections of basic types of artefacts and to use the data as evidence of the material culture of the period.

Industrial archaeologists at present, therefore, concentrate on the interpretation of sites, structures and landscapes rather than artefactual material. This does not, of course, mean that they are excused from working within a theoretical framework but that the data used is rather different from that of the prehistoric archaeologist. The various approaches used by archaeologists are intended to provide a means of extracting the maximum information from material remains by making observations within a framework of inference. Yet industrial archaeologists have usually contented themselves with a functional analysis of sites and structures, or by giving them an economic or technological context. The necessity of locating the earliest example of a particular process, or the most complete surviving site for the purposes of listing and scheduling, as discussed earlier, has inevitably led to an approach which concentrates on the positive aspects of human progress and therefore has much in common with the processual school of the new archaeology. Yet the majority of sites in the industrial period provide structural evidence for the social upheaval and redefinition of the class system which accompanied the process of industrialisation. A Marxist approach would be more appropriate in many cases, since the period under study certainly witnessed contradictions between the forces and the relations of production, i.e. between capitalist organisation utilising new technology and the social organisation of the workforce who were forced to adapt to a new working and often also a new domestic environment. Looked at in this way, the introduction of a new steam engine to a previously water-powered mill, a common phenomenon in the nineteenth century which can be identified both from physical and documentary evidence, probably involved the workforce both in learning new skills and also in more rigorous shiftwork, since the owner would wish to recoup his capital expenditure by keeping the engine working on a continuous basis. The resolution of this conflict between the new technology and the social organisation of the workforce which operated it would be, in Marxist terms, an example of the way in which society advanced.

Of course, not all sites of the industrial period lend themselves to this kind of approach. Many mundane structures, such as lime-kilns or buddles, seem far removed from conflicts within human society. They have usually been examined typologically to assess technological development (Palmer and Neaverson 1989; Stanier 1993), yet any industrial structure is not an isolated monument but part of a network of linkages relating to the methods and means of production. In these instances, Ian Hodder's use of 'contextual archaeology' is relevant, 'the full and detailed description of the total context as the whole network of associations is followed through' (Hodder 1986: 143). These associations include not only the economic ones of sources of raw materials, methods of processing and transport networks which industrial archaeologists do normally consider, but also the social context of production. Industrial archaeologists have the advantage of documentary as well as material evidence, and should not be afraid to use it to help explain the sites and structures with which they are dealing. The social context of production has frequently figured in the display material accompanying museum or conservation projects, but has less often formed part of the agenda for recording industrial sites. It is, however, a vital element in understanding the relationship between the different components of complex sites and also their social symbolism.

From the point of view of the entrepreneur, his industrial empire could be used as a vehicle for the expression of personal prestige. The mill-owner adopted new fashions in architecture, from the Palladianism of the late eighteenth century to the Gothic and Italianate traditions of the late nineteenth. Boulton and Watt in 1765 employed Benjamin Wyatt to design their manufactory at Soho, Birmingham, which for a time became the largest of its kind in Europe. The Palladian façade disguises the more mundane reality of the forges, rolling mills and other aspects of the production carried out by this international firm. The Italianate style became popular for textile mills in the north of England, where several magnificent mill chimneys were modelled on Italian campaniles. A supreme example is Manningham Mill in Bradford (Plate 1), designed by local architects for Messrs Lister, manufacturers of velvet and other fancy cloths. The six-storey mill, with its campanile chimney 249 feet [75.9 metres] high, dominated the Bradford skyline, and enabled its owners to maintain their position in relation to other local entrepreneurs such as Sir Titus Salt, whose model community and huge mill had been built twenty years before. Similar fashions were also often adopted in the homes of the mill-owners: the wealthy cotton-spinning family, the Fieldens of Todmorden, had the vast pile of Dobroyd Castle constructed for themselves in the 1860s as well as providing their town with a town hall, the scale of which was designed to reflect their own prestige rather than to be in keeping with the rest of its buildings. These symbols of power are as important to the understanding of the dynamics of nineteenth-century society as the personal possessions of the elite are to that of Bronze Age Wessex.

**Plate 1**  The dominant Italianate chimney stack of Manningham Mill, built 1871–3 on a hilltop site, which helped to establish Lister's as a landmark in Bradford, West Yorkshire.

Many industrial sites developed over time as sources of power and methods of technology changed, and have primarily been analysed in these functional terms. But these sites can also indicate the changing social dimensions of production, the landscape of weavers' cottages with isolated fulling mills representing a different type of organisation from that of Sir Titus Salt's model community of Saltaire (Plate 2). The spatial layout of the purpose-built industrial complex, which was typical of much industrial society from the late eighteenth century onwards, shows how time was regulated in the interest of the maximisation of profit. Continuous production, whether powered by the waterwheel or

*Plate 2* Workers' housing in William Henry Street, Saltaire, West Yorkshire, built 1854. The varied façades mirror the social hierarchy within the mill. The tall end blocks were intended for boarding houses, while the elaborate stone lintels and front gardens of the terraced houses reflect the status of the overlookers who occupied them. The cupola of Sir Titus Salt's elaborate Congregational church can be seen in the distance.
RCHME, © Crown Copyright.

steam engine, necessitated a degree of social control by the entrepreneur over his workforce. This can be observed by the industrial archaeologist in the organisation of space both for the actual processes of production and in the provision of living accommodation. In the iron industry, for example, the furnace was often in blast for campaigns of over a year and demanded continuous attention. The ironworks were arranged to enable easy movement of raw materials to the furnace and to allow for shifts of men continually on site, occasionally living in cottages contrived under the charging bridge of the furnace itself. In the new cotton industry of the late eighteenth century, the entrepreneurs appreciated the value of social control from the very beginning. Menuge (1993) has shown how the entrance to Arkwright's first cotton mill in Cromford, erected in 1771, was only from within the mill yard: the site was provided with a high perimeter wall, and no ground-floor windows overlook the mill road. Documentary evidence indicates that Arkwright was very concerned over the secrecy in which his newly patented machines operated, but the layout of the mill yard also enabled close supervision of the workforce: this was perhaps symbolised by the dominant position of his new home, Willesley Castle, in relation to his works. This is equally true of the earlier Derby silk mill, for which the layout of the great circular throwing machines and the power transmission have recently been reconstructed by Calladine (1993) (Figure 1). This stood on an island in the River Derwent, closed off from prying eyes by elegant wrought-iron gates. Access into these mills by the work-force was therefore more closely supervised than had ever been possible in the proto-industrial 'putting-out' system of organisation which had preceded them.

Inside the buildings, the workforce operated in a controlled space, made necessary by the ratio between the narrow width of the building to admit maximum light and its length which was determined by horizontal systems of power transmission. They no longer had the power to dictate their own working conditions, and the spatial layout of each floor of the mill made supervision very easy. The overlooker could ensure that no one wasted the time paid for by their employer, the mill-owner. Using the technique of access analysis, Markus (1993) has attempted to delineate the relationship between social and spatial structures in a number of early textile mills but all too quickly reverts to straight historical analysis. More will be said on the use of this technique in Chapter Three. However, looked at in this way, these early flagship mills become less monuments to technological development than controlled spaces in which a wholly new system of social relations had to be worked out.

*Figure 1* A reconstruction drawing of Lombe's pioneering silk mill at Derby as it may have appeared in 1721. The workforce operated in a space dictated by the circular and transverse silk-throwing and -twisting machines, which were themselves dependent on the power of the great waterwheel. RCHME, © Crown Copyright.

Arkwright had advertised for 'weavers with large families' to come and work in Cromford, and the village symbolises a new era in gender relations: female and child labour in the mills, with the houses he built for his workforce containing workshops for the men. The close proximity of the housing to the mills, as in other model communities such as Belper, New Lanark and Styal, may suggest benevolence on the part of the mill-owner but in spatial terms it symbolises the discipline of the factory, needing a contiguous workforce who were available to meet the demands of a continuous power source. This spatial relationship could, however, be more widespread. The stocking knitter or handloom weaver, working in his garret, or the nail-maker in his back-yard workshop, was subject to the discipline imposed by an entrepreneur even though direct supervision was not possible and the worker retained the illusory independence of working at home. The linkages between the provider of raw material, whether factory-spun yarn or mill-produced bar iron, and the producer of the finished goods need exploration if it is to be understood how the nineteenth-century outworker was usually equally part of a capitalist form of production (Palmer 1994a).

What this suggests is that an important theoretical stance for the industrial archaeologist is one that acknowledges the role of the individual in the creation of material culture – that objects or structures are the result of deliberate choice rather than environmental determinism. Of course, environmental factors like the presence of raw materials, the existence of a good water-power site and the immediate topography all influence the location of a particular structure, but human agency is ultimately responsible both for its existence and for its form. Typological study of a series of structures may enable generalisations to be made about their development and may also help to establish the position of a particular object in a chronological sequence, but the role of the individual cannot be omitted from the equation. As Ian Hodder has argued (1982, 1986), material culture is not a passive reflection of society but an active constituent of it. It can be deliberately used by individuals to negotiate social position and bring about social change. For example, the adoption of 'polite' architectural styles for textile mills, discussed above, may well have been intended to prove that those in trade were as well versed in current trends as the builders of country houses and to facilitate the admittance of the entrepreneur into the ranks of landed society, as indeed frequently happened.

Unlike colleagues working in pre-literate periods, the industrial archaeologist has an advantage here in that documentary evidence may help to put a name or a face to some of the innumerable shadowy individuals who have made these choices throughout human history. A surviving lime-kiln in north Derbyshire departs from the functional norm in having openings resembling Gothic windows in the façade: documentary evidence shows that it was built on the estate of Samuel Oldknow, an entrepreneur who was an associate of Richard Arkwright and one with equal pretensions to emulate the landed gentry. Although constructed alongside the Peak Forest Canal, one of whose objectives was to enable the cheap carriage of limestone, it was in fact run by Oldknow at a loss for a period of only fourteen years and, like many other pretentious structures of the industrial period, is a monument to a failed enterprise.

Finally, it is important to recognise that objects and structures do not necessarily retain the cultural meaning they had when first created, but that this may change over time. Landowners utilised ruined abbeys and castles as romantic images in designed landscapes in the course of the eighteenth century, giving them a totally different meaning from that of their builders. Industrial structures have achieved this transformation only in the latter part of the twentieth century, now being seen as icons of an innovative industrial past rather than as functional structures operating within a manufacturing environment. They are regarded as objects in themselves rather than part of the culture-historical process. It is partly for this reason that industrial archaeologists have become so divorced from the human aspect of industrialisation by accepting the contemporary meaning invested in the structures and not seeking that of their original creator and builders.

To summarise, as in any other field archaeology, the material evidence prompts a series of questions which the industrial archaeologist is often fortunate in being able to answer from documentary evidence. But a broad range of questions will not be asked unless there is a theoretical agenda which embraces not only functional and technological questions but also those concerned, for example, with social relations and the symbolic meaning of structures. If it is to be accepted as a credible aspect of archaeology, industrial archaeology has to adopt a more theoretical stance and will become richer in the process. It will be responsible not only for recording the appearance of structures and artefacts of the recent past, and for attempting to set them in an economic and technological context, but also for trying to explain how they indicate change or continuity in human behaviour. In this way, industrial archaeology may make a distinctive contribution to an understanding of the development of human society.

## THE INTERNATIONAL CONTEXT

The origins of industrial archaeology are considered to be essentially British by the rest of the world, yet in some respects its study had commenced elsewhere before becoming generally accepted in Britain. In many instances there were elements of government support for the creation of inventories of monuments, including those of industry. Some were politically motivated, such as the establishment of the Historic American Buildings Survey (HABS) in the

1930s as a means of providing work for unemployed architects. A pioneering survey of New England textile mills was undertaken by HABS in 1967–8. This programme still continues with industrial buildings now being recorded by the Historic American Engineering Record (HAER), established in 1969 under the aegis of the National Park Service, which itself dates back to 1916. HAER utilised a technique similar to the NRIM in England, producing a card index of industrial sites in each state to determine what was worthy of more detailed recording (Figure 2). The records are maintained by the Library of Congress in what is termed 'preservation by documentation', a concept similar to the British National Monuments Records (NMR). Whereas the NRIM in England utilised amateur enthusiasts in the recording process, the HAER surveys are undertaken by university staff and students working under contract to the National Park Service. They have usually been architects and engineers: only after twenty-five years of activity did the National Park Service first employ an archaeologist on a HAER project, a survey of a hard-rock mining site in the Mojave Desert of California, and they envisage further co-operation between the various disciplines (Andrews 1994). Recording has not always ensured preservation and the HAER records form an invaluable inventory of the industrial built environment of the USA (Burns 1989).

In Europe, the value of the physical remains of industry took rather longer to be appreciated. Although French historians had for a long time been interested in industrial history, little notice was taken of industrial sites until the 1970s and the first national study of industrial archaeology in France was not published until 1980 (Daumas 1980). The *Inventaire Générale*, established in 1964 to create a record of the French cultural heritage, began to include industrial sites in 1983 with the foundation of an industrial heritage group within it, the Cellule du Patrimoine

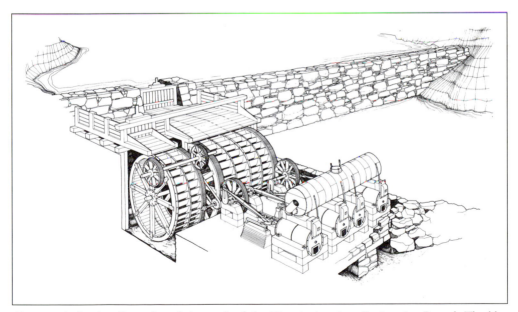

*Figure 2* A drawing illustrative of the work of the Historic American Engineering Record. The blast machinery and dam of the Adirondack Iron and Steel Company in Tahawus, New York, were in a ruinous condition when recorded in 1978, but have been graphically re-assembled to produce this interpretative drawing of the original plant. No attempt was made to reconstruct the building which once covered the machinery.

Reproduced by permission of HAER. Drawing by Barry A. Richard, 1978.

Industriel. Various thematic surveys are being undertaken by this group and several regional publications have emerged (Belhoste *et al.* 1984; Belhoste 1988, 1991). A long-term project to create a national database of French industrial sites was initiated in 1986. The same year, a similar database project was begun in the Netherlands. While the French surveys go back into the post-medieval period, the contrasting industrial development of the Netherlands is recognised in this survey which concentrates on architecture and town planning between 1850 and 1945 (Nijhof 1991). Responsibility for the industrial heritage has now passed to the Projectbureau Industrieel Erfgoed (PIE) which was created in 1992. In Belgium, various categories of industrial building have been surveyed, particularly watermills and windmills, and a national survey published (Viaene 1986). The Scandinavian countries have an important industrial heritage which is increasingly being recognised by their governments. In Norway, buildings and sites of industrial interest have been recorded both by the Council for Culture and the Norwegian Technical Museum, while in Sweden the Central Office of National Antiquities is monitoring various recording initiatives. The ending of the Cold War has resulted in various countries of eastern Europe having greater contact with western traditions and recognising the wealth of their industrial heritage. Further afield, industrial archaeology has made rapid progress in Australasia since the 1960s with National Trusts in each state including industrial sites and buildings in their registers (Donnachie 1981).

The conservation of many industrial sites preceded the compilation of systematic inventories but undoubtedly these have helped to determine priorities for more selective preservation in the future. In both America and Europe, voluntary effort and enthusiasm have been responsible for saving many sites which have often later passed into public guardianship.

At an international level, the General Council of the United Nations Educational, Scientific and Cultural Organisation (UNESCO) has adopted a policy of designating important cultural and ecological sites as World Heritage Sites. Around 300 have now been accorded this status, but only a handful are industrial sites. These range from the Ironbridge Gorge in Britain to the Potosi tin mines in Bolivia and a salt mine at Wieliczka in Poland. The International Committee for the Conservation of the Industrial Heritage (TICCIH) was established in 1973 and has led to increased awareness of the importance of the industrial past. It is seeking a more formal organisation and consultation by UNESCO on further industrial World Heritage Sites.

In the USA, sites of national significance are designated as National Historic Landmarks but may be maintained by the National Park Service or a variety of state and other local organisations. For example, America's recent Industrial Heritage Project in South-western Pennsylvania is a community project

***Plate 3*** Two of the blast furnaces at Tannehill in Alabama, USA, which were built to supply arms to the Confederate armies in 1863 but destroyed two years later by the Union armies. These have been totally rebuilt and even fired: despite their reconstructed state, they have been declared a National Metallurgical Engineering Landmark. They stand in a Historical State Park, which also includes some of the housing for the 600 slaves who worked the furnaces, and a museum of ironmaking.

designed to commemorate the significant contribution of the region's iron and steel, coal and transportation industries to the industrial growth of the USA through a series of heritage trails around conserved sites. The iron industry of the eastern states of the USA was a key factor in their economic development and its importance has been recognised through the designation of a wide range of structures as National Historic Landmarks. Only two, the Saugus Ironworks in Massachusetts and Hopewell Furnace in Pennsylvania, are in the care of the National Park Service and consequently well maintained and interpreted. Two other Pennsylvanian furnaces are preserved as isolated structures, Greenwood within a state park and Scranton by the state museums service. By contrast, the Sloss furnaces in Birmingham, Alabama, a vast complex dating from the 1920s, survive in entirety and are maintained by the city: no comparable examples have been preserved in Britain. There is little hesitation in the USA over the heavy restoration and even rebuilding of particularly important structures: Saugus was America's first integrated ironworks, built in 1646, but the present site is an almost total rebuild based on extensive archaeological excavation. The Tannehill furnaces in Alabama, suppliers of armaments to the Confederates, were totally destroyed by Union armies but have been reconstructed and even refired at the centre of a state park (Plate 3). Canada's first ironworks, Les Forges du St Maurice, are similarly preserved by Parks Canada.

In Europe, the conservation of industrial monuments is more haphazard. They have increasingly figured in schedules of historic structures, but there is no real equivalent to the comprehensive schemes operated by the National Park Services of North America. The decline in the numbers of Dutch windmills after the First World War led to the foundation by a group

*Plate 4* In no other place in the world can a landscape of windmills be more appreciated than at Kinderdijk, north of Dordrecht in the Netherlands. Two ranges of tower drainage mills, eighteen in all, lift water by means of scoop wheels from the Alblasserwaard polders into channels which flow into the River Lek.

of enthusiasts of the Association for the Preservation of Windmills in 1923. Their efforts have been rewarded in that over a thousand windmills now enjoy a degree of protection, many of which are fully operational like the splendid landscapes of the Kinderdijk drainage mills near Dordrecht (Plate 4) or the industrial mills at Zaandam north of Amsterdam. The Dutch founded the Netherlands Open Air Museum at Arnhem in 1912, which contains several rural industrial buildings such as a paper mill and a horse-driven oil mill that were moved on to the site. The more recent museum at Enkhuizen was opened in 1983 to perpetuate the vanishing maritime life of the now infilled Zuiderzee. A similar motive encouraged the creation of the Écomusée in 1974 at Le Creusot in Saône-et-Loire, France. This ironworking complex was established in the 1780s under the direction of an Englishman, William Wilkinson, brother of the better-known John. The works were later taken over by the Schneider family and became the largest in France.

*Plate 5* The original Henrichenburg ship lift on the Dortmund–Ems Canal, one of several sites preserved by the Westphalian Industrial Museum. This impressive structure was built in 1899 to transfer boats, mainly coal barges, through 14 m from the Dortmund branch to the main canal to Emden. This is now the centrepiece of a unique canal landscape, which demonstrates alternative means of overcoming differences in level. The first lift was supplemented in 1917 by a lock which is now also an industrial monument: this was followed by a second larger lift in 1962: and finally in 1989 by an even larger lock to accommodate standard European 1350-tonne [1328-ton] barges.

The Écomusée pioneered a novel approach, now adopted elsewhere in Europe, of involving the local community in the interpretation of their own environment, in this case an industrial one.

Belgium followed Britain in the change to industrial production in the late eighteenth century and had become a major industrial nation one hundred years later. An early museum of iron and coal was set up in Liège, and an Écomusée has been created around the colliery village of Bois-du-Luc near La Louvière. Generally, industrial buildings received no legislative protection until the 1970s and responsibility is now divided between the Flemish and Walloon areas of the country. In the Flemish area, much important conservation work has been carried out by the Vlaamse Vereniging voor Industriële Archeologie, a volunteer organisation established in 1979.

The importance of heavy industry to the German economy was recognised as early as 1930, when the Deutsches Bergbau-Museum was founded in Bochum on the initiative of the mining industry. Now housed in a striking modern building, this internationally important collection includes artefacts from all periods of mining activity. The heavily industrialised area of the Ruhr was the key to Germany's economic prosperity from the second half of the nineteenth century and the province of North Rhine-Westphalia has financed the preservation of several important monuments. These include the architecturally impressive Zollern II–IV coal mine complex, the Henrichenburg ship lift on the Dortmund–Ems Canal (Plate 5) and several of the Malakoff winding towers which once dominated the coalfield. Of greater international significance are the retention of the iron-cased blast furnaces at Völklingen in the Saarland and the Thyssen AG plant at Duisburg-Meiderich, since few twentieth-century steelworks are preserved anywhere else. By contrast, in the Harz Mountains of Lower Saxony, the illustrations from Agricola's *De Re Metallica* are brought to life in the lead and silver mines of St Andreasberg and the Rammelsberg (Agricola 1556). Here, wooden waterwheels, headgear and man-engines vividly recall the techniques of metalliferous mining practised in early modern Europe.

Austria was also an important centre of mining, and a heritage trail, the Styrian Iron Trail, has been created to link a series of ironworking sites and blast furnaces in the Erzberg. Similar mining landscapes have been conserved in Scandinavia, dating from the seventeenth century when much of Europe's copper was produced in this area. At Falun in Sweden, a vast open pit, the Stora Stöten, was caused by the collapse of extensive underground workings. The Stora company itself realised the importance of their mining remains and a mining museum was opened in the 1920s. Especially striking is the miners' housing district, the Elsborg, in which the wooden houses stand on foundations of copper slag blocks and are painted with iron-based Falun red paint. Several early blast furnaces are also preserved in Sweden, notably the estate ironworks at Engelsberg where both the owner's eighteenth-century house and those of his workers remain. Company housing is an equally outstanding feature of the mining town of Røros, in Norway. The small wooden houses have grassed roofs and are dwarfed by massive slag heaps of copper-smelting waste while, by contrast, the town is dominated by the Baroque company church (Plate 6). The initiative for a local museum came from local trade unions, and the displays in the underground hall are particularly informative on working conditions. Røros became one of the first industrial complexes to be designated as a UNESCO World Heritage Site in 1982.

*Plate 6*   Copper-mining and -smelting have dominated the Norwegian town of Røros since its foundation in the late seventeenth century. Below the slag heaps are the ramshackle wooden workers' houses with
their grassed roofs, while the company town is dominated by the late eighteenth-century Baroque church.
Mining continued in Røros well into the twentieth century, but the importance of the town's historic
remains was recognised and they were carefully conserved and accorded World Heritage status in 1982.

The emphasis placed on the human element in these Scandinavian sites is not always found elsewhere. In Britain, as discussed above, technological achievements have often been stressed at the expense of human effort, perhaps understandably in a country where so many developments were pioneered. Yet, in the 1960s, a leading industrial archaeologist could write:

> Industrial archaeology is, of course, ultimately concerned with people rather than things: factories, workshops, houses and machines are of interest only as products of human ingenuity, enterprise, compassion or greed – as physical expressions of human behaviour. From whatever standpoint the subject is approached, man is the basic object of our curiosity.
>
> (Smith 1965: 191)

Some notice has now been taken of this approach in Britain, with displays, for example, in the Kelham Island museum of working conditions in the Sheffield cutlery industry and often nostalgic glimpses of life below ground in various museums of coal-mining. In the United States, on the other hand, equal weight has been always been given to both technological and human achievement. The rapidly expanding textile towns on the Merrimack River in Massachusetts made extensive use of female labour from farming districts in the mid-nineteenth century. The women lived very regulated lives in boarding houses, the essence of which is captured in excellent archival displays and conserved buildings in both Lawrence and Lowell. Later in the century, the labour force was vastly augmented by European immigrants, who were again highly regimented. Labour troubles were rife, notably the 'Bread and Roses' strike of 1912, which dominates the displays in the interpretation centre at Lawrence. The iron and steel industry of Pennsylvania also had its share of labour problems in the nineteenth century, notably the Homestead strike in Pittsburgh in 1892. Recent moves to conserve industrial monuments in this area have concentrated on their relevance to the labour movement as well as their place in technological development. In the southern states, the employment of Negro labour in iron-works as well as many other industries is a recurring theme in schemes of interpretation. Congress in 1991 authorised a National Historic Landmark Theme Study on American labour history, with a view to adding significant sites to those already in the care of the National Park Service.

Industrial archaeologists in Europe have also drawn attention to the need to consider the human dimension of past industrial activity. Manuel Cerdà, the president of the Associaió Valenciana d'Arqueologia Industrial, would go so far as to suggest that the study of industrial archaeology is mainly concerned with the period when worker–master social relationships changed as a result of the beginnings of factory production, a view echoed in the policy state-ment on industrial archaeology published by English Heritage (English Heritage 1995b). Cerdà argues that:

> Industrial archaeology must treat the study of the physical remains of a specific historical period of capitalist industrialisation, since it is from this moment on that society establishes new forms of organisation based upon new relationships among the main factors affecting production, i.e., capital and labour, which allow for the formation of new social classes.
>
> (Cerdà 1991: 407)

He rightly stresses that documentary evidence is sadly lacking for the study of working-class housing because of the illiteracy of that class, and that the study of physical remains is therefore essential. However, it is precisely this aspect of the built environment which has undergone most destruction, not least in Spain where there is no national policy towards the industrial heritage. Areas of housing associated, for example, with the textile town of Alcoi in Catalonia and the copper-mining and -processing areas of Rio Tinto do remain but, certainly in the latter case, are the houses of the immigrant English overseers and not truly representative of the working classes. This is also the case in Britain, where the status of Conservation Area has been granted to exceptional enclaves of working-class housing such as the textile villages of Cromford or New Lanark or garden cities such as Port Sunlight, but typical urban terrace or tenement housing have, understandably, been cleared away. The industrial archaeologist is often limited to sources such as maps and photographs, which are selective in themselves, for the study of the working-class neighbourhoods that mushroomed around mills and factories.

Industrial archaeology is really a way of looking at a period of human history using all the evidence available and not just the documentary. The parameters of that period have not been strictly defined, since industrialisation began earlier in some industries than others, but it is probably true to say that industrial archaeology concentrates on the period when the manufacture of goods ceased to be at the level of domestic or craft production and moved into industrial or capitalist production. However, this form of production was not entirely factory-based, many goods still being manufactured on a part-time, domestic basis but normally under the control of an outside entrepreneur as in the case of handloom-weaving or nail-making. The essence of industrial archaeology is the analysis of surviving field evidence but this is enhanced by the use of a variety of other sources. It also has to be accepted that certain aspects of human activity lend themselves to this type of analysis better than others, and the study of political elites or religious belief, which play a major role in other periods of archaeology, are perhaps best left to the historian of the industrial period.

It was concern for the survival of field evidence which first prompted the creation of the discipline of industrial archaeology, and the rate of destruction has been such that industrial archaeologists have had to be more concerned with the preservation movement than archaeologists of other periods. The recent establishment of inventories of industrial sites in both Europe and America has been prompted by the need to establish priorities in a time of scarce resources. But industrial archaeology is a discipline which has matured in the last decade to look beyond the industrial monument to a consideration not just of its significance in technological and economic terms but also of its cultural meaning as a symbol of changing human relationships. The two chapters which follow attempt to analyse the two major areas of field evidence, first the landscape and townscape and second the buildings, structures and machinery, while the other chapters concentrate on the practical techniques of the discipline, including documentary research. The final chapter returns to the difficult question of the conservation of the industrial heritage and considers examples of what the authors regard as good practice.

*Chapter Two*

# Landscapes and townscapes

Industrial archaeology has until recently been constrained by its origins, when the need to conserve the vanishing physical evidence of early industrialisation led to an over-emphasis on the concept of an industrial monument. Recent work has followed the normal archaeological pattern of paying more attention to the context of the material remains of industry. Context in this instance should comprise both the immediate physical environment and the wider cultural one, although the latter has often been neglected. The same considerations apply to the study of whole landscapes and of townscapes.

Landscape, like context, is a term that is not easy to define. It is often taken to mean natural scenery to which the onlooker reacts aesthetically. To the historian and the archaeologist, however, landscape is the physical manifestation of changes wrought by man in both space and time and can be interpreted by the trained eye. Most previous studies of the landscape have concerned themselves with patterns of cultivation and settlement over a long period of time. It is perhaps only in the last 250 years that industrial development has superimposed itself on this already man-made landscape and its effects have often been cataclysmic by comparison, despite the shorter time dimension. Many have echoed John Ruskin in decrying this new transformation of the landscape, yet it is a vital resource in understanding the origins of modern industrial society.

There has been a great increase in the number of surveys of industrial landscapes undertaken in the last decade, largely because of the increasing attention being paid to management and conservation. Some of these surveys have been initiated by those involved with managing the landscape for heritage purposes, as in the National Parks and large open-air museum complexes such as the Ironbridge Gorge. Others have been concerned with recording what are classed as derelict and contaminated landscapes, often those of past mining activity, in advance of reclamation. The economic regeneration of rundown urban areas has also involved rapid surveys to identify historically important structures; for example, in the Urban Development Corporation Areas. The result of all these surveys has been a greater understanding of the inter-relationship of the factors that have shaped past industrial landscapes.

## ANALYSING THE LANDSCAPE

There are three stages in the process of analysing the industrial landscape: determining the reasons for the location of particular industrial enterprises; interpreting the changes to them through time; and examining their spatial relationship both with each other and with the development pattern of settlements and transport systems. It is the task of the industrial archaeologist to interpret physical features in the landscape by the normal archaeological means of survey, perhaps excavation and the typological ordering of both artefacts and structures.

# The location of industry

The location of industry in the landscape has been the subject of considerable research among historical geographers (e.g. Smith 1971; Grant 1987). The existence of industrial activity in a particular area is normally governed by the interaction between three groups of factors: the presence of natural resources, topographical features and the human agencies which harnessed these for industrial production.

Raw materials for industry are both extracted from the earth or grown on its surface. In the case of extractive industries, the physical evidence for the local presence of raw materials is relatively easy to determine. Quarry faces and open pits, often overgrown, are evidence for past extraction of building material and its type can usually be determined from the local vernacular buildings. Adits, shafts and tips indicate the existence of past underground mining activity, while examination of any surface plant may help identify the mineral being processed. For manufacturing industries, the availability of local raw materials was often not such a key factor in their location. Before the advent of efficient transport networks, most communities produced the essentials for their own basic needs. Corn was ground, ale was brewed, and shoes and clothing were made, all of which can leave physical traces in the form of corn mills, maltings, breweries, tanneries and workshops. The pattern of industrial production was therefore highly dispersed, a situation that was to alter only from the eighteenth century onwards with the construction of a turnpike road system, improved river navigation, canals and, later, railways. These enabled raw materials to be taken to sites with topographical advantages or potential markets, as, for example, with early cotton mills which used imported materials but were often located a long way from the port of entry. The presence of raw materials, therefore, may not always be the predominant locational factor.

The major topographic feature utilised by industry is the natural gradient of the land which influences the provision of both power and transport. The availability of running water has been a key factor in the location of industry since the Roman period, and continued to be so even after the introduction of other forms of power. Water can be collected in a reservoir for use in manufacture or channelled to a waterwheel for powering a corn mill or other machinery. The actual mechanism for the collection of water can vary considerably according to the size of the water course. Fast-flowing rivers can be channelled directly to a waterwheel sited at a natural fall or where an artificial fall can be created; a series of mills can be spread along a river at a suitable spacing to prevent the back-up of water in flood conditions. Smaller rivers can also be utilised for power but require more ingenious husbanding of the resource by the creation of artificial leats leading to storage ponds upstream of a mill. In regions of low rainfall, or at high altitudes, water may have to be collected over a vast area. Many miles of leats with a slight fall in their gradients have been dug along the hillsides, sometimes with short tunnels, leading to artificial storage reservoirs.

Another use of a natural gradient may be for transport, using an inclined plane with rails for conveying waggons or even boats from one height to another. This may be achieved by means of gravity or by the application of power from human, animal or other power source. The coalfields of north-east England were the first to be exploited on a large scale because coal from outcrops on the hills could be lowered by means of these gravity railways down to the Rivers Tyne and Wear for shipment to the London market. In less favourable situations heavy loads had to be moved both up and down slopes, and for this purpose powered winders were used. Inclined planes of this kind formed a part of many of the early long-distance railway systems of the early nineteenth century.

Natural slopes were also important in the siting of a variety of industrial structures. Prevailing wind currents up a suitable slope were used to provide the draught for primitive boles or smelting hearths (Willies and Cranston 1992). Chimneys were placed on a hillside to provide an artificial draught, with a sloping flue between the furnace and the stack. In some cases, such as lead-smelting, these flues may be very long and also serve a secondary purpose of allowing vaporised metallic ores to condense on their inner surfaces. These stone-built flues are a striking feature of the landscape of Swaledale, running from smelting mills situated in valleys for use of water power to chimneys on the hilltops. Similar flues were used elsewhere in the world; for example, on the Sierra de Almagrera in southern Spain (Plate 7). Long flues, often with condensing chambers or labyrinths, are also employed in the calcining of tin ores to extract the volatile arsenic. Where suitable topography was not available, the long flues were replicated by labyrinthine chambers built on horizontal sites. A spectacular example of this technique may be seen on the clifftop at Botallack on the St Just peninsula in Cornwall. Natural topography was also usefully employed in the location of lime-kilns and blast furnaces. Both were charged from above and emptied at the base, and were therefore built against a hillside wherever possible. The range of five early nineteenth-century blast furnaces being consolidated by Cadw at Blaenavon in South Wales is a classic example of careful siting to make use of the natural terrain.

Environmental determinism is, however, not solely responsible for the location of industry: human agency has been equally influential. In Britain, the landed elite generally had the power to exploit all the resources of their estates, both above and below ground. This resulted in a pattern of exploitation of mineral resources which reflected seigneurial initiative as much as the existence of raw materials. The distribution of iron furnaces in South Derbyshire in the late eighteenth century, for example, bore more relation to the estates occupied by the Hastings, Burdetts and Ferrers than to purely geological considerations. Landowners might also deter the establishment of manufacturing industry on their estates, preferring to retain the integrity

*Plate 7* The extensive lead-condensing flues snaking across the barren landscape of the Sierra de Almagrera in southern Spain.

of their closed villages by not encouraging immigration. The Dukes of Rutland prevented the introduction of the domestic hosiery industry into the Vale of Belvoir, which therefore presents a totally different landscape from the industrialised villages of the Vale of Trent.

It is not only the great landowners who have been responsible for shaping the industrial landscape. The unemployed often squatted on common land and eked out a precarious living by small-scale mining and quarrying. Such settlement was frequent on the fringes of major coal-fields, where scattered houses in isolated plots rather than nucleated villages are often still the norm. The right of ordinary men to exploit natural resources was both recognised and regulated in certain areas, notably the mining districts of the Forest of Dean, Derbyshire and Cornwall. In the latter, the tinners had the right to divert streams, cut fuel and prospect for tin without hindrance from the landowner. Their disputes were settled by the Stannary Courts and they paid for their privileges by a proportion of their product after smelting. Their stream workings are still an obvious feature on Bodmin Moor and Dartmoor.

## Change through time

Most industrial landscapes, once established, evolve through time and the present landscape is a palimpsest of past changes. The task of the industrial archaeologist is to determine the sequence of events and to account for the changes which have taken place since the initial establishment of an industry on a particular site. It is clear, for example, that water power played a major role in the location of many post-medieval industries. A site chosen for its water-power potential was then often developed by the construction of leats and storage ponds or by lowering the tailrace level below the mill in order to increase the head of water across the wheel. The construction

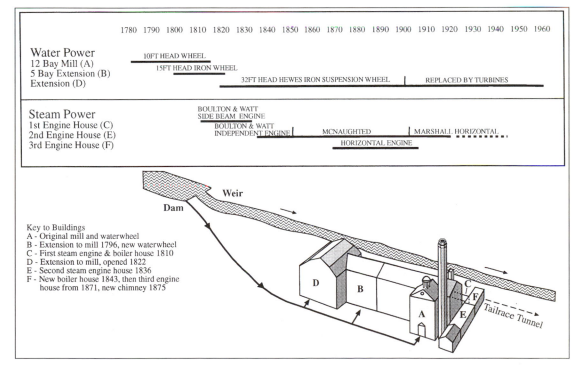

*Figure 3* The development of power systems at Quarry Bank Mill, Styal, Cheshire. More efficient types of water power continued to be used alongside steam power.

*Plate 8* The dramatic façade of Cheesden Lumb mill near Rochdale in Lancashire, one of ten water-powered cotton mills which once operated along the valley of the Cheesden Brook.

*Plate 9* A rare survival, the breastshot waterwheel *in situ* at St Mary's Mill, Chalford, in Gloucestershire. The machinery of this former woollen mill was driven by gearing from the internal rim of the wheel and by an auxiliary Tangye steam engine which also survives.

and size of the waterwheel itself could be improved through the use of cast iron and rim instead of axle drive. This type of development can be appreciated at Quarry Bank Mill at Styal in Cheshire (Figure 3), a cotton mill now operated by the National Trust. The original wooden wheel was replaced by an iron wheel, and the head of water across the wheel was increased by 5 feet [1.5 metres] after the building of a weir on the River Bollin. The second wheel was replaced by a large iron suspension wheel and a tunnel dug for the tailrace to create a head of water three times the original. After nearly one hundred years of operation, the third wheel was replaced by two turbines which continued in use until 1959. Turbines also replaced wheels in the numerous large textile mills on the massive Merrimack River in Massachusetts, USA. In the towns of Lowell and Lawrence, weirs constructed across the river diverted water into canals or leats running parallel to it. The mills were erected on the bands of land between the three water channels and are examples of the ultimate in water-power technology.

The most efficient water-power installations can be jeopardised by drought, frost or even flood. Once steam power became available, many sites added an auxiliary steam engine to maintain their operations under these conditions. Initially, steam pumping engines were erected in order to pump water from the tailrace back into the headrace for reuse on the water-wheel. The invention of the rotative beam engine in the 1780s enabled steam power to be applied directly to drive machinery. One obvious effect was the appearance of tall factory chimneys which provided draught for coal-fired boilers for steam raising. New buildings also appeared, engine and boiler houses adjoining the mills as well as coal storage areas.

However, transport costs for coal were expensive and many isolated water-powered mills began to close down in the face of newly built steam-powered mills. These were located in places where coal could be cheaply brought by canal or railway, especially in urban areas where labour was plentiful. This migration from the river valleys has in many cases left a fossilised landscape such as that west of Rochdale in Lancashire, where ten mills mostly processing cotton waste once operated along one mile of the Cheesden Brook but are now only evocative ruins (Plate 8). Even the addition of steam engines to these mid-nineteenth-century mills did not always ensure their survival. In Gloucestershire, with its old-established water-powered woollen cloth industry, there were over 170 mills around 1820 but only 79 by 1840 and 20 by 1901. During the nineteenth century, thirty water-powered factories lined a 5.5-mile stretch of the River Frome upstream from Wallbridge Mill in Stroud, a section of river with only a modest gradient (Tann 1967). Steam power was introduced in some mills to supplement the river as a power source, and St Mary's Mill in Chalford still retains both its waterwheel and steam engine (Plate 9). In the iron industry, too, the use of steam power for blowing blast furnaces combined with the use of coke instead of charcoal as a fuel resulted in the migration of the industry from wooded hilly areas such as the Lake District and the Forest of Dean to the coalfields. This has left relict landscapes where the interrelationship between fuel supply, power sources and production can still be appreciated because of the lack of subsequent development. The size of the charcoal storage barns at Duddon furnace in Cumbria gives some idea of the scale of exploitation of the adjacent woodlands. On a 14-year coppicing rotation, 10 acres [4 hectares] of woodland were needed to

*Plate 10* The River Derwent powered several mills here at Belper in Derbyshire. The small T-shaped North Mill on the right, built in 1804, is one of the earliest cast-iron framed buildings to survive and was powered by an internal breastshot wheel. It is dwarfed by the East Mill of 1912, built on a steel frame and powered by electricity generated both by steam and turbines making use of the available head of water.

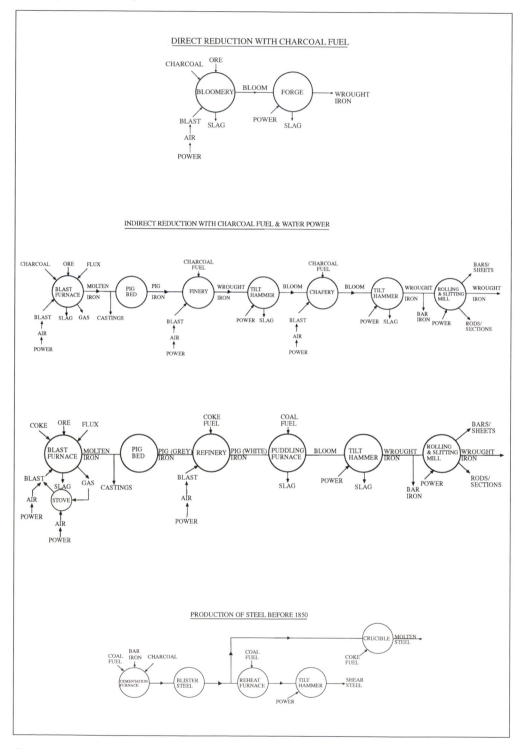

*Figure 5* Diagram illustrating the evolution of processes in the manufacture of iron and steel, showing the transition from charcoal fuel and water power to coke and steam power.

The dispersed pattern of early industry created a similarly dispersed pattern of settlement. People had to live within walking or riding distance from their workplace. Isolated mines and quarries relied on their labour force being prepared to live in barracks at the sites, only returning to their homes at weekends. The ruins of these spartan dwellings can still be found, for example, at many Welsh slate quarries. Industrialists also constructed rows of houses in order to attract labour, particularly to isolated water-power sites, mines and quarries. Some became the nucleus of new villages; others remain as derelict reminders of past industry. A few employers founded model villages associated with their mills and factories, displaying their benevolence yet at the same time exercising social control over their workforce. Their own houses reflect the social aspirations of the new entrepreneurial class and reinforced the gulf between employer and employee. The study of settlement patterns is therefore an essential element in the analysis of the industrial landscape, revealing much about the nature of industrial organisation and the social differentiation it created.

## TYPES OF INDUSTRIAL LANDSCAPES

Nearly every landscape has some industrial element within it, but an industrial landscape is one where industry has been the dominant factor in its creation. Within such a landscape, the components can represent a single phase of industrial development or several hundred years of activity. Industrial landscapes can be categorised by the dominant influence which initially shaped them, whether it be, for example, extraction of minerals, manufacture of textiles or food-processing industries. This section will examine three types of industrial landscape to illustrate the interrelationship between the various elements which contributed to their formation.

## Linear landscapes

Early industrial development often took a linear form, utilising either water-power sites along streams and rivers or methods of transport. Previous research has tended to concentrate on either a single site or the transport element itself, ignoring the totality of the landscape with its inter-dependent features. New standards were set with the publication of two books from the Royal Commission on Ancient and Historic Monuments of Wales (RCAHMW), one on horse-drawn railways in the Brecon Forest and the other on the Montgomeryshire Canal (Hughes 1988, 1990). In both cases, the linear feature forms the basis for the study of industrial development and settlement patterns along its length.

From the early Middle Ages onwards, streams and rivers have been harnessed for power. The tiny streams of the Outer Hebrides provided power for primitive Norse mills, serving individual farms. Although used in recent times, the strings of small mills recall a different cultural pattern which existed before corn milling became part of the manorial system. To visit Sandvaat or Tolsta Chaolais, with their ruins of stone-built mills and leats and isolated millstones, is to step back several centuries. By contrast, most mainland mills with their guaranteed income from the milling soke, were larger and more technologically advanced. The type of waterwheel they used depended on their location along the river gradient. Figure 6 shows the River Sence in west Leicestershire, a small river with a reasonable fall of over 20 feet [6.1 metres] per mile in its 13.5-mile length where the use of leats and storage ponds enabled ten corn mills to continue working into the twentieth century. The three upper mills had overshot wheels and the remainder breastshot wheels. Each mill originally served a village, but the growing population in that part of the county as a result of coal-mining activity enabled them to survive and even to modernise, some of the wheels being replaced by turbines.

As the pace of industrialisation quickened, corn mills were converted to other uses and new types of mill constructed. As David Crossley has shown:

> There can be few districts in Britain where rivers have been as intensively used for power as in and around Sheffield. On almost 30 miles of five streams and their tributaries, there are upwards of 115 places where mills have stood, some employed for corn milling, paper-making or snuff-grinding, but the great majority used by the metal trades, whose water-wheels drove grindstones, forge-hammers, rolling-mills and wire-mills.
>
> (Crossley 1989)

One of the most intensively used of the Sheffield streams was the Porter and its main tributary, the Mayfield Brook. The watercourse fell 450 feet [137.1 metres] in a little over 4 miles and powered twenty mills, ranging from a corn mill at the upper end through grinding and wire mills to the Sharrow snuff mill. The latter survives, together with the Shepherd Wheel where blade grinding is still demonstrated – a last remnant of the 'little mester' system of independent producers which once dominated the Sheffield scene. Rivers further north in the Pennines were intensively exploited for textile production from the early nineteenth century onwards. Mills had been erected earlier for fulling and carding woollens, followed by larger spinning mills. Tributary streams were also utilised for power such as the Brook in the Luddenden valley running into the River Calder to the west of Halifax. Three storage reservoirs or dams on the moors gathered water to supply two corn mills, a paper mill and seven textile mills (Giles and Goodall 1992). An alternative method of conserving water was utilised in the Coalbrookdale valley in Shropshire, where waterwheels powered blowing engines, forge hammers and grinding mills in a distance of half a mile or so. Here, a tunnel was driven back upstream and water returned to the Upper Furnace Pool by means of a steam-powered pumping engine (Alfrey and Clark 1993). These examples indicate how the intensive study of a river as a power source can put individual sites into a meaningful context.

Rivers were, of course, also a means of transport and many were improved for this purpose from the seventeenth century onwards. This caused conflict with millers anxious to keep their head of water, as is indicated by the existence of locks by-passing the weirs which diverted water into the mills on most river navigations. The Nene in Northamptonshire was made navigable in the first half of the eighteenth century but had numerous watermills along its sinuous course between Northampton and Peterborough. These mills were by-passed by staunches and pound locks: the staunches have been replaced and the locks are now conspicuous by their bottom guillotine-type gates

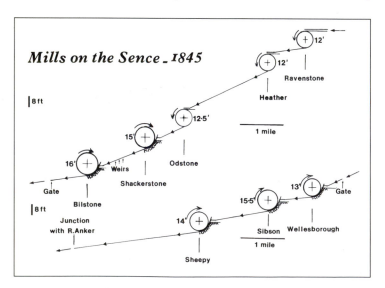

*Figure 6* The small River Sence in west Leicestershire powered ten corn mills (eight here shown) in its 13.5-mile length. This section, based on a survey of 1845, illustrates how overshot wheels were used near the source, with high falls and small volume, and breastshot wheels downstream where the volume was greater and the available head smaller.

(Palmer and Neaverson 1992). In low-lying East Anglia, an important grain-growing area, millers jealously guarded their water rights when rivers were made navigable from the coast to inland market towns. Along the upper reaches of the River Bure, made navigable from Coltishall to Aylsham, disused locks may still be found alongside the white-painted, weather-boarded mills at Buxton Lammas and Oxnead among others. River navigations presented a greater problem where the gradient was steeper and the only means of providing a transport link was by means of an artificial canal along the river valley. In the Colne valley, west of Huddersfield, the river is harnessed by means of leats and storage ponds to numerous spinning mills and is paralleled and even crossed by the Huddersfield Canal. Small villages, such as Marsden, Slaithwaite, Linthwaite and Milnsbridge, became mill towns with densely packed mills and houses filling the available space in the valley bottom (Plate 11). Another canal which paralleled a river was the Swansea Canal along the Tawe valley which, unusually, combined the functions of a water supply leat with those of a transport artery. The available water supply encouraged the growth of over forty mills or works, mainly connected with metal-working, while coal mines in the valley were provided with access to the coast (Hughes 1979). There are other instances of the water from artificial waterways being used for both power and transport in Britain and Europe, while in the United States, the extensive leat systems used to power textile mills in Lowell and Lawrence were also used for bringing coal to them. These elements in the landscape demonstrate that harmony could exist between mill-owner and boat-owner on the same stretch of water.

Where there were no suitable rivers for improvement for navigation, the increasing demand for coal, limestone and other bulky goods in the second half of the eighteenth century prompted the construction of artificial waterways. The history of these has been extensively studied, particularly by Charles Hadfield, but their contribution to the landscape in promoting linear industrial growth has rarely been considered. For example, the Peak Forest Canal was constructed to exploit a rich, but inaccessible, source of limestone in northern Derbyshire. At its northern end it connected to the canal network to Manchester and across the Pennines, while from its southern terminus at Bugsworth Basin a horse-drawn waggonway was constructed to the Dove Holes quarries. The canal encouraged the further development of the cotton industry along its length from New Mills to Ashton-under-Lyne, while substantial lime-kilns were constructed on its banks and at Bugsworth Basin itself. A number of transit warehouses were built in vernacular style with integral boat-loading docks. Traffic for Manchester from the Peak Forest Canal passed through Ashton and Ancoats where the waterway was fringed with cotton mills, iron-works and other industrial premises, some with their private canal branches. A southern connection to the East Midlands by water proving impossible, a railway was eventually built from Whaley Bridge, near Bugsworth Basin, right across the White Peak to join the Cromford Canal and a through route to

*Plate 11* Stone-built mills lining the River Colne in Milnsbridge, west of Huddersfield in West Yorkshire.

the River Trent. The Cromford and High Peak Railway was a hybrid enterprise of inclines worked by stationary steam engines and level sections operated by horses which were eventually replaced by steam locomotives (Figure 7). Many quarries were opened up as a result of the railway but it had minimal effect upon the settlement pattern because of the bleakness of the terrain it traversed. Since the railway operated until the 1960s, the archaeological evidence for its method of operation is still visible in the landscape and much of its route has become a long-distance footpath. A similar hybrid transport system was used to cross the Allegheny Mountains in Pennsylvania, where the canal boats themselves were moved on wheeled trolleys hauled by steam engines. The remains of this system are protected by the National Park Service.

Some of the more ambitious canal schemes introduced striking features into the landscape, in the form of embankments, cuttings and aqueducts. On the Birmingham Canal Navigations, a system which remained viable well into the twentieth century in conjunction with railways, the sequence of development can be identified in the landscape. Three separate canal lines in Smethwick, for example, display the increasing ingenuity of engineers to shorten journey times (Andrew 1995). Flights of locks were eliminated and replaced by deep cuttings, spanned by elegant bridges and aqueducts. Locomotive railways had an even more dramatic impact upon the landscape because of their need for low gradients. Broad river estuaries were bridged, mountains pierced by tunnels and valleys crossed by spectacular viaducts, monuments to the confidence of the engineers who designed and built them. Many of these utilitarian structures are emphasised

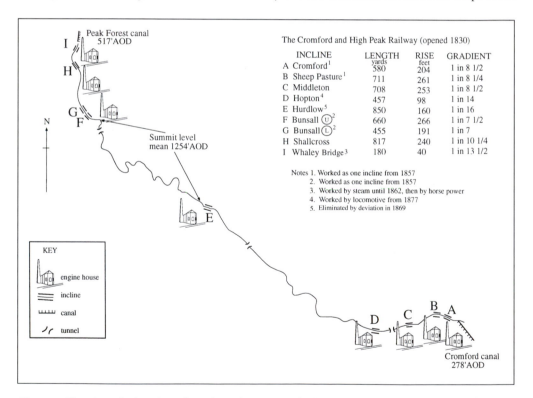

The Cromford and High Peak Railway (opened 1830)

| INCLINE | LENGTH yards | RISE feet | GRADIENT |
|---|---|---|---|
| A Cromford[1] | 580 | 204 | 1 in 8 1/2 |
| B Sheep Pasture[1] | 711 | 261 | 1 in 8 1/4 |
| C Middleton | 708 | 253 | 1 in 8 1/2 |
| D Hopton[4] | 457 | 98 | 1 in 14 |
| E Hurdlow[5] | 850 | 160 | 1 in 16 |
| F Bunsall (U)[2] | 660 | 266 | 1 in 7 1/2 |
| G Bunsall (L)[2] | 455 | 191 | 1 in 7 |
| H Shallcross | 817 | 240 | 1 in 10 1/4 |
| I Whaley Bridge[3] | 180 | 40 | 1 in 13 1/2 |

Notes 1. Worked as one incline from 1857
2. Worked as one incline from 1857
3. Worked by steam until 1862, then by horse power
4. Worked by locomotive from 1877
5. Eliminated by deviation in 1869

Peak Forest canal 517'AOD

Summit level mean 1254'AOD

N

KEY
engine house
incline
canal
tunnel

Cromford canal 278'AOD

*Figure 7* The Cromford and High Peak Railway in Derbyshire was constructed across the southern Pennines to connect the Cromford Canal to the Peak Forest Canal at Whaley Bridge. The railway, opened in the 1830s, was typical of its era in making use of a series of inclines worked by stationary steam engines and level sections on which horse-drawn haulage was later replaced by steam locomotives. It remained operative into the 1960s.

by statuary, crests and other ornamental features, reflecting the pride of railway and canal companies in their achievements or, occasionally, their need to placate a landowner for their intrusion on to his estate. The portal at the eastern end of the Sapperton tunnel on the Thames and Severn Canal faces into Cirencester Park, home of Earl Bathurst, and is an elaborate classical structure compared with the simple portal at the western end. Lord Anson gained a crenellated portal to a railway tunnel to add to his collection of classical monuments already on his estate at Shugborough in Staffordshire.

The facility of a railway within a national network attracted industrial development, particularly for food-processing and the storage of goods in transit. Large malting complexes built alongside railways in eastern England gathered barley from the surrounding countryside to process it for delivery to London and Burton-on-Trent breweries. In the Jurassic ironstone belt of the East Midlands, the railways themselves helped to make the low-grade ores commercially viable as branches could be built right up to the quarry face and blast furnaces built alongside them. The former Midland Railway through Northamptonshire was once the central artery of a whole network of ironstone railways and flanked by many steel-cased furnaces. These have long disappeared, but their former existence is still visible in the form of isolated bridges, cuttings and slag heaps. Railways became corridors of industry rather than merely a means of transport from one place to another.

Settlement patterns were also affected by railway development. Stations, signal boxes, locomotive sheds and warehouses were built in a uniform style by individual railway companies, giving a unity to new linear landscapes. Similar styles were often adopted for rows of railway workers' cottages, while planned towns, such as Swindon and Crewe, were grafted on to existing villages when the railway passed through them (Cattell and Falconer 1995; Drummond 1994). In the USA, railways opened up vast uninhabited tracts of land and towns such as Birmingham, Alabama, and Altoona, Pennsylvania, were deliberately created because of the railway. New modes of transport have since superseded railways and it is often only the style and uniformity of the settlements which betray their former association.

The study of linear landscapes, generally the immediate hinterland of intensively exploited rivers, canals and railways, reveals their importance in the process of industrialisation. Most of the documentary evidence is concerned with the lengthy process for obtaining Acts of Parliament to enable construction to proceed and the minute books of the companies set up to finance the operation. The landscape, on the other hand, indicates how these transport routes acted as a magnet to a range of industrial enterprises beyond the dreams of their initial backers. Nor do bare financial accounts do justice to the magnitude of the structures which became features in the landscape, themselves monuments to generations of navvies who left no written records.

## Metalliferous mining landscapes

The surface evidence of past mining activity is a fragile resource for the archaeologist but one which is increasingly threatened by environmental considerations. The 'green' movement is demanding the reclamation of derelict areas and the removal of contaminated waste tips, which can provide short-term funding for archaeological work but the eventual loss of the resource. This is threatening previously untouched mining landscapes in the remoter areas of Britain, whilst pressures for building land in more populous areas can be equally destructive. Fortunately, this destruction has generated an increasing realisation of the value of the resource and prompted schemes of evaluation such as the Monuments Protection Programme funded by English Heritage. Our understanding of mining landscapes has, as a result, advanced considerably in recent years.

The location of mining activity is geologically determined but the decision to work mineral deposits depends upon human agency. Minerals are a valuable asset and their exploitation has at different times been the privilege of the Crown, of proprietors of landed estates or of lesser individuals. The workings of the latter were often haphazard, consisting of fruitless trial shafts and adits as well as small-scale, successful operations. The Crown and landowners were able to invest more capital in larger-scale operations, although many mineral rights were leased to companies of adventurers in return for royalties on produce. These longer-term projects involved the construction of more permanent buildings and plant, often to attract further investment even though the underground potential did not always justify it. These contrasts of scale are nowhere better observed than in the Derbyshire lead-mining landscape. The area round Brassington is pock-marked with hundreds of shafts, together with the ruins of 'coes', where miners stored their clothing and tools, and the remains of horse-powered, ore-crushing circles. Individual mines were accorded evocative names such as 'Paupers Venture', 'Children's Fortune' and 'Perseverance', while the organisation of mining was governed by the Barmote Court. Near Sheldon, the upstanding buildings of the Magpie Mine represent large-scale investment by companies of adventurers, one of whom introduced Cornish technology in the form of steam pumping and winding engines whose remains are now an alien element in the Derbyshire landscape (Plate 12). Similar contrasts can be observed in many other mining areas of Britain.

The availability of water for power and ore-dressing was vital and ensuring its supply has brought about major changes in the landscape. Water from storage ponds on hilltops was released to expose mineral veins by means of hushing, the repeated sudden force of water dislodging the

*Plate 12* The surface features of Magpie Mine on Sheldon Moor in Derbyshire. The engine house on the right was built for a Cornish beam pumping engine, but coal costs forced the owners to revert to the traditional Derbyshire practice of sough drainage in the 1870s. The small headgear reflects a twentieth-century reworking using an electric winder housed in a corrugated iron shed. The buildings on the left were the agent's house and smithy. The site is maintained by the Peak District Mines Historical Society.

mineral itself along with gangue (waste) material. Water power then drove crushing machinery which reduced the ores to a smaller size so that they could be separated from the gangue by means of gravity after mixing with water. The former presence of a dressing floor may now only be indicated by various horizontal levels, together with a series of waste tips consisting of material in gradually reducing particle size as the gradient is descended. In many cases the water after use for dressing was collected in storage ponds along the valleys to allow any remaining mineral content to settle out before discharge into the natural water-course. These landscapes dominated by a water-powered mining industry are characteristic of Wales and the Pennines in Britain and some hilly regions of Europe such as the Hartz Mountains. They indicate the survival of a comparatively primitive technology long after more sophisticated forms of power, such as steam, had become available. The latter, however, proved invaluable in areas lacking sufficient water power, such as Cornwall, where the mining landscape is characterised not by leats and wheelpits but by numerous engine houses and chimneys. The comparative study of field evidence reveals the varying levels of technology employed within the same chronological period. Mines processing the same ores used either innovative or outdated equipment depending on location, profitability and mine management (Palmer and Neaverson 1989).

Spatial analysis of mining landscapes may help to reveal the organisation of mining activity. The source of water power for pumping and winding shafts was not always available close at hand. Remote waterwheels often drove lines of flat rods which transmitted power over considerable distances to these shafts, and the gullies in which the rods ran can often be traced back to disused wheelpits. Bucking floors and primitive buddles at the shaft head indicate rough dressing to eliminate the more obvious waste material before the ore was taken elsewhere for powered crushing and concentration. Many lead mines have rows of ore bins where the ore raised by each gang of miners could be kept separate, reflecting a system of payment by result which continued even on large concerns (Plate 13). Smelting mills are rarely found in association with individual mining or dressing sites but more often served a group of mines, indicating the sale of the ore from the mines for processing by specialists. These mills were located either near to water power or with access to adequate fuel supplies. This distribution pattern can be observed in the Yorkshire Dales National Park, where there are good survivals of smelting hearths for lead ore along various streams. Adjacent to many of the mills are barns or open-sided sheds for the storage of peat fuel. The mines themselves are scattered over a wide area, following the ore veins which had often been revealed by the hushing process. A similar analysis explains why the Cornish landscape is dominated by the remains of steam-powered mine pumping and winding engines rather than smelting mills. The county is lacking in good water-power sites, although intensive field survey in remote

*Plate 13* The row of ore storage bins at High Stoney Grooves lead mine in North Yorkshire. These were also known as bouse teams, since they served to keep separate the bouse, or ore, raised by each team of miners.

areas of, for example, Dartmoor has revealed several of the earlier blowing houses for smelting tin ores. Generally, however, the copper ores which formed the bulk of the output in the late eighteenth and early nineteenth centuries were smelted in South Wales, close to the source of fuel, and return cargoes of coal brought back to Cornwall for its steam-powered mining industry.

As can be seen, the spatial distribution of the components of the mining and smelting process required the use of a transport system. The landscape evidence suggests the continuing use of packhorses or carts which followed evenly graded tracks. In Germany, horse-drawn waggonways had served metalliferous mines since the sixteenth century whereas in Britain these were mainly used for transporting the more bulky products of coal-mining and limestone quarrying. Only rarely during the nineteenth century did larger mines group together to construct them, an example being the Redruth and Chacewater Railway in Cornwall. The greater scale of metalliferous mining activity overseas called for more extensive railway development such as the Rio Tinto Railway in southern Spain which shipped the massive pyrites deposits down to the port of Huelva. This railway also provided a link between the various open-cast workings and the dressing plants and smelters as well as several of the company settlements. The style of company housing varied from the primitive Spanish adobe-style of Alto de la Mesa which housed the local miners to the Anglicised colonial suburb of Bella Vista for the British staff, useful indicators of the hierarchy within the workforce.

Company settlements in Britain were more a feature of coal-mining than of metalliferous mining areas. Isolated metal mines provided barracks for weekday use, but the scarcity of these suggests that miners walked or rode considerable distances to work. Their home villages often expanded to house an increasing workforce, such as the single-storey whitewashed cottages built in Leadhills and Wanlockhead, high up in the Lowther Hills of southern Scotland. Settlement patterns often indicate the part-time nature of mining, the isolated cottages with large allotments showing that mining and smallholding continued to be carried out in conjunction well into the nineteenth century. The scattered cottages around Camborne and Redruth in Cornwall are the result of a deliberate policy by the landlord to improve his rather barren estate by awarding additional plots to mining tenants who made good use of their original holdings.

Analysis of the landscapes of metalliferous mining can therefore reveal a great deal about the organisation of mining and the nature of the workforce. Such analysis also indicates the extent of technological inertia in the mining industry, some regions retaining primitive but well-tried equipment long after more efficient methods were available. Study of the documentary evidence alone is entirely misleading, since the need to impress shareholders often led to the publication of glowing accounts of technological innovation which field evidence often indicates were totally unfounded. Industrial archaeology has greatly refined our understanding of past metalliferous mining by revealing the extent of continuity as well as change.

## Landscapes of the textile industries

A similar understanding of the extent of continuity, as opposed to change, and the unreliability of documentary evidence, has also been the result of industrial archaeological work carried out in the textile industries. The manufacture of textiles in Britain has, like metalliferous mining, a long history of being carried out as a domestic industry in conjunction with agriculture. In the late Middle Ages, woollen manufacture became an industry serving both home and foreign markets with regional areas of specialisation. Systems of industrial production developed which were nevertheless still based upon home manufacture. Only in the course of the eighteenth century was power applied to specific processes within the industry, initiating a system of factory production which affected not only woollens but also silk and linen. The innovative cotton industry was organised in a factory system from its inception and created new areas of textile manufacture. But study of the landscape would suggest that these developments were not uniform throughout each branch of the industry and that there were considerable regional variations in the pace of change. It is, however, primarily in the textile industries that new forms of industrial organisation were introduced which in turn brought about change in the settlement pattern of many regions of Britain.

One of the best surviving landscapes of the textile industry is that of West Yorkshire, specialising largely in woollens and worsteds with enclaves of linen and cotton production. Analysis of the landscape indicates both the changes brought about by technological innovation and the continuity of established methods. Most of the weavers' cottages are in hillside locations, often in groups around a farmhouse which were known as 'weaving folds' (Plate 14). Although some are of seventeenth-century date, others were built during the nineteenth century and emphasise the continuity of domestic-based handloom-weaving. Mills down in the valleys made use of water power, first for fulling cloth as early as the twelfth century and for carding and spinning by the end of the eighteenth. This spatial distinction between the powered and hand processes created paired settlements, with mill communities such as Hebden Bridge in the valleys and weaving villages like Heptonstall on the hilltops. This kind of pairing was gradually brought to an end in the second half of the nineteenth century by further technological innovation as steam power replaced water power and integrated, valley-bottom mill complexes were built which

*Plate 14* A typical weaving fold at New Tame, Delph, in the parish of Saddleworth in Greater Manchester. Around the nucleus of a seventeenth-century farmhouse, itself adapted for weaving by the insertion of long mullioned windows, a series of cottages with loomshops was added in the late eighteenth century. The three-storey building in the right foreground had a top-floor loomshop, while the 'taking-in' door on the middle floor enabled yarn to be received for weaving without intrusion into the ground-floor living quarters.

included all processes from carding to weaving and dyeing under one roof. Cotton-producing areas, such as Lancashire, present a very different landscape because of the use of the factory system from the very beginning. This helps to account for the rash of spinning mills which were built first in rural locations on the slopes of the Pennines and later on the coalfield. Even in the cotton branch, however, the presence of handloom weavers' houses of nineteenth-century date indicates that not all processes were immediately mechanised.

The spatial distribution of buildings also reveals the changes in industrial organisation within textile production. Daniel Defoe's description of the landscape between Rochdale and Halifax in 1724 suggests a pattern of scattered settlement in which a meagre subsistence from agriculture was augmented by spinning and weaving:

> the nearer we came to Halifax, we found the houses thicker, and the villages greater in every bottom; and not only so, but the sides of the hills, which were very steep in every way, were spread with houses; for the land being divided into small enclosures, from two acres to six or seven each, seldom more, every three or four pieces of land had a house belonging to them . . . hardly a house standing out of speaking distance with each other, and as the day cleared up, we could see at every house a tenter, and on every tenter a piece of cloth, kersie or shalloon.
>
> (Defoe 1724–6)

This settlement pattern can still be seen in the West Yorkshire landscape. These independent clothiers, responsible for the production of a piece of cloth from carding the fibres to weaving and finishing, made use of a network of paved packhorse tracks to transport their products to the piece halls in the larger villages and towns where their cloth was sold.

The effect of the intrusion of the entrepreneur into this system of domestic production can best be seen in the landscape of the west of England. Here, large clothiers' houses of seventeenth-century date can be found in towns such as Bradford-on-Avon and Trowbridge, from which the clothier organised a workforce of individual spinners and weavers who continued to work at home. The construction of large houses in West Yorkshire illustrates the growing prosperity of some yeoman clothiers who eventually developed a similar putting-out system to that in the west of England. The landscape evidence, however, suggests that the independent clothier continued to exist alongside the new generation of entrepreneurs who were later to finance the first water-powered textile mills. Some entrepreneurs, particularly in the cotton industry, attracted labour to the remote locations in which these mills were built by the construction of company housing. The best known of these mill villages are New Lanark in Scotland, Styal in Cheshire and a group of them in the Derwent valley of Derbyshire which owed their origins to the Arkwright and Strutt enterprises. These are whole communities with public buildings as well as housing, whereas elsewhere single rows of purpose-built weavers' houses or mill cottages suggest that speculators took advantage of the need for worker accommodation in hitherto undeveloped areas. Similar developments can be observed in the hosiery districts of the East Midlands, rows of cottages with large-windowed workshops being erected on the outskirts of villages. Their occupants operated within a similar putting-out system to that of West Yorkshire, obtaining their yarn via middle-men from urban spinning mills. Map evidence suggests a further method of financing textile workers' housing during the nineteenth century, when symmetrical terraces of cottages with cellar workshops, like the Club Houses at Horwich in Greater Manchester, were built for the workers themselves by means of a terminating building society.

Contemporary written accounts therefore clearly over-emphasise the immediate adoption of a factory system in textile production. The field evidence indicates differentials in the levels of technological progress both between the processes themselves and within the various branches of the industry. The settlement patterns in the textile districts enable the changing methods of industrial organisation to be detected, from the independent producer to the integrated factory system. Once again, the methods of the industrial archaeologist enable a more refined picture of industrial development to be presented than would be possible from documentary evidence alone.

## Townscapes

The industrial archaeologist faces a similar problem in towns to the mainstream archaeologist: the continuity of settlement in one place which makes the determination of sequence a difficult task. The stratigraphy of industrial development is often indicated through adaptations to the built environment, either to individual buildings or to their context. However, the rapid growth of towns in the industrial period placed a premium on land values and often led to the destruction of earlier phases. This has continued into the twentieth century on an even larger scale, and so the sequence of industrial development in towns can be pieced together only by a combination of fieldwork and the use of topographical sources such as maps and plans.

The continuity of settlement in towns meant that industrial undertakings had to be grafted on to pre-existing communities. Most towns had been established with a market function, resulting in the establishment of a wide range of craft industries serving the local area. These operated within the domestic environment or in small workshops where the role of human labour was more important than the availability of raw materials. The importance of human resources in the urban context continued in the period of industrialisation, many towns and cities developing specialist craft areas serving much wider markets but retaining their domestic modes of production. Workshops crammed into small spaces were a feature of cities such as London, Birmingham and Sheffield. The Spitalfields area of London still possesses many of its top-floor workshops for silk-weaving, while small, high-value goods such as watches and jewellery were produced in Clerkenwell. In Birmingham, small metal wares were manufactured in similar workshops, the most distinctive area of these being the Jewellery Quarter, where hand crafts are still practised. Other Black Country towns also produced small metal wares ranging from lorinery (for animal harness) to nails and chains, domestic workshops continuing to be built throughout the nineteenth century. Sheffield followed a similar pattern, as the manufacture of cutlery and edge tools continued within the town, often in workshops making use of a central steam engine (Plate 15).

Many towns were situated on rivers and had made use of water power for corn milling or metal-working since medieval times. During the eighteenth century,

*Plate 15* The multi-storey workshop complex known as Butcher's Wheel in Arundel Street, Sheffield, South Yorkshire. Three boilers in the courtyard supplied steam to three engines which provided power for the grinding wheels and other machinery. (See Figure 50.) RCHME © Crown Copyright.

*Plate 16* Abbey Mill, the last of the west of England woollen mills, was built in Bradford-on-Avon, Wiltshire, in 1874. It is an attractive stone building, with Gothic windows and an elaborate cornice: the original engine house can be seen on the right. The mill survived, like others in the town, through adaptive reuse for rubber manufacture and, more recently, for housing.

some of these sites were adapted for other forms of manufacture and were developed to their maximum power potential. Towns had been centres of the cloth industry in the medieval period, but this had often migrated to rural locations after the introduction of water-powered fulling. The application of water power to spinning resulted in the re-establishment of many urban cloth mills; for example, those in Stroud, Trowbridge and Bradford-on-Avon in the west of England and others on Yorkshire rivers, as in Milnsbridge and Sowerby Bridge (Plate 16). This trend to urban cloth production was intensified with the introduction of steam power to both spinning and weaving. Independence from water power meant that manufacturers could site their mills in the centres of population rather than attract the workforce to remote rural locations. The classic mill town of the north of England began to take shape, a mixture of mills, chimneys and terraced housing which has been immortalised in the paintings of L. S. Lowry. The task of the industrial archaeologist is to use both surviving physical evidence and topographical sources to chart the changes in the townscape which have been brought about by technological development.

Some towns are dominated by buildings of distinctive form which indicate the industry in which they specialised. Burton-on-Trent, for example, still retains most of the tower breweries, water storage towers and maltings which made it the centre of the British brewing industry, together with a canal and railway system which enabled the widespread distribution of its products. The towns of the Potteries area of Staffordshire, now sadly mutilated, were charac-terised by the tall curving outlines of the potkilns, both free-standing or incorporated into groups of multi-storey buildings or potbanks (Baker 1991). Their warehouses have impressive street façades to facilitate selling, with the functional area of workshops and kilns grouped around a courtyard to the rear, as, for example, at the Gladstone Pottery Museum in Longton. The monotonous rows of red-brick terraced houses interspersed with small factories in Kettering in Northamptonshire or Stafford, for example, indicate the planned layout superimposed on them by the boot and shoe manufacturers. The spatial distribution underlines the economic organisation of the industry, in which leather was cut out in the factories, distributed to back-garden workshops behind the houses and returned to the factories for finishing. The close integration of house, factory and warehouse was therefore fundamental to the boot and shoe industry (Figure 8). Knowledge of the functional forms of buildings for specific manufacturing processes therefore enables the industrial archaeologist to interpret the built environment.

The spatial patterning and styles of houses in towns can provide an insight into the type of development which has taken place. The material evidence can often be supplemented by documentary evidence in the form of maps and building plans. Areas with a considerable variety

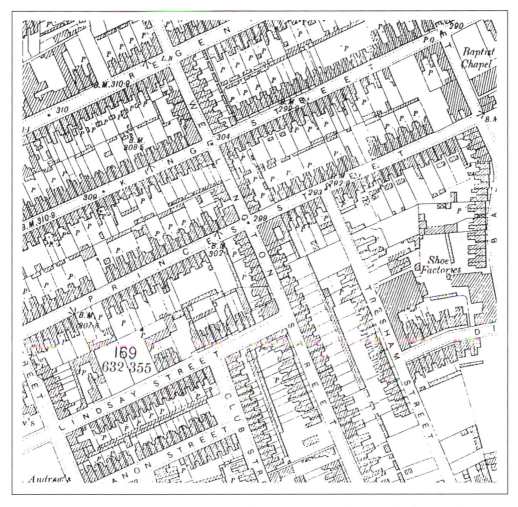

**Figure 8** An extract from the 25-inch OS map of Kettering showing the urban landscape in the 1880s. Rows of terraced houses are interspersed with small factories in which leather was cut out, whilst outworkers stitched shoe uppers in workshops against back-yard walls. The layout illustrates the continuation of domestic alongside factory production.(Sheet XXV.10, 1886)

of housing, including courts with narrow street access, can indicate the infilling of the gardens and orchards of larger properties to accommodate an industrial workforce within the confines of an old-established town. In Nottingham, the refusal of the corporation to enclose the Common Fields created a land shortage which was reflected in the infamous 'rookeries' where houses and workshops were built back-to-back around alleys and courts and even above communal privies. Little now survives after recent slum clearance, but investigation of the rear elevation of rows of houses can reveal their former industrial use, often for lace manufacture. Areas with housing of uniform layout and style, on the other hand, suggest planned development. If associated with a particular industrial or transport enterprise, the development could be company housing such as that provided in Derby by the Midland Railway or by Jedediah Strutt, who provided terraced rows and cluster houses for his mill workers in both Belper and Milford in the Derwent valley. Wealthy landowners could also influence development, as in the three west Cumbrian towns of Maryport, Whitehaven and Workington where the Senhouses, Lowthers and Curwens respectively vied with each other in creating ports for the export of their coal to Ireland. The planned layout of these three towns contrasts with the organic growth of most other Cumbrian towns.

Accommodation for the majority of the industrial workforce was, however, left to the mercy of the speculative developer, who bought or leased land and erected houses for renting. The style of housing he provided could range from the squalid back-to-backs of northern towns such as Leeds to the lofty tenements so characteristic of Scottish burghs. Once building regulations were introduced in the middle of the nineteenth century, more through houses were built in terraces which made up the greater proportion of the housing stock of Victorian industrial towns. Many of these survive and the hand of individual builders can be detected by means of breaks in the terraces, together with changes in the patterns of brickwork and ornamentation and occasionally datestones. Workshops and even factories were incorporated into these speculative developments, thereby creating new industrial suburbs. Other suburbs, where the housing is dominated by large villas and semi-detached properties, indicate how the entrepreneurs and professional classes insulated themselves from the industry which provided their livelihood. Most were established on the fringes of towns once the introduction of horse-drawn trams made them accessible, such as Roundhay in Leeds, Edgbaston in Birmingham and the Park Estate in Nottingham. The spatial patterning of urban housing is therefore an important source for determining the increasing social differentiation which accompanied industrialisation.

The growth of the nineteenth-century town created new kinds of structures, the buildings and artefacts connected with public utilities. Overcrowding and pollution caused widespread disease, although the connection between infection and polluted water was not established until the middle of the century. Early attempts to supply towns with pure water emulated the pattern of Roman aqueducts, bringing water from rural areas by open conduits. These date back to the late sixteenth and early seventeenth centuries, when Drake's leat carried water from Dartmoor to Plymouth and the New River scheme supplied London from Hertfordshire. This pattern was continued in the nineteenth century with the construction of storage reservoirs in high rainfall areas and the transmission of water by pipeline. The elegance of the dams, take-off towers and treatment works associated with these schemes symbolises the Victorian attitude towards the provision of clean water. This attitude was also expressed in the large steam-powered pumping stations which were built both to extract water from the rivers above towns, as at Chelsea on the Thames, and also to tap underground aquifers. Many must have been built as

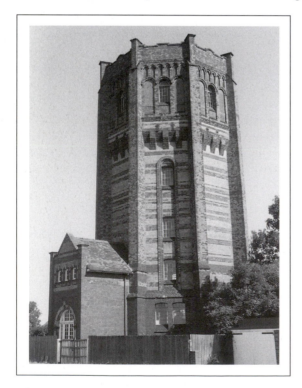

*Plate 17* An elaborate polychromatic brick water-tower at Finedon in Northamptonshire, erected 1904–5.

show-pieces for the newly created municipal undertakings. An example of the latter is the pumping station at Papplewick, built to supply Nottingham in the 1880s. The exterior is ornamented with terracotta, the windows contain stained glass and the beam engine entablatures are decorated with iron filigree work depicting aquatic plants and fish. Like many other pumping stations, the surrounding area is landscaped with open cooling ponds and filter beds arranged in geometrical patterns and the whole planted with specimen trees. The water was pumped to storage reservoirs and then flowed by gravity to Nottingham, but in flat landscapes storage towers were used, many as ornamental as the pumping stations themselves (Plate 17). The treatment of sewage required similar civil and mechanical engineering solutions, which were accorded equal architectural embellishment, as were the buildings associated with the provision of gas and electricity. The buildings serving these mundane purposes are as much a symbol of Victorian civic pride as the more visible town halls, libraries and museums.

The market charters which had led to the original foundation of many towns were also given physical expression in the Victorian era by the creation of covered market halls. The attractive pannier markets, such as those in Barnstaple and Dartmouth in Devon, were built to house the produce previously brought by local people in panniers or baskets to be sold on the streets of the town. Elsewhere, large halls of glass and iron construction accommodated the market stalls previously erected in the open air. These were general markets, but others had a specialist function, such as the row of thirty-three shops known as Butchers Row, built in Barnstaple in 1855 and retaining the age-old tradition of grouping butchers' shops in 'shambles', as in York. Specialist wholesale markets were constructed in major distribution centres, such as Covent Garden fruit, Billingsgate fish and Smithfield meat markets in London. Industrial products needed similar outlets, the first of which were probably the cloth halls of the Yorkshire Pennines where the individual yeoman clothiers sold their cloth to merchants. The earliest date from the seventeenth century, but the most splendid survival is the Halifax Piece Hall dating from 1779. As the scale of production grew, equally elaborate structures were designed to attract buyers, both home and overseas. Good examples are the worsted warehouses in the Little Germany quarter of Bradford, the Lace Market in Nottingham and the cotton warehouses of Manchester (Plate 18). In many industries, urban warehouses performed the central function of distributing raw materials to domestic outworkers and collecting finished goods. They therefore symbolise the maintenance of the relationship between the town and its hinterland which had characterised towns since their foundation.

This relationship was further fostered by improvements in the transport network. Because of

*Plate 18* The warehouse built for Thomas Adams, a Nottingham lace manufacturer, one of several in the Lace Market. It was designed by a well-known local architect, T. C. Hine, with the intention of impressing visiting buyers, but also incorporated lace-finishing rooms in the attic storey, together with welfare facilities for the workforce.

its administrative and market function, the town had always been the focus of communications and this was usually enhanced when new methods of transport were introduced in the eighteenth and nineteenth centuries. The improvement of the parish-maintained road systems by turnpiking only served to direct traffic into towns, where large numbers of coaching inns and stables met the travellers' needs. Carriers' carts distributing goods to the surrounding neighbourhood were also based upon the inns. Tollhouses provide some visual indication of the existence of previous turnpike roads, although most have been swept away in redevelopment and rural examples are more common (Plate 19). In towns, they were situated at busy junctions like the stone-built Cainscross tollhouse which still survives at Stroud in Gloucestershire. The turnpikes leading out of towns created a framework for urban expansion. New link roads between them provided access for new housing and factories, often in a gridiron layout very different from the still medieval pattern of the town centres. Many of these remained unchanged and consequently congested until the twentieth century, encouraging new suburban industrial development. A good example of this type of growth is the quarter in north Stafford between the turnpikes to Stone and Eccleshall, where an integrated landscape of terraced housing and shoe factories can still be found.

A prime objective of many canal proposals was to pass through industrial towns. The Leeds and Liverpool Canal forced a route through the Pennines by means of daring engineering to link the Yorkshire woollen towns of Leeds, Shipley and Skipton with the Lancashire cotton towns of Burnley, Blackburn and Chorley and the port of Liverpool. Such direct links were not always possible because of topographical considerations but canal companies constructed branches to towns off the main routes. Examples of industrial towns served in this way were Bradford, Coventry, Leek and Stockport. The urban canals had a dramatic effect on the townscape in terms both of the routes they took and the buildings attracted to their banks. The Leeds and Liverpool Canal entered Burnley by means of an embankment almost a mile long before passing through a canyon of tall textile mills built on either side. Warehouses sprang up on canal banks to store goods for distribution and shipment, as at Shardlow on the Trent and Mersey Canal in Derbyshire.

Canals brought coal to the towns much more cheaply than before, resulting in the sudden growth of steam-powered corn mills, textile mills, breweries and iron foundries, often situated by the canal for convenience. In Loughborough, where the price of coal dropped by a half when the Soar Navigation was opened in 1778, worsted spinning mills and iron foundries developed on the banks. The later extension to Leicester around the rapidly developing town gave it a new eastern boundary, the area being infilled by houses and factories. The canals themselves promoted whole new towns, such

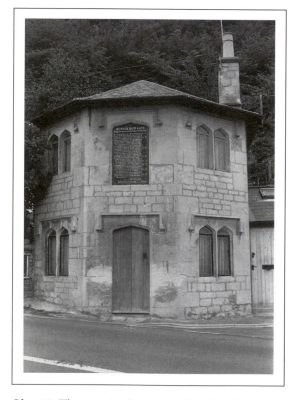

*Plate 19* The attractive Butterrow toll-collector's house at Rodborough in Gloucestershire. The octagonal house, built of local ashlar, is complete with its toll-board showing the authorised rates. It was built *circa* 1825 for the new turnpike road from Bowbridge, on the Thames and Severn Canal, up to Rodborough.

as Stourport where the Staffordshire and Worcestershire Canal linked to the navigable River Severn. The small town was centred around basins fringed with warehouses, timber and boat-building yards and a series of locks giving access to the river. The planned town of Goole in south Yorkshire grew up on drained marshland in the early nineteenth century to act as a terminal for coal exports brought down the Aire and Calder Navigation. The cranes and tub boat hoists on the docks dominate the flat landscape of the town.

The widespread development of railways in the mid-nineteenth century involved their super-imposition on what were by then large settlements, often with dramatic effects. Where the terrain was difficult, the railway was taken through towns by viaducts, tunnels or cuttings. Particularly dramatic is the viaduct dominating the Cheshire town of Stockport, with textile mills nestling beneath its arches on the banks of the River Mersey. The North Midland Railway passed through the recently laid-out textile community of Belper by means of a deep cutting which involved ten overbridges in a mile for the grid pattern of streets. At the end of the nineteenth century, the Great Central Railway faced in Nottingham a fully developed town. In order to have its station in the centre, the company was involved in wholesale demolition of property, boring tunnels and making deep cuttings before its line could go on to London on a long blue-brick viaduct across the Trent floodplain. This sequence of events can be traced on the early editions of large-scale Ordnance Survey maps as well as on the ground, and the situation was replicated in many other English towns and cities. The railways also sterilised large areas of towns with their vast land requirements for goods and carriage sidings, locomotive sheds and warehouses, as can still be seen in the town of Derby.

On the other hand, the power and prestige of railway companies were symbolised by the new build-ings they added to the townscape. Many urban railway stations were built in monumental style, like the vast classical structure in Huddersfield or the Gothic edifices of Shrewsbury and Bristol stations. The increasing number of travellers needed accommodation, and rail-way companies were responsible for the construction of large hotels such as the Jacobean North Stafford

*Plate 20* The North Staffordshire Railway Company contributed this Jacobean-style station to the townscape of Stoke-on-Trent in 1850. On the opposite side of Winton Square is their prestigious hotel, while the adjacent railwaymen's houses are in a similar style.

Hotel in Stoke-on-Trent, in the same style as the railway station (Plate 20). The army of railway workers also needed housing, and its provision created new settlements on a scale far greater than had been the case with canals. Railway housing was distinctive both in style, often peculiar to a particular company, and in construction, since the transportation of materials from outside the region presented no difficulty. The Great Western Railway created a separate suburb in the Wiltshire town of Swindon for its workforce, together with vast engineering works, and similar developments can be found elsewhere.

Studies of the evolution of the cultural landscape all too often make only passing mention of industrialisation, regarding it as destructive of an idealised rural environment. W. G. Hoskins, for example, saw the whole process of large-scale industrialisation as the replacement of a qualitative culture by a quantitative one: in Wigston Magna, the subject of *The Midland Peasant*, by 1901 fifteen times as many families could get their living off the same area of land than had been possible in the fourteenth century, but he felt that the essential nature of the community had been lost. But, as Hoskins himself acknowledged in his later work, industry had long been integrated into the rural environment. Corn and fulling mills were clustered along rivers, while streams powered blast furnaces and forges, themselves linked by sledways to charcoal-burning sites concealed within the woodlands. Many industrial structures were sited to take advantage of natural features such as gradients or the direction of the prevailing wind, while the dispersed pattern of settlement ensured that most available natural resources like brick clay and limestone were worked locally on a small scale.

From the late seventeenth century onwards, the pace of change increased and wholly industrial landscapes began to evolve, both rural and urban, as indicated in this chapter. Unattractive as these may appear to people who feel that landscape should be an aesthetically pleasing experience, we cannot ignore their existence if we are using the landscape as a means of determining change in the human condition. The barracks of an isolated mine or quarry; a weaving hamlet high up in the Pennines; a planned company village – these are as indicative of a type of human existence as the more generally recognised archaeological monuments of settlement such as Skara Brae on Orkney or Chysauster in Cornwall, and need to be recognised as such.

## Chapter Three

# Buildings, structures and machinery

The essence of industrial archaeology in the 1960s was the need to protect a selection of buildings and other structures associated with early industrialisation. The lack of any established criteria for the selection process has led to the preservation of a random sample of industrial buildings, often those containing prime movers or being associated with key people or events. The establishment of survey programmes to create national inventories is attempting to make the selection process more representative of the whole range of industries, but the emphasis is still on the preservation of monuments rather than the scientific study of industrial buildings and structures in order to learn more about their technological and social contexts.

Industrial buildings are the visible symbol of the processes of production in both space and time. The analysis of these buildings requires the use of the archaeological concepts of function, context and typology. The industrial archaeologist has to learn to recognise the buildings characteristic of particular industries in order to determine their function. For an individual building, its function may be ascertained both by examining its form and by considering its topographical context. Once the purpose of a building has been determined, then its relative date can be established by placing it within a known typological sequence as with any other archaeological artefact. The final stage of the analysis involves the study of the building in its cultural context, attempting to understand its symbolism in terms of power structures and employer–worker relationships within the industry with which it was associated.

The procedure outlined above represents the ideal, and should always be attempted. Inevitably, however, the reality is far more complex than it may first appear. Whereas the function of many industrial buildings, such as potbanks and malthouses, is immediately obvious, others, particularly factory buildings, were adaptable to alternative processes and frequently served several functions in their useful life: their cultural meanings therefore changed over time. The topographical context of buildings may have changed drastically as a result of, for example, open-cast mining, derelict land clearance or wholesale demolition of their built environment. Often a single building or structure survives, devoid of its ancillaries, like Washington 'F' Pit winding engine house and head gear in Tyne and Wear or the Catcliffe glass cone near Sheffield, which have been retained as monuments amid new housing developments. Few typological sequences for industrial buildings have yet been established, and those which have tend to be regional in their application, such as the Cornwall Archaeological Unit's Engine House Assessment (Sharpe *et al.* 1991), or a recent survey of Dorset lime-kiln types (Stanier 1993). The rate at which new technology was diffused varied regionally, affected by levels of capital investment and individual entrepreneurship (Palmer and Neaverson 1989). The current development of listing criteria for industrial buildings should go some way towards creating typological sequences which, used with care, will correct the previous random selection and enable classes of building to be better understood.

Many industrial buildings constructed after the middle of the eighteenth century contained both prime movers, like waterwheels and steam engines, and machinery for production processes, such as carding and weaving. Only rarely do the machines survive *in situ*: most have been dismantled for scrap although some have found their way to industrial museums, where they are rarely displayed in any typological sequence or realistic context. An understanding of the development of machinery can be derived from technical literature but the problem for the industrial archaeologist is to understand the type of machinery originally installed and the way in which the building was designed to accommodate it. The increasing weight and size of, for example, textile and boot and shoe machinery were instrumental in the changing designs of factories, particularly the move into single-storey sheds in the later nineteenth century. In the case of prime movers, the system for the transmission of power to the individual machines was also important and has rarely been studied, with some notable exceptions (e.g. Stratton and Trinder 1988; Calladine 1993; Williams 1993). It is only by relating established technological sequences to surviving buildings and structures that their form and function can be fully understood.

The remainder of this chapter will consider some classes of industrial buildings to illustrate the essential relationship between form, function, context and change through time. Space does not permit the consideration of the whole range of industrial buildings, but the methodology suggested is applicable beyond the examples given.

## KILNS AND FURNACES

One of the most widespread types of structure surviving from the industrial period was concerned with effecting chemical changes in materials by means of heat. Kilns and furnaces were built to transform clay into bricks, tiles and pottery; limestone into lime or cement; metallic ores into pure metal and a variety of raw materials into glass. The actual difference between kilns and furnaces is difficult to define, but generally the structures used for smelting metals or melting glass are referred to as furnaces while those needing less heat for processing clay and limestone, etc. are referred to as kilns. The structures were of necessity robust, particularly iron furnaces which had continuously to withstand high temperatures – up to 1600°C in some cases. This temperature could be achieved only by means of an artificially created draught and so their location was determined by available power sources, especially water, as well as the local supply of fuel and an adequate transport network for bulky materials.

The form of kilns varied according to the type of material being processed but also developed over time, generally changing from an intermittent to a continuous mode of working. The form of furnaces underwent a similar development but was more affected by the use of different fuel supplies and power sources, which also resulted in considerable changes in their distribution. The typological development of kilns and furnaces reflects the increasing sophistication of society, which generated a demand for variety as well as increased quantity of goods. The transition to continuous production created a full-time workforce, unlike the earlier intermittent production which enabled the labourer to put in some time at the kiln when other agricultural work permitted. Nevertheless, primitive forms of both kilns and furnaces survived in some areas, presumably whilst they remained economically viable.

The post-medieval production of bricks and tiles was accelerated both by shortages of structural timber and by improvements to the transport network, particularly the development of river navigations and canals for the transport of heavy goods. Paradoxically, however, the growth of canals, and also railways, stimulated the most primitive form of brick production by the use of clamps on the sites of new structures such as bridges, tunnels and aqueducts. The clamps survive only as burnt areas or earthworks but are often associated with overgrown or water-logged clay pits; for example, those beside the Grand Union Canal south of Leicester. There are documentary references to the use of clamps as late as the construction of the Great Central Railway in the last decade of the nineteenth century. Generally, though, during the eighteenth and early nineteenth centuries, bricks and tiles were made in permanent, but still intermittent, kilns in forms which ranged from the circular beehive kiln to the rectangular Scotch kiln and its variants (Figure 9). The Scotch kiln, which continued in use in smaller brickworks well into the twentieth century, had no permanent roof and the green bricks were covered with turves for each firing cycle. The robustness of the kiln structures has led to their survival whereas the ancillary buildings which surrounded them have disappeared in many cases. These included the clay-preparation, brick-making and drying sheds such as those which still exist at the South Cove brickworks in Suffolk. Horse power, driving edge runners and roller mills, was often used for grinding the clay and the circular horse track may still remain. Examples of the actual machinery are rare, but a horse capstan and roller mill survive, together with a Scotch kiln, at Ticknall on the Calke Abbey estate in Derbyshire.

Steam power replaced the horse on larger brickworks during the nineteenth century. Hand-moulding processes were superseded by wire-cut and machine-moulded bricks, whose uniformity of appearance helps to account for the monotony of the terraced rows of nineteenth-century urban expansion. Chimneys became a feature of large brickworks, partly for the steam boilers and partly for the new continuous kilns introduced in the 1850s to meet the increasing demand. The most common of these was the Hoffman, usually circular or elliptical in plan, in which a series of chambers were arranged round a central flue so that the firing process proceeded sequentially from chamber to chamber, the heat from cooling bricks being used to pre-heat the green bricks (Figure 9). These have generally been replaced by continuous tunnel kilns where the bricks travel on trolleys through the kiln, but the characteristic form of Hoffman kilns can still be found, a good example surviving as part of the mining museum at Prestongrange in East Lothian, Scotland. Brick- and tile-making were frequently associated with coal-mining during the nineteenth century and many collieries ran their own brickworks.

Until the advent of the tunnel kiln, brick-making demanded hard, physical labour in all aspects, from the digging of clay through the hand-moulding of bricks to the loading and unloading of the kilns. The workforce was generally male, although after the mid-nineteenth-century Acts forbidding women to work in coal mines, many of them transferred to the equally arduous, but less politically emotive, environment of the brickworks. Shift work meant that they had to live close at hand, and large brick companies built housing estates for their labourers, thereby establishing a reliable rather than a shifting workforce.

Beehive kilns had been used for firing pottery since the Middle Ages, but the distinctive form of the bottle oven was introduced in the eighteenth century to reach the temperatures necessary to fire glazes. Bottle ovens are double-skinned structures, the outer cover or hovel enclosing the inner oven in which the pottery was placed. As with brick production, ancillary buildings were required for preparation and these were usually grouped around the kilns in a complex known as a potbank. In some cases, the kilns were incorporated within buildings and only the protruding necks betrayed their presence. Kiln bases of this type have been excavated within complexes used for making ceramic tiles in the Ironbridge Gorge, and a classic potbank has been preserved in nearby Coalport. By far the largest concentration of potbanks was in the Potteries area of Staffordshire, and some of those which still exist have been recorded by RCHME (Plate 21) (Baker 1991). They were often situated on the banks of canals since water was ideally suited for the transport of the fragile product. RCHME also recorded much of the extensive terraced housing in the 'six towns' of the Potteries, where in the mid-nineteenth century many of the

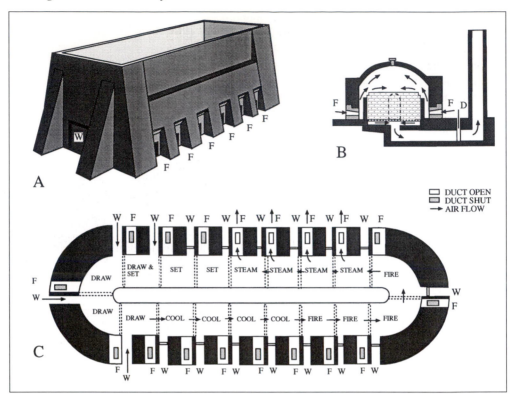

*Figure 9* Some common types of brick-kiln.

(A) A typical Scotch intermittent kiln. This updraught brick-kiln was open-topped and rectangular in plan with apertures or wickets (W) in either end for loading and unloading. The side walls, tapered from top to bottom, had a series of fire grates (F) at the base. The green bricks were stacked with air gaps between them, the wickets bricked up and the charge covered during firing. The initial slow firing (*circa* 3 days) dried the bricks, the temporary roof was then removed and the draught increased for faster burning (2–3 days), after which the fires were allowed to burn out, all air supply was cut off and the bricks allowed to cool (7–10 days) before being removed from the kiln.

(B) Section of a beehive downdraught kiln. This circular kiln was smaller but more controllable and was used to produce better-quality bricks. Heat from the fire grates (F) was directed upwards and deflected by the domed roof down through the stacked bricks. Several kilns were often connected to a common chimney stack.

(C) Plan of a Hoffman continuous kiln showing the firing sequence. Each chamber has its own wicket (W) and fire grate (F) and is separated from the next by means of a temporary partition. A chimney is used to pull air through the kiln. This air is pre-heated by cooling bricks before entering the chambers being fired; the hot air then steam-heats the green bricks ready for firing, thereby increasing the efficiency of the kiln.

workforce lived in appalling squalor in an atmosphere polluted by the very industry in which they worked. Both men and women were involved, since many of the tasks required dexterity rather than sheer physical strength, especially in the decorating departments. The novels of Arnold Bennett help in understanding the original cultural context of the potbanks, since their present role is as memorials to a vanished manufacturing process.

Visually, and even archaeologically, it is easy to confuse the physical evidence of the pottery industry with that of glass manufacture. The production of glass required similar high temperatures both to melt the raw materials in a special crucible and to maintain the glass in a molten state for blowing or moulding. Medieval glass production was based in woodland areas, such as the Weald of Kent and Sussex (Crossley 1994) but the transition to coal as a fuel during the seventeenth century resulted in the gradual relocation of the industry to coalfield areas. The use of coal also resulted in changes to the form of the furnace, with the fire directly below the crucibles and draught provided by underground flues. Sometime in the eighteenth century, the furnace was covered by a cone similar to that of a bottle oven although much larger in diameter and height, and the resulting structure was known as a glass-house. In a bottle oven, there is little space between the hovel and the inner kiln, whereas in a glass-house the space between the outer cone and the inner furnace formed the working area. The overall diameter of the glass-house seems to have been about twice that of the bottle oven. A good surviving example is at the Red House glassworks near Stourbridge, where the preserved glass-house has a diameter of 18.5 metres [60.5 feet] and a height of 30.5 metres [100 feet]: the glass furnace itself is 7.6 metres [24.6 feet] diameter giving a

*Plate 21* The courtyard of the Gladstone Pottery at Longton in Staffordshire, now the Gladstone Pottery Museum. The potbank includes kilns which are both free-standing and incorporated within workshops. RCHME, © Crown Copyright.

working space around it 5.4 metres wide [18 feet]. There were arches in the outer cone which gave access to other areas, including an annealing kiln or lehr and a glory hole or small furnace for re-heating glassware during working. The crucibles were pre-heated in a separate furnace in the pot arch. The now cool and sanitised interior of the Red House cone does not enable the visitor to appreciate the incessant activity inside a working glass-house, as blobs of molten glass had to be taken from the crucibles to the craftsmen as quickly as possible to prevent them from cooling. The heat must have become unbearable at times, and beer shops were an essential part of the environment of a glassworks.

The huge glass cones were unstable and many collapsed, and so the glass-house developed into a much more anonymous structure in the form of a large multi-storey building with a central chimney to which the furnaces were connected. A glassworks, like a potbank, was a complex of numerous buildings whose purpose can often be deduced from large-scale maps and engravings.

An iron furnace fulfils a similar function to a glass furnace in attaining high temperatures to reduce the ores to metallic iron. First introduced into Britain in the fifteenth century, the blast furnace was basically a substantial stone-built structure of square section with an interior firebrick-lined shaft tapering downwards to a crucible in which the molten iron collected. The necessary temperature to produce molten iron could be reached only by means of an artificial blast of air, usually provided by water-powered bellows or cylinders driven from an adjacent waterwheel. The base of the furnace contained two or three arches, one or two of which contained tuyères through which the air blast was piped into the furnace and the other of which served to tap off the molten iron. The furnace was usually built against a bank or provided with a bridge by means of which the charge could be fed into the top of the shaft. These features can all be seen at Duddon Furnace in the southern Lake District, which continued operation until 1867 (see Plate 35 and Figure 27). A similarly well-preserved furnace remains at Bonawe near Oban in Scotland. Their woodland location was typical of early blast furnaces because of the need of charcoal as a fuel, which was stored, along with iron ore, in large barns. The existence of most upstanding early blast furnaces in Britain is now known (Riden 1993) but some were reused for other purposes. At Guns Mills in the Forest of Dean, a seventeenth-century iron furnace was transformed into a paper mill and capped with a timbered building but its original structure is still obvious. The continuous operating cycle of the blast furnace required constant supervision and so the workforce needed to be close at hand. There is evidence of settlement at both Duddon and Bonawe, for example, but the best-preserved early charcoal ironworks settlement is probably that associated with Hopewell Furnace in Pennsylvania which remained in operation from 1771 to 1883.

The iron industry in Britain, like other similar undertakings, was forced to seek alternative sources of fuel because of the dearth of wood from the seventeenth century onwards (see Figure 5). The use of coke became practicable from the middle of the eighteenth century and water power for blowing was replaced by steam power, resulting in larger furnaces located near coal-fields. Large blowing engine houses became part of the ironworks complex, supplying banks of

*Plate 22* The Sloss Ironworks in Birmingham, Alabama, USA, which have been preserved by the city as a National Historic Landmark. The works were founded in the 1880s although these two furnaces date from 1927 and 1931. The mechanical charging conveyor can be seen on the right-hand furnace, where the attached casting hall has been converted into an auditorium. The six cylindrical hot blast stoves dominate the scene.

blast furnaces rather than single ones, as can be seen at Blists Hill in the Ironbridge Gorge or Blaenafon in South Wales. At the latter site, too, the living as well as the working environment of the ironworker can be appreciated in the form of Stack Square, three rows of terraced houses which were once grouped around the main chimney stack for the complex. These houses, together with Engine Row, date from the 1790s and symbolise the change in living conditions for the workforce made necessary by continuous production. Lowe has suggested that their generous size indicates that the houses were in fact built for the foremen and craftsmen whose presence was essential to the working of the furnaces (Lowe 1977: 9) and for whom the immediate environment of their living quarters was a necessary evil.

The introduction of hot blast in the early nineteenth century resulted in additional structures within the ironworks, most notably the cylindrical heat exchanger stoves with their associated pipe-work. By this time, many of the furnaces themselves were steel-cased rather than masonry structures, charged by means of mechanised conveyors. The furnace was now only one element in an integrated complex which included casting houses, rolling mills and stores, all served by a railway network. Because of their sheer scale, many of these complexes have been demolished following the decline of the industry and only the housing which formerly accommodated the workforce remains. Attempts have been made both in Europe and the USA to retain examples of this generation of ironworks structures as icons to the era of heavy industry (Plate 22), but in Britain most have been swept away in attempts to re-create the more rural landscape which, in modern eyes, is a more acceptable image of the past.

Other types of furnaces were used to turn wrought iron into steel which was in demand for edge tools, weapons and springs. Wrought iron was converted into blister steel in a cementation furnace, resembling a pottery kiln in shape. The wrought-iron bars were packed into chests with charcoal and heated with a coal fire, the wrought iron absorbing sufficient carbon to produce blister steel. For better-quality steel, the product was then re-melted in a crucible furnace in a process which distributed the carbon throughout the steel. This was achieved by placing broken bars of blister steel in special crucibles which were heated to high temperatures in a coke fire.

To create the necessary draught, tall rectangular chimney stacks were used which, along with the conical stacks of the cementation furnaces, produced the fumes which once blackened the city of Sheffield. The rural settings of the surviving cementation furnace at Derwentcote in County Durham (Plate 23), in the care of English Heritage, and the Abbeydale crucible steelworks on the outskirts of Sheffield give a misleading impression of the true nature of the steel industry, which for the majority of the workforce was far from being a rural idyll.

The smelting of non-ferrous metals has also left structural remains in the archaeological record. Generally, non-ferrous metals required lower temperatures than iron for the

*Plate 23* Derwentcote cementation furnace in County Durham after restoration by English Heritage. The central furnace, which had two chests in which wrought iron was converted to blister steel, is flanked by buildings providing work space and charcoal storage.

half a mile up a hillside were constructed both to remove the fumes from the vicinity of the smelt mill and to condense the vaporised lead. This could be retrieved only by manual labour, and the size of many of the flues suggests that children were sent through to scrape off the solidified lead. The isolated nature of the smelt mills meant that the fate of these children did not attract the same public sympathy as chimney-sweeps' boys and little documentary evidence survives. The mills were usually located in valleys to make use of water power. Most were built of stone, as were the large peat barns which were normally open-sided to allow the peat to dry. In the Pennines, the smelt mills continued in use long after the introduction of the cupola elsewhere and so there are several good survivals. For example, Old Gang and Surrender mills have been excavated and consolidated by the Yorkshire Dales National Park (Plate 24). The peat store at the former is marked by two rows of rubble pillars which once supported the roof. The smelt mill at Surrender contains several hearths whose flues unite in one long flue on the hillside to the rear. At both Old Gang and Surrender mills, the original flues were lengthened and new chimneys built, presumably to improve the condensation of the lead vapour. Our knowledge of these and many other ruinous smelt mills in this area is greatly enriched by the pioneering recording work of R. T. Clough, carried out in the 1940s and 1950s (1962, 1980). The most complete hearths to survive are those which have been restored at Wanlockhead in Dumfriesshire.

As with tin-smelting, the ore hearth was replaced in some areas by the reverberatory furnace or cupola using coal. The furnaces were contained in stone or brick buildings, but can be differentiated from other reverberatory furnaces by the multiple flue systems associated with them which served for condensing any vaporised lead. There are fewer remains of cupolas than ore hearths, the best survivals being at Alport and Stonedge in Derbyshire, the latter claiming to have the oldest industrial chimney in existence, dating from *circa* 1770 (Willies 1991).

The smelting of copper was a more complex process than that required for tin or lead, partly because of its higher melting point and partly because of the complex sulphide ores which required several treatments to produce the refined metal. There are no substantial remains in Britain of the water-powered shaft furnaces, which were replaced by reverberatories in the late seventeenth century. These were situated close to coalfields, the earliest being in Bristol with other sites in Cornwall, Cheshire, Staffordshire and the Swansea valley in South Wales. The only real archaeological evidence for their existence is the slag blocks incorporated into walls; for example, in the docks in Hayle and the houses of Vivianstown in Swansea. In the Swansea valley, where the greater proportion of Cornish copper ore was smelted, widespread damage was caused by fumes from the process and the total clearance of this area in the Swansea Valley Project was in itself an act charged with symbolic meaning. Only documentary and pictorial evidence can attest to former copper-smelting activities. Pure copper itself was too soft for many practical purposes but alloyed well with other metals, particularly with tin to produce bronze and with zinc to produce brass. The former, so important in prehistoric times, had ceased to have much practical value by the post-medieval period apart from its use for bell metal. Bronze had largely been replaced by brass, which could be cast, drawn into wire or beaten into vessels. The latter was carried out in battery works, the most characteristic structure of which was the annealing furnace in which the vessels were heated to relieve stresses created during hammering. The surviving furnaces in the Bristol area at Saltford and Kelston are tapering square stone stacks about 10 metres [33 feet] high with open arches for charging and firing on opposite sides of the base. On the charging side a long slot above the arch allowed the vertical movement of a counter-balance arm which controlled the firebrick-lined door. Brass manufacture was also carried out in other areas of Britain and fragmentary remains may be found in Staffordshire and the Greenfield Valley of Clwyd (Day 1973, 1991).

The largest surviving class of kilns is that concerned with the roasting of stone to change its chemical composition and enable further processing. This involved the removal of moisture and impurities such as sulphur and phosphorus and carbonaceous matter to reduce the bulk of materials prior to transport elsewhere. Most iron ores were roasted, which could just be carried out in heaps in the orefield. More efficient, and less environmentally damaging, were roasting kilns which ranged from structures like small brick kilns to large hoppers with steel shutters such as those which remain in ruins at Rosedale in the North York Moors. Coal was transformed into coke in a similar manner and large batteries of beehive ovens were a feature of many coalfields. Their ephemeral nature has meant that few survive, but a range of top-loading coke ovens near Rowlands Gill in Tyne and Wear has been scheduled. Small kilns were also used for shattering the crystalline structure of flint before grinding for use in pottery-making. These were similar to the lime-kilns discussed below, brick or stone structures containing a bowl-shaped pot with a draw arch at the base through which the burnt flints were removed. The flints were layered in the pot with small coal and burnt for several days, but required grinding before use for strengthening and whitening pottery. An interesting survival is the flint-grinding mill at Cheddleton in Staffordshire, where flint transported along the canal system from East Anglia was unloaded into brick-lined kilns set in the bank of the Caldon Canal. Bone, another constituent of pottery which required grinding, was treated in a similar manner to flint and the Etruscan Bone and Flint Mill at Etruria, also in Staffordshire, combined both processes. The calcined flint and bone were mixed with water before grinding to lessen the amount of dust, which was injurious to health, and so small drying kilns form part of a grinding mill complex, often with square or circular stacks which can easily be mistaken for the pottery kilns themselves.

By far the most widespread kind of kiln was that used for calcining limestone, chalk or even sea shells to produce quicklime which was in great demand both for agriculture and for the making of mortar, especially during the nineteenth century. These were basically larger versions of the flint kiln described above, but often had more than one draw hole within one or more draw arches. The pot was usually brick-lined and could be sunk into the ground or built within a brick or stone structure (Figure 11). Since the pot was charged from above, it was convenient to locate the kiln on a quarry bench or against a bank so that both the pot and draw arch were accessible. It was essential to keep burnt lime dry owing to its violent reaction with water to form slaked lime. For this reason, many draw arches were of large size to protect the product and might even contain pits or blind arches for storage. In banks of kilns, the draw arches often opened into a continuous covered way for removal of the lime. In East Anglia, a particular type of kiln evolved in which the draw holes of a single kiln opened into an annular underground chamber with an arch leading to the outside.

The spatial distribution of lime-kilns is partly related to geology, the

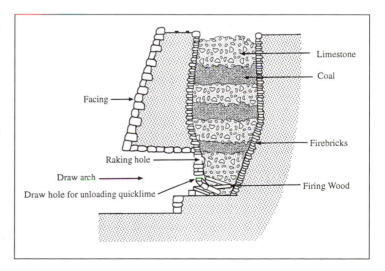

*Figure 11* A section of a lime-kiln built against a bank, allowing ease of charging and emptying the kiln.

majority of kilns being built in limestone or chalk areas. However, lime was badly needed for agricultural purposes on other types of soil, particularly the sandy heathlands brought into cultivation at the time of the Enclosure Acts passed by Parliament in the late eighteenth and early nineteenth centuries. Because quicklime was corrosive, limestone or chalk was often burnt where it was needed and so the distribution of kilns is also related to the transport network. Every small harbour in south-west England and Wales had its lime-kiln, many of them now preserved as landscape features. Similarly, kilns were built by the roadside, on the banks of navigable rivers or canals and later beside railways. These means of transport were also used for bringing in fuel for the kilns, usually small coal, and some collieries set up kilns especially to use their slack coal.

The form of lime-kilns developed in a similar fashion to other kilns, moving from a single intermittent kiln to a battery of kilns in continuous operation. Lime-burning became a full-time task, as can be seen from nineteenth-century census returns. However, local needs ensured the survival of the intermittent field kiln, worked by farm labourers as part of their normal routine, into the twentieth century. Its form varied with regional preference and so it is difficult to classify intermittent kilns into types, although attempts have been made using the criteria of number and style of draw arches (Stanier 1993) and the profile of pots and hearth shapes (Marshall, Palmer and Neaverson 1992). Continuous kilns, often known as draw kilns, were introduced in the late eighteenth century to meet increased demand. Their pots were lined with firebrick or hard stone to withstand long firing cycles. Most were built in groups, usually either at quarries or beside the transport network, and often have elaborate arrangements for charging and unloading the kilns. The latter included water-powered inclines, remains of which can still be seen at Moorswater in Cornwall and at Closeburn in Dumfriesshire (Clarke 1987), and ramps incorporating railways with tracks for tipper trucks at the kiln mouths. A good example of a rail-fed system can be seen at Millers Dale in Derbyshire beside the old Midland Railway to Manchester, now consolidated and interpreted by the Peak District National Park. These larger kilns usually had fire grates at the base of the pots and iron doors to the draw holes to control the draught. A group of kilns at Charleston harbour in Fife preserves these features. Some batteries of kilns, such as those at Marsden in Tyne and Wear, illustrate a typological sequence of kilns on a single site. The final stage in the development of continuous kilns was the adaptation of the Hoffman brick kiln for lime-burning. These were generally located in large quarries and examples may be found at Llanymynech beside the Montgomeryshire Canal and at Langcliffe beside the Settle to Carlisle railway (Trueman 1992).

Some kilns were developed for special purposes, such as the chalk-kilns of the North Downs which were free-standing, tower-like structures rather than the conventional type. These made use of forced draught and powdered fuel, a technique also adopted in twentieth-century lime-burning where the Hoffman kiln was not used. A superb, although under-researched, collection of these kilns survives

*Plate 25* A sophisticated conical lime-kiln at Sulejow in Poland, which was at work until the 1980s. The kiln was charged by means of a lift in the adjacent concrete tower.

at Sulejow and Rudniki in Poland, a typological study in themselves (Plate 25). These kilns were built alongside the railway network, and doubtless in eastern Europe many more examples remain to be discovered.

The manufacture of cement from argillaceous limestone demanded higher temperatures and so kilns resembling bottle ovens were built, especially along the Thames estuary. Some elaborate kilns of this type have been preserved at Coplay in Pennsylvania. A similar type of kiln was used for calcining sea shells in the Netherlands, a country badly in need of lime manure but lacking limestone. A group of bottle kilns from Akersluit have been preserved within the Enkhuizen museum. Most British lime-kilns were unpretentious structures, but occasionally the owner asserted his individuality by incorporating decorative features such as Gothic arches on kilns at Tenby in South Wales, arches resembling traceried windows at Mellor in Derbyshire and, most elaborate of all, a battery of kilns at Llandybie in South Wales modelled in ecclesiastical style by the Victorian architect R. K. Penson. These are, however, exceptions to the normal typology of lime-kiln development which would benefit from a national recording study.

## FOOD-PROCESSING

Although the British diet was a mixed one, the processing of grain crops for bread, animal feed and drink has left more structural remains in the landscape than the processing of animal products for food. Grinding corn by means of querns was labour-intensive, and it is not surprising that this was one of the first processes to make use of forms of power other than human. The origins of the watermill and the windmill have been the subject of much debate (Kealey 1987; Holt 1988) but it is fairly certain that, although the watermill is of pre-Roman origin, the windmill in its modern form was a North European development of the twelfth century. The two worked alongside each other until the late nineteenth century, when increasing consumption led to massive imports of hard wheat. Large-scale steam mills, involving capital outlay in roller milling and dressing machinery to produce the white flour then in demand, brought about the concentration of corn milling at ports or alongside waterways or railways. Most rural watermills could not afford to re-equip and the windmill had neither the power nor the space to incorporate roller milling plant. As a result, many mills of both types have disappeared although watermills, in attractive settings, have proved amenable to conversion to residential uses.

The oldest type of watermill to survive is the horizontal wheeled mill, often known as a Greek or Norse mill. Simple in form, the upper stone is directly mounted upon a vertical shaft, at the lower end of which is the tirl or set of paddle blades (Figure 12). Water is channelled by leat into

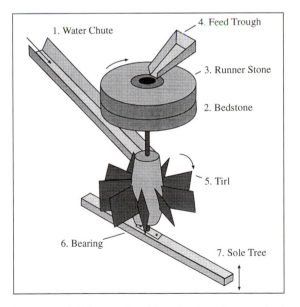

*Figure 12* A Norse mill with a horizontal waterwheel driving a single pair of stones.

a chute and directed on to the paddles in a chamber below the bedstone. The wooden structures of the water course survived well in the eighth-century mill excavated at Tamworth in Staffordshire (Rahtz 1981). In the mills of northern Scotland, the millstones were contained

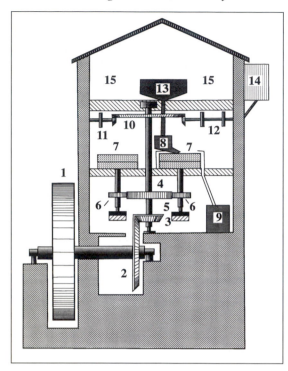

*Figure 13* Diagrammatic section of water-powered corn mill with a vertical wheel driving several pairs of stones and auxiliary machinery via gearing. 1 – Waterwheel, 2 – Pit wheel, 3 – Wallower, 4 – Main shaft, 5 – Great spur wheel, 6 – Stone nuts, 7 – Millstones (upper driven), 8 – Grain hopper and feed shoe, 9 – Meal bin, 10 – Crown wheel, 11 – Auxiliary machine drive pulley, 12 – Sack hoist and auxiliary machine drive pulleys, 13 – Grain bin, 14 – Lucam, 15 – Grain storage.

within a small rubble-stone building, often oval in plan. Only a small amount of water was required, and many mills could make use of the same stream. Norse mills catered for a single farm or hamlet, usually in areas of dispersed settlement.

Where nucleated settlement predominated, as in lowland Scotland and much of England, the village or manorial mill served the community. The Domesday Survey of 1086, although not completed for the whole country, recorded a total of some 6,000 watermills. In the medieval period, their spatial distribution was governed more by the right of the lord of the manor to force his tenants to grind their corn at his mill than by topographical considerations. The medieval mill usually made use of a vertical wheel from which the drive was transmitted by gearing to the millstones (Figure 13). Higher speeds and increased power were possible and several sets of stones could be worked from one wheel, resulting in a greater output of flour than was possible in the simpler Norse mill. The water-mill became an important component of the village settlement and as such was a permanent structure, usually built in the local vernacular tradition. The type of wheel used was governed by the gradient of the water course on which the mill was situated, overshot wheels predominating where there were high falls of water as on the Pennine slopes and undershot on the sluggish rivers of East Anglia. The mill buildings became larger in the post-medieval period because of the introduction of ancillary equipment, such as a kiln for drying grain and dressing machines for purifying the flour. Large granaries were frequently built alongside, together with the miller's house.

Where a suitable tidal range and long coastal inlet coincided, mills making use of the rise and fall of the tide could be built. The most characteristic feature of tide-mills was the dam constructed across the inlet containing gates which allowed the incoming tide to be ponded. The stored water was then released through the wheel on the ebb tide. A house adjoining the mill was essential because of the unsociable hours at which milling frequently took place. Tide-mills were subject to storm damage and few survive, but their previous existence can often be determined by the remnants of the dam which also served as access to the mill. Many of these can be seen around the coasts of Brittany and south-west England (Plate 26). Working tide-mills remain at Woodbridge in Suffolk and Eling in Hampshire, while the Pembrokeshire Coast National Park is restoring the tide-mill associated with Carew Castle.

The earliest form of windmill found in Britain was the post mill, illustrations of which can be found in medieval manuscripts. The body of the mill, or 'buck', built of wood, contained the stones and had to be turned manually into the wind by means of a tail pole. The buck turned on a vertical post, braced by quarter bars, which was mounted on a cruciform timber frame (Figure 14). In early mills, this was usually set in an earthen mound to increase the height and, where mills have disappeared, their former presence can often be detected by earthworks and crop marks. Because the wooden frame rotted in the ground, it was set on masonry piers in later mills and the whole base structure enclosed in a round house to increase storage space. Post mills were vulnerable to gales and fire and were frequently rebuilt or even moved to new sites. From the end of the eighteenth century, they were being replaced by the sturdier brick or stone tower mills which survive in much larger numbers. Only the cap needed turning into the wind, either manually from a gallery or mechanically by means of a fan tail (Figure 15). The increased space and height available within the tower mill meant that more sets of millstones as well as dressing machinery could be accommodated, while multiple sails gave increased power. A third variant was the smock mill, where the tower was constructed of timber instead of brick or stone to lessen the weight. The smock mill was useful on unstable ground as in the case of the Dutch polder drainage mills or could be mounted on a brick base or another building to increase the sail height for corn milling. The tower mill reached the zenith of its development in the first half of the nineteenth century and many surviving examples can be seen, particularly around the North Sea in Holland, Lincolnshire and East Anglia (Plate 27).

As can be seen, the introduction of steam power in the late eighteenth century did not mean the

***Plate 26*** A squat stone-built tide-mill on the Gulf of Morbihan in Brittany, France. The mill is built into the causeway which also serves as the water storage dam. The two sluices, one for filling the pond and the other providing the feed to the waterwheel, can be seen.

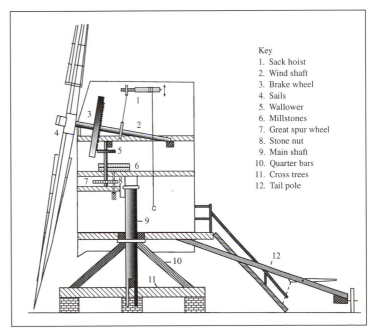

Key
1. Sack hoist
2. Wind shaft
3. Brake wheel
4. Sails
5. Wallower
6. Millstones
7. Great spur wheel
8. Stone nut
9. Main shaft
10. Quarter bars
11. Cross trees
12. Tail pole

***Figure 14*** A section of an early post mill, with a tail pole and open trestle.

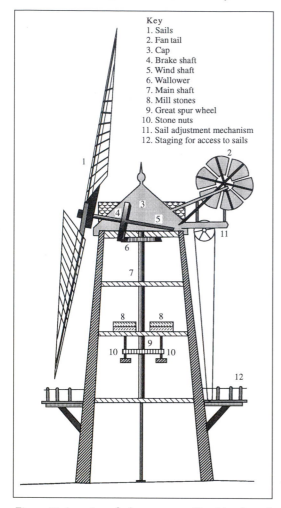

Key
1. Sails
2. Fan tail
3. Cap
4. Brake shaft
5. Wind shaft
6. Wallower
7. Main shaft
8. Mill stones
9. Great spur wheel
10. Stone nuts
11. Sail adjustment mechanism
12. Staging for access to sails

*Figure 15* A section of a later tower mill, with a fan tail which turned the cap into the wind automatically.

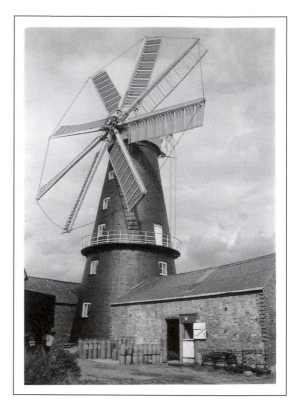

*Plate 27* A rare survival of an eight-sailed tower mill at Heckington in Lincolnshire.

automatic demise of the water- and windmill, since their power sources were free, although variable. In many places, the miller continued to hold the important place in the village community which he had enjoyed for centuries, despite his frequent unpopularity for mulcting his clients of excessive amounts of flour in return for his services. However, the increased demand by a rising population in the course of the nineteenth century meant that Britain could no longer be self-sufficient in grain and the import of corn led to the construction of steam mills, especially in ports as well as alongside navigable waterways and railways. The mills were rectangular multi-storey brick or stone structures, with loading doors on each floor and hoists housed in a lucam on the upper storeys. Large granaries stood alongside. The change in scale of flour production can be appreciated by comparing the Norse mill at Dounby on the Isle of Orkney, dating from 1825, a single-storey building the height of a man, with the six-storey Spillers' mills on the docks at Birkenhead, built less than a century later. The two buildings also reflect totally different economic systems, the former producing enough flour for a single household and the latter for an entire town.

As well as a watermill, many villages had a maltings and even a small brewery attached to the inn, the centre of village life. Malt was produced by steeping barley, allowing it to germinate and then arresting the germination by roasting the grain. A maltings was a distinctive functional building, having two or three long low storeys with small louvered windows and a pyramidal-topped kiln at one end (Figure 16). This was surmounted by a fixed or movable cowl which turned into the wind by means of a vane. The grain was spread on the floor to a depth of not more than 8 inches [20 cm] and turned periodically by hand, hence the headroom of each storey needed to be only around 6 feet [1.83 metres]. Like the water-mill, the village maltings reflected vernacular building tradition and examples survive in clunch, flint, brick and stone, all now in alter-native uses. The malting process was lengthy and as demand grew in the late nineteenth century, new means of speeding it up were found in the form of box and drum

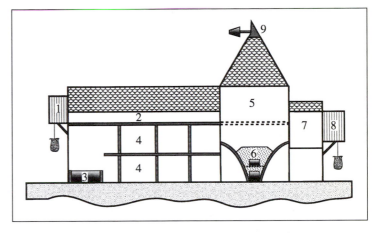

*Figure 16* Diagrammatic section of a three-storey floor maltings with two growing floors. 1 – Barley intake hoist in lucam, 2 – Barley store and screens, 3 – Steeping cistern, 4 – Growing floors, 5 – Kiln floor, 6 – Kiln furnace, 7 – Malt store, 8 – Malt delivery lucam and hoist, 9 – Cowl for kiln airflow.

maltings. Mechanical turning of the grain eliminated the need for the large growing floors, but headroom was increased to accommodate the machinery. The characteristic kiln was retained but groups of them were needed to roast the more rapid output. In the brewing towns, such as Burton-on-Trent, and in the grain-growing areas, such as Sleaford in Lincolnshire, brewing companies grouped several large malting blocks together around a central steam engine house and a characteristic water-storage tower. Even these large maltings have been superseded by faster processing and their redundant buildings pose difficult problems as to their adaptive reuse.

Another essential ingredient for bitter beer was the hop, first imported from the Continent around 1400 and grown in parts of England from the sixteenth century onwards. Unlike barley for malt, hops were processed on the farm where they were grown since they needed less specialised attention. After picking, the hops were dried in kilns which were normally part of a farm complex and were known as 'oasts' in the south-east and 'kells' in the West Midlands. The characteristic farm oast-house consisted of two floors, one for storage and the other for bagging up the dried hops, while one or more kilns were either built into the structure or linked to it. Like a maltings, the oast-house kilns had a variety of shapes and cowls. The hops were often marketed through urban hop exchanges, such as those surviving in Worcester and London.

Malt and hops came together in the brewing of beer, which also needed pure hard water, sugar and yeast. Beer was an important drink in the days when water was impure and imported tea and coffee expensive. As demand accelerated in the early nineteenth century, the small breweries attached to village inns were unable to cope and the characteristic urban tower breweries took over. Their form was dictated by the nature of the process, since gravity was utilised to transfer the liquor from mash tun on the top storey to the copper and then to fermenting vessels on the lower floors. The upper storeys of the tower were ventilated by means of louvered windows and the façades frequently enlivened by the use of terracotta or brick mouldings. It was an archi-tectural symbol of the wealth and prestige of the brewery, often dominating the urban skyline and proclaiming the name of the particular firm in a position where it could be seen by all. But the tower was only one element in the large brewing complex, which included a boiler house, steam engine for pumping, cooperage, bottling plant, cart sheds and stabling for the dray horses which delivered the product. Later in the nineteenth century, first steam and then electric power was used to pump liquor between vessels laid out on one level and the tower became redundant.

An alternative use of malt liquor was in the production of whisky, in which it was distilled in closed copper vessels after fermentation. Peaty water was preferred for single malt whisky, and the British industry was located in the Highland zone of Scotland where many small distilleries survive (Plate 28). The distilling process, seeming to turn water into a highly desirable product, had a mystique of its own which the distillers have always been keen to exploit in their advertising. The complex included a maltings, the distillery and a warehouse where the raw spirit matured in oaken casks for long periods. The tiny, barred windows in these buildings indicate the tight security under which whisky was stored, since it was subject to a heavy excise duty. The warehouses where such dutiable goods were stored were known as bonded warehouses. The production of blended whisky took place in the barley-growing areas of eastern Scotland and much of the blending was carried out in large warehouses, such as those in Leith, near Edinburgh. Rye and maize were also utilised for whisky production, especially in North America where similar bonded warehouses were constructed.

Meat came to play a larger part in British diet due to the improvements in animal-breeding during the eighteenth century, but the buildings for processing animal products are, generally, not so distinctive as those for grain products. However, the dovecotes, which provided a source of fresh meat, are an exception. Once a jealously guarded privilege by lords of the manor, the keeping of doves became more widespread in the early modern period and these attractive buildings remain a feature of the rural landscape, usually echoing the local vernacular tradition. They were usually rectangular or circular with cupolas incorporating entrance holes for the birds. A similar type of structure was the game larder, a small building often raised off the ground as a protection against vermin and with louvered sides for ventilation. Both these types of building can still be found on country estates.

*Plate 28*  The whisky distillery at Dalwhinnie in Scotland, dating from the late nineteenth century. A range of low buildings, the roof-line of which is broken by the pagoda-like vents of the malt-kilns and the louvered vents over the still-rooms.

Cattle markets often reflected the civic pride of the municipalities which constructed them, with buildings unnecessarily elaborate for their mundane function. Slaughter houses were usually built alongside, recognisable by their louvered roofs, and could also be found, on a smaller scale, in many villages. Skins were removed by fellmongers and sold through purpose-built hide and skin markets, usually having open-sided covered sheds with drained floors. One of the most unpopular, although widespread, industrial activities was the tanning of leather: the unpleasant smell inherent in the process often led to tanneries being confined to the outskirts of towns, although they became incorporated within them as a result of urban sprawl in the nineteenth century. Tanneries were also characterised by louvered windows and roofs, and contained large areas of stone tanks sunk in the ground as the tanning process was of long duration. Chemical methods introduced in the late nineteenth century speeded up the process and made the tanks redundant, but ventilation was still essential. Power was necessary to drive newly introduced machinery and an engine house and chimney were added to the buildings. The tanned leather was finished by curriers, often in large, multi-storeyed dressing mills, before being passed to wholesalers or manufacturers.

Fish played an important role in diet, often for religious reasons, and fish ponds or earthworks of abandoned ones abound as landscape features. Many harbours were developed for the fishing industry, with a range of characteristic buildings which included net and sail lofts, as well as storage cellars. Before the invention of ice-making machinery, natural ice was imported from Scandinavia and stored in deep wells in the same way as local ice was utilised in the ice houses which were a feature of many houses and estates (Beamon and Roaf 1990). The bulk of the fish catch was, however, preserved by salting, smoking or pickling. Curing houses were usually two-storey buildings with vents in the roof ridge, and a cooperage was often established alongside to produce barrels and boxes for the product. These methods of preservation were less widely used after the introduction of ice-making plant in the 1850s, which became a feature of many harbours as did a wholesale market for disposing of the much greater catches. Preservation by canning became important for certain kinds of fish, notably salmon, pilchard and tuna, and canneries were established in many fishing ports, especially on the west coast of North America (although 'Cannery Row' now usually has heritage rather than industrial connotations).

Salt was a vital commodity for the preservation of foodstuffs and was extracted from sea-water in coastal salterns, pumped from inland brine springs or mined as rock salt. At a characteristic Cheshire saltworks, brine was pumped to the surface by means of a steam engine, evaporated in large iron tanks and allowed to crystallise. The corrosive nature of

*Plate 29* A rare survival, the massive wooden structure of the salt gradation tower at Ciechocinek in Poland.

salt meant that buildings were constructed of timber rather than brick or iron and regular repairs were necessary. The Lion saltworks at Marston, near Northwich, is the last remaining complex of these ephemeral buildings, set in a sunken landscape created by the brine extraction. Subsidence was such a major problem that by-laws in the 1880s insisted on timber-framed construction for new buildings in towns like Northwich, creating a Tudoresque townscape that is nineteenth- rather than sixteenth-century in date.

The most spectacular monuments to the salt industry are those constructed in eastern Europe, especially Germany and Poland, to process weak brine solutions pumped from below ground. The brine solution was first concentrated by means of huge wooden structures known as 'gradation towers', much longer than they are high, as can be seen in Plate 29. Three of these towers, built in the first half of the nineteenth century, survive at Ciechocinek in Poland; all are 15 metres [46 feet] high and the longest is 719 metres [2,360 feet] in length. The towers are packed with brushwood, through which the brine trickles down after being pumped up to the top by wind power. Air flowing horizontally through the brushwood evaporates some of the water and so concentrates the brine without expensive coal fuel, whose use is confined to the more traditional concentration pans used later in the process. A side effect of the gradation process was the creation of an atmosphere rich in iodine, and so at Ciechocinek a spa town grew up around the industrial processing plant, the visitors breathing in both the mineral-laden air and the smoke from the saltworks!

## TEXTILES

The buildings of the textile industry are a very complex class but it is possible to classify them in terms of technological change and the organisation of production, as can be seen in Figure 17. In

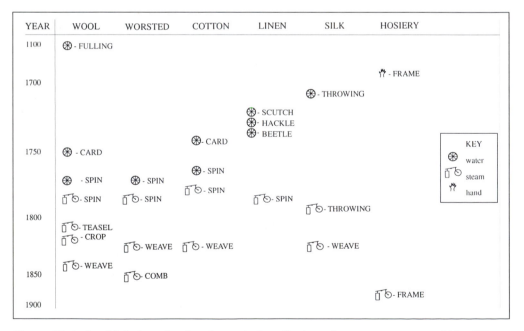

*Figure 17* A simplified chart showing the gradual application of power to processes within different branches of the textile industry. The replacement of one power source by another did not necessarily mean the extinction of the earlier one for all processes.

all branches of the industry, the earliest phase was one of domestic production, often as a secondary employment to agriculture. Cottages were adapted to house spinning and knitting machines and looms, their main characteristic being the insertion of long or large windows to allow maximum light into the working area. As machines became larger, they were grouped together in small purpose-built workshops with similar fenestration either on one floor of a house or in the back yard or garden. Changes in the organisation of capital investment, with the intervention of a middleman between the producer and the market, led to the grouping of machines in multi-storey, purpose-built workshops although the machines remained hand-powered. The final phase was the adoption of power, first water and then steam, gas and electricity, which resulted in the large multi-storey mills and factories which provide a rich collection of industrial buildings in many parts of the world. The sequence is in reality far more complex than this, since new technological developments took place at different times in various branches of the industry. The transition to large workshops or powered factories also did not mean the automatic replacement of previous production processes and different phases of buildings coexisted even within the same branch of the textile industry.

The woollen industry is the oldest of Britain's textile industries. Many of the stages of production remained hand-powered until well into the nineteenth century and the built environment of a domestic textile industry can be fully appreciated in the Pennine districts of Yorkshire and Lancashire. Carding and spinning were universal domestic employments and have left little physical trace apart from the outdoor first-floor galleries which gave both light and shelter, some still remaining on farms in north-west England. Carding was water-powered from the 1770s and the new machines were either added to existing fulling mills or installed in new scribbling mills built to accommodate them. The spinning process was adapted to power from the 1790s, utilising the technology developed for the cotton industry which will be discussed below. The movement of spinning into first water-powered and then steam-powered mills broke up the domestic system of production practised in the Pennine areas, whereby the individual yeoman clothier had been responsible both for making a piece of cloth and marketing it. Women and children were employed in the spinning mills whereas weaving remained largely a male preserve. Clothiers' houses had usually contained long rows of mullioned windows to throw light on the loom and weaving, in fact, remained on a domestic basis, even growing in the early decades of the nineteenth century to process the rapid increase in mechanically spun yarn. Loomshops were added to existing farmhouses and rural folds as well as being built adjacent to new spinning mills. Terraces of houses incorporating top-floor loomshops were built in many Pennine villages. Not until the mid-nineteenth century was steam-powered weaving accepted in the woollen industry, and room was often found for the new power looms in existing mills although in some instances single-storey north-light sheds were built (Giles and Goodall 1992; Giles 1993). In south-west England, renowned for its broad-cloth production, large-scale capital investment at a much earlier date than in the Pennines resulted in a different type of organisation, with workshops attached to the elegant houses of master clothiers who managed all the processes of production. Water-powered spinning mills were built in the late eighteenth century, often along the ornate lines of the clothiers' houses, but in this area the industry had already begun to contract in favour of Yorkshire. Two particular types of building characteristic of the south-west are the circular stone stoves for drying the wool and the ventilated handle-houses for drying the teasels used in the gig machines for raising the nap on the finished cloth (Plate 30).

Woollen cloth was fulled after weaving in water-powered mills driving wooden fulling stocks, a process which had been divorced from the domestic environment since the thirteenth century. Fulling mills and corn mills competed for the available water supply, and the former were only

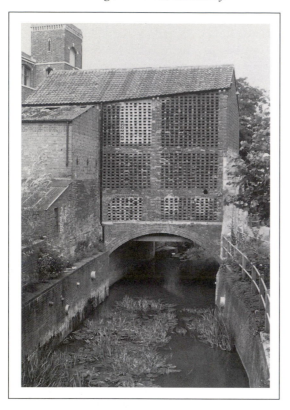

*Plate 30* The 'handle house' at Studley Mill, Trowbridge in Wiltshire, a rare survival of a building characteristic of weaving communities. The perforations in the brickwork provided a draught of air for drying teasels after their use for raising the nap on damp woollen cloth.

widespread in areas with ample water-power sites as in, for example, Wales. The buildings used for marketing cloth also indicate the contrast in organisation between Yorkshire and the south-west. The yeoman clothier originally sold his cloth on stalls in weekly street markets and eventually in specially built markets or 'piece halls', where his goods could be displayed in individual rooms. The superb Piece Hall in Halifax, built in 1779, has some 315 rooms arranged in galleries around a quadrangle (Plate 31). The piece halls became obsolete with the decline of the yeoman clothier system of production and were replaced by wholesale warehouses. As in other branches of the textile industry, these were often more ornate than the mills in order to impress the buyers. Little Germany in Bradford is a good example of a warehouse quarter devoted to the sale of worsted cloth. There are no comparable buildings in the west of England, where the cloth seems to have been marketed direct by the clothiers.

As a comparatively new industry, the production of cotton yarn led the way in technological development at the end of the eighteenth century and pioneered new systems of industrial production which are reflected in the built environment. Water power was first applied to spinning in the cotton industry by Richard Arkwright and his buildings were the exemplars for the first generation of textile mills. They were two or more storeys high, about 70 feet [21.3 metres] long and 30 feet [9.1 metres] wide to allow maximum light on to the machines. Since the more accessible water-power sites were already in use by other industries, Arkwright and his fellow entrepreneurs were obliged to construct their mills in remote areas unless existing water rights could be purchased. It was usually possible for the mills to operate continuously and steps had to be taken to accommodate the workforce nearby. New settlements were grafted on to existing villages, as at Belper and Cromford in Derbyshire, or new model communities were created like Styal in Cheshire and New Lanark in Strathclyde. Since employment in the mills was predominantly for women and children, alternative employment had to be found for men; this could be weaving, as indicated by the loomshops in Cromford and cellar loomshops in Styal, or existing crafts such as the nail-making which was promoted in Belper. Mention has already been made of the strict social control operated in these model communities, both within the mills where the ratio of length to width made supervision of the workforce on each floor a relatively easy task, and within the company settlements where the emphasis was on moral education and where drinking was discouraged by the exclusion of public houses and beer shops.

Within two decades, it was possible to replace a waterwheel by a rotative steam engine for driving cotton-spinning machinery, but the cost of coal encouraged many mill-owners to maximise the potential of water power by improving waterwheels or later by introducing turbines. Even so, a new generation of red-brick textile mills grew up on or near the coalfields, their power source indicated by attached engine houses and boiler chimneys. A particular hazard of cotton preparation and spinning was fire and many early mills were destroyed. Iron-framed construction was developed in the last decade of the eighteenth century, textile mills leading the way in its adoption (Figure 18). The use of iron beams and the availability of gas lighting enabled wider mills to be built and larger machines to be accommodated. A third era of new building followed the end of the cotton famine caused by the American Civil War in the 1860s, and many of the new mills were designed by specialist architects for the first time, enabling their owners to demonstrate their tastes in architectural style. Power was originally transmitted to the various floors of the mill by means of gearing and shafts, but in the 1880s the advent of rope drive enabled a more flexible mill layout to be used. These large mills were built on green-field sites on the fringes of existing mill towns, often at the centre of a network of streets of monotonous terraced housing.

*Plate 31* The Piece Hall at Halifax, West Yorkshire, in which pieces of cloth were displayed for sale. Built in 1779, this prestigious structure symbolises the competition between the textile towns of the West Riding and is the only major survival.

Textile mills were also a feature of many European and American towns, although Britain dominated the cotton industry for much of the nineteenth century. Mention has already been made of the water-powered mills on the Merrimack River in Massachusetts, which made use of turbines to maximise the potential of the available power source. Many German towns were dominated by textile production, notably Augsburg, where a huge proto-industrial cotton factory was built in the 1770s and still stands as a monument to the putting-out system, while Aachen also had a pre-industrial woollen industry which developed a factory system early in the nineteenth century. The province of Catalonia was among the most industrialised regions of Spain, with a cotton industry making use first of water power and later of steam power. The River Molinar in the town of Alcoi is lined with cotton mills, some dating from the late eighteenth century, while the workforce were housed in large tenements, a common housing type in Continental industrial centres which contrast with the company villages of England. A final example is the town of Łódź in Poland, which developed a cotton industry as a result of government incentives, specifically, to begin with, a domestic industry rather than one based on factory production. Cottages were built for spinners and weavers, and these later served to house a different kind of workforce once water- and steam-powered factories were introduced by

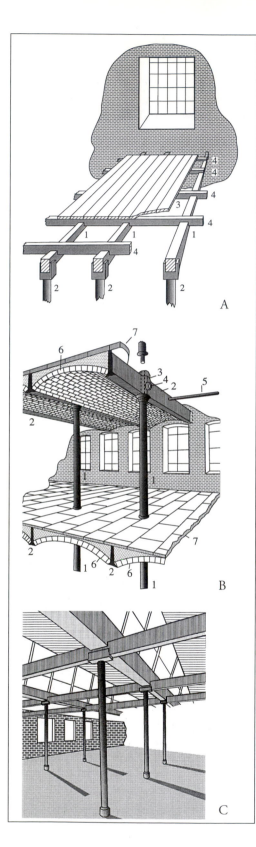

*Figure 18* Typical textile mill building construction:

(A) Diagrammatic section of the first floor of a typical timber-framed mill building: transverse beams (1) are supported by cast-iron columns (2) and at either end in sockets in the wall; a timber floor (3) is located on longitudinal beams (4).

(B) Diagrammatic section of the first and second floors of a typical cast-iron-framed fireproof mill: the cast-iron columns (1) have a spigot at the bottom, and an annular recess and a socket at the top to interlock together. The transverse cast-iron beams (2) have half sockets on the ends (3) which seat in the column recesses. Lugs on either side of the half sockets are clamped together round the column by means of shrink rings (4). The transverse beams are linked by wrought-iron tie rods (5). The gaps between the beams are filled by brick arching (6) and the spaces above the arching are filled with rubble over which a stone-flagged floor (7) is laid.

(C) Diagrammatic section of a single-storey weaving shed. The timber-built, north-light roof is supported by cast-iron columns. This form of building allowed the accommodation of the heavier and larger power looms and was the precursor of most modern factory construction.

the mid-nineteenth century. Prussian capital financed many huge mills and adjacent tenement housing, until by the late nineteenth century Łódź came to be known as the 'Polish Manchester'. The early development of the textile factory in Britain must not blind the industrial archaeologist to the fact that many other countries caught up fast and developed different systems for housing a rapidly growing workforce.

As in the woollen industry, cotton-weaving remained on a domestic basis into the nineteenth century. Handlooms were accommodated in the cellar or ground-floor workshops of houses, humidity being necessary for cotton-weaving. In areas of Lancashire, rows of houses with raised steps to the ground floor and cellar windows at pavement level indicate this former use. Power was applied to looms for cotton-weaving from the 1820s and single-storey sheds were incorporated into existing spinning mill complexes, often filling every available space. An aerial view of Gidlow Works, Wigan, shows a strong link between building form and function, with the multi-storey warehouse and spinning mill together with sheds for weaving (Plate 32). Yet documentary evidence indicates the continuation of handloom-weaving in cellar workshops at the same time as these integrated mills were being constructed, illustrating the importance of considering both the structures themselves and available written sources in the interpretation of buildings.

The manufacture of linen was widespread throughout Britain but particularly concentrated in Northern Ireland and Scotland. The nature of flax fibre required different processes, and therefore a different range of buildings, from either the woollen or the cotton industry. The soaked

*Plate 32* Gidlow Mills at Wigan in Greater Manchester: an example of a late nineteenth-century integrated textile complex with multi-storey spinning mill and single-storey weaving sheds crowding the available site.
RCHME, © Crown Copyright.

*Plate 33* The scutching machinery in a derelict water-powered mill at Cleggan in Northern Ireland: the central iron rim and the wooden wiper blades, known as a scutching handle, would have been enclosed on one side to protect the operatives who held the bunches of flax against the rotating blades.

flax was broken up or 'scutched' by means of large wooden blades driven by water power in small mills (Plate 33). After drying, the flax was taken to a different mill where carding, known as 'hackling', and spinning took place, also using water power. Weaving was not powered until the 1840s; previously, since the yarn required damp conditions similar to those for cotton, cellar workshops had been utilised. The cloth was then finished by pounding with hammers to produce the sheen characteristic of linen fabric. The process was known as 'beetling' and was also water-powered. Consequently, many of the streams in Northern Ireland were lined by sequences of small mills, each performing a different process in the manufacture of linen. The dispersion of the mills accorded well with the settlement pattern of Northern Ireland, villages and hamlets providing the necessary workforce. Steam power was applied to flax-spinning in the 1820s, and some linen manufacturers were pioneers in iron-framed fireproof mill construction. In fact, the first such mill was constructed for flax-spinning in Shrewsbury by Charles Bage in 1791 and still survives. Multi-storey mills became characteristic of the linen industry by the mid-nineteenth century and dominated the townscapes of Belfast and Dundee, although many in the latter changed to jute- and hemp-processing. The major use for spun hemp was in rope manufacture, originally carried out in open rope walks but by the nineteenth century often contained within long low buildings. Many of these were built in ports to provide ropes for shipping, the best-known being the double rope walk at the naval dockyard in Chatham, 1,140 feet [347.4 metres] long.

Silk thread had already been spun by the silkworm, but needed twisting and doubling before it could be knitted or woven. The twisting process was known as 'throwing' and, surprisingly, was the first process in textile manufacture to be water-powered in the first two decades of the eighteenth century. Lombe's mill in Derby was the fore-runner of many more during the nineteenth century (Calladine 1993). Silk-weaving remained hand-powered much longer than in other branches of the textile industry, first in garret workshops of purpose-built terraced houses and then in mills such as those which dominate the towns of Macclesfield, Congleton and Leek. Both the workshops and mills illustrate the introduction of the Jacquard loom in the 1820s which required additional headroom for the punched cards which determined the pattern of the fabric (Calladine and Fricker 1993). The deep and wide garret windows of houses in Coventry and adjacent villages indicate the use of a narrow Jacquard loom for the production of fancy ribbons and tapes, a speciality of the area. Coventry also witnessed an experiment to utilise steam power in the garrets of terraced houses, supplied by line shafting from a central engine house (Prest 1960). This 'cottage factory' allowed the worker to remain in the domestic environment, but does not seem to have been widely adopted elsewhere.

The textile industry to remain longest in a domestic setting was the knitting of hosiery, and a study of the buildings associated with it illustrates the phases of development. The knitting frame was invented late in the sixteenth century and timber-framed houses were adapted to create workshops with large windows. By the late eighteenth century, demand was such that speculative builders were providing terraced houses with workshops for rent by knitters. These had large windows at the front and rear of the workshop, which could be situated either on the ground, first or even second floor. Many remain in the East Midlands where 90 per cent of the industry was located. Larger machines meant that a domestic environment was no longer possible but, as in the boot and shoe industry, small workshops with maximum window area were built in back yards. Hosiery workers, like others who carried out manufacturing processes in a domestic environment, therefore had to rationalise the relationship between living and working space or, as Campion

**Figure 19** Elevations of a master hosier's house in Hucknall, Nottinghamshire; the juxtaposition of living space and working areas is evident from the different styles of windows, the long segmental-headed windows providing light for the knitting frames.

Drawing by courtesy of Garry Campion.

(1996) has put it, 'to reconcile the tension between structural envelope, habitation and production'. He has used the technique of access analysis to study that relationship in buildings representing different phases of production, the domestic house with integral workshop, the hosier's house with attached workshop (Figure 19) and the proto-factory in which machines were grouped together, but no power provided. It is clear that little differentiation was made between living and working space in the domestic house, but in the hosier's house great care was taken to provide the outworkers with their own entrance and working areas: they did not penetrate the living space of the hosier's family. The technique could well be applied to other types of proto-industrial structures, as Markus (1993: 282–3) attempted, but Campion stresses the importance of considering each building on its own merits or, put archaeologically, within its own context.

The knitting frame was not mechanised until the middle of the nineteenth century and so the hosiery industry never passed through a water-powered phase. Even the transition to steam power was a slow one, and the red-brick hosiery mills that dominate East Midlands towns are generally a product of the 1880s and later. This late mechanisation has meant the survival of many of the domestic workshops. The machine lace industry, centred in Nottingham, developed from the hosiery industry and its most characteristic buildings are the huge multi-storey tenement factories in which machine holders could rent room and power for their machines. As the latter became larger and heavier, single-storey factories were built to accommodate them. Lace required careful finishing, usually carried out in separate dressing mills with well-lit attics. Similar attic premises for inspection and mending were also a feature of the warehouse quarter in Nottingham, where a sweated female labour force toiled away behind the elegant façades which were designed to attract buyers.

The buildings of the textile industry therefore reveal much about the technological, industrial and social organisation of its various branches. A general transition can be seen from manufacture carried out in the home to the provision of separate, but still hand-powered, workshops and finally the mill with its central power source, employing a workforce finally divorced from their domestic environment. The buildings also indicate the increasing size, complexity and weight of the machinery during the nineteenth century, often resulting in single-storey sheds covering vast areas. Fire was a particular hazard and it was textile manufacturers who pioneered the use of large, fireproof structures incorporating new materials such as cast iron and reinforced concrete.

## STEAM POWER

The earlier phases of industrialised production were dependent upon water power and this continued to be developed even after the successful use of the steam engine on mines and in factories and mills from the late eighteenth century. Good accounts of the development of the steam engine already exist (Buchanan and Watkins 1976; Hills 1967, 1989) but archaeologists will more usually be faced with the remains of engine houses and foundations from which to interpret their former use. Stationary steam engines were first developed for pumping water out of mines but their use for rotative power greatly widened their application. Rotative engines were used for winding men and materials from mine shafts, crushing minerals as well as driving a whole range of machinery in manufacturing industry. Steam power was also applied to haulage, first as stationary engines on railway inclines and then for traction in the form of the locomotive. These numerous uses of steam power created a whole range of buildings from mine engine houses to the elegant Victorian municipal pumphouses for water supply and those incorporated within textile mills and factories.

The impetus for the production of a steam engine came from the need to drain the mines both for coal and metallic ores. Existing means of pumping by manual, animal or water power had limited scope and it was the invention of the atmospheric beam engine of Thomas Newcomen in 1712 which provided a solution. Essentially, this consisted of a heavy rocking beam pivoted by bearings on top of a wall. To one end of the beam was connected the rod of a piston in an open-topped vertical cylinder supplied by steam from a coal-fired boiler mounted underneath the cylinder. To the opposite end of the beam a pump rod was attached which went down the mine shaft to a lift or plunger pump. The action of the engine depended on filling the cylinder beneath the piston with steam from the boiler; the weight of the pump rod in the mine shaft normally lifted the piston to the top of the cylinder. The working stroke of the engine was achieved by shutting off the steam, injecting cold water into the cylinder, condensing the steam and creating a partial vacuum beneath the piston. At this point the pressure of the atmosphere on the top of the piston was sufficient to force it downwards and rock the beam, lifting the pump rod and raising a quantity of water. Originally, manually operated valves controlled the steam-emission and steam-condensing actions but eventually this could be achieved automatically by means of valve rods also connected to the beam.

In the field, a Newcomen engine house can be distinguished from later beam engine houses by its extra height and lack of a cylinder base, the cylinder being mounted on wooden cross-beams. A feature of all beam engine houses was the extra thick 'bob'-wall on which the rocking beam was carried: this wall is usually the last to disintegrate in a derelict engine house. Another feature, common to all mine pumping applications using pump rods, is the 'balance bob' pit by the top of the shaft. A weighted box on a beam pivoted in this pit and was connected to the pump rod to balance the weight of the pump rod so that the only work which had to be done was to lift the water. In Britain, the only Newcomen engine to survive in its original engine house is at Elsecar in South Yorkshire and even this has been modified by the addition of a separate condenser. An empty engine house remains at Rockley, also in South Yorkshire, whilst others at Furnace pit at Moira in Leicestershire and several on the Shropshire coalfield have been converted to dwellings. At the Black Country Museum at Dudley a working replica of the original 1712 engine at Dudley Castle has been built. The Newcomen engine continued in use, both for pumping and winding, long after more efficient engines were available but really only coal mines could afford its excessive coal consumption.

Improvements to the basic Newcomen engine were made by James Watt, some of which had a direct effect upon engine-house design. The most important was the introduction of the separate condenser in which the steam from below the piston was drawn into a separate vessel or condenser which had been exhausted by means of an air pump; there it was condensed, producing the vacuum which allowed steam pressure on the top of the piston to force the piston down for the pumping stroke. This, together with jacketing the cylinder, greatly increased the engine efficiency with immediate fuel savings. In addition the Watt engine used steam at higher pressure, replacing the 'haystack' boiler by the wagon boiler which was mounted in a separate boiler house. The modifications by Watt brought changes in engine-house design: first, a separate boiler house, usually adjoining the engine house, allowed the latter to be reduced in height; second, the cylinder assembly was usually mounted upon heavy stone blocks, often of granite, with large holes for holding-down bolts and these cylinder mountings are a prominent feature in many derelict engine houses. Measurement of these enables the diameter of the cylinder once mounted there to be estimated. Another feature of the Watt-type engine was the well in the floor, either in front of the cylinder mounting block or immediately in front of the bob-wall, which contained a tank of water in which the condenser and air pump were immersed (Figure 20).

The fuel efficiency of the Watt engine was such that it found ready acceptance in the metal mines of south-west England and elsewhere, and created an

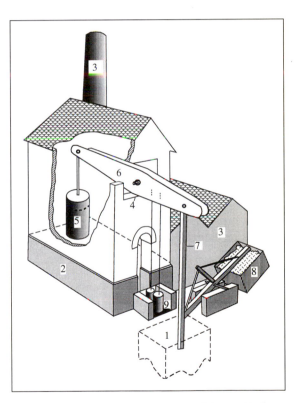

*Figure 20* Simplified arrangements of 'Cornish' beam pumping engine. 1 – Mine shaft, 2 – Engine house, 3 – Boiler house and chimney, 4 – Bob-wall supporting rocking-beam trunnion, 5 – Steam cylinder, 6 – Rocking beam, 7 – Pump rod into shaft, 8 – Balance bob with weighted box to balance weight of pump rods, 9 – Condenser tank with air and water feed pumps linked to beam.

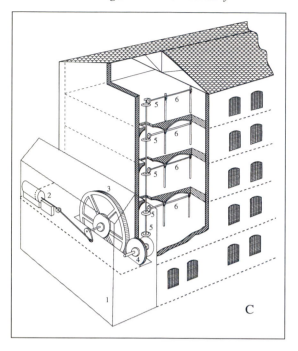

*Figure 22* Diagrammatic representation of a horizontal steam engine in a separate engine house attached to a multi-storey mill. A pinion driven from the flywheel rim transmits power via bevel gears to line shafting on each floor. 1 – Engine house, 2 – Steam engine, 3 – Flywheel, 4 – Pinion gear, 5 – Bevel gear, 6 – Line shafting.

engine turned upon its side. The cylinder and crankshaft were mounted on the same bedplate which itself was located on masonry foundations. The horizontal engine was available in many sizes and was easily portable in its smaller versions. The effect on engine-house form was immediate, as height was no longer essential. The engines were placed in long single-storey buildings, their former presence often confirmed by bolt holes for fastening the bedplates and recesses in the foundations. A common application was the twin cylinder horizontal engine for mine winding, which was in effect two singles side by side but connected to a common crankshaft. The space between the foundations was wide enough to contain the winding drum which was often driven by gears from the crankshaft. Normally, two ropes were wound on to the drum, one connected to each cage in the mine shaft. One rope reeled on to the top of the drum and the other to the bottom so that one cage descended while the other ascended. This arrangement left two slots in the front wall of the engine house at different horizontal levels which are often stained from oil and grease off the winding ropes or chains.

The horizontal engine could also be applied to pumping from a shaft by connecting the pump rods to an angle bob from which a 'flat rod' or link ran to the end of the piston rod. This configuration was used in many later public water-supply installations. The power and efficiency of steam engines was increased by means of compounding and placing engines in tandem. These large horizontal engines provided the drive for many multi-storey textile mills and much manufacturing plant.

Whilst the engine houses on mines and pumping stations were separate buildings, albeit with boiler houses and chimneys attached, the engine formed an integral part of the whole building in many factories and mills. In the latter, early steam engines were installed to supplement water power and the engine house was an add-on structure but subsequently buildings were designed especially for the use of steam power. In some production processes – for example, in rolling mills – the engine was mounted on the factory floor with no separate building. In multi-storey textile mills, engine houses were built at one end of the mill and originally connected to the conventional upright shaft and bevel gearing to line shafting on each floor (Figure 22). A new innovation was the friction rope drive, whereby the flywheel was very wide having grooves machined on its rim which carried long circular-section cotton ropes formed into loops which drove pulleys located on horizontal shafts on each of the mill floors (Figure 23). This introduced a new feature in mill buildings, the 'rope race', a vertical void the full height of the mill containing the ropes and pulleys. The engine house was built on to one wall of the mill, again at one end. Such were the ambitions for expansion in cotton-spinning that many owners installed engines with extra power which were capable of driving a second mill so making a double-length mill. Former engine houses can often be distinguished by their tall round-headed windows and situation in the mill complex (Figure 24). The final phase of development of the textile mill steam engine was its use to drive electricity-generating plant to power large motors on each floor. Only when public mains electricity and small individual electric motors became available was the heavy capital cost of steam engines and power transmission systems eliminated.

An attempt has been made by Markus (1993) to explain the relationship between spatial structure and power transmission within a textile mill by means of the concept of homology, the relation of corresponding parts forming a series in the same organism. He sees mill buildings developing to become like machines, with both static and dynamic systems within them. The static systems, i.e. the buildings themselves, changed over time, using different building materials and methods of construction, especially the introduction of cast-iron framing. The machinery within the buildings, however, made them liable to movement, to become dynamic systems in themselves, and Markus shows how refinements were introduced to adjust them, such as the levelling devices on the basement supports in Strutt's Belper North Mill of 1804. The other dynamic system within the buildings was for movement – of people, material substances and energy. The static systems for movement, such as staircase towers, were replaced by lifts and hoists, dynamic systems in which people and objects became static in moving space. With power transmission, he suggests that the early system of a

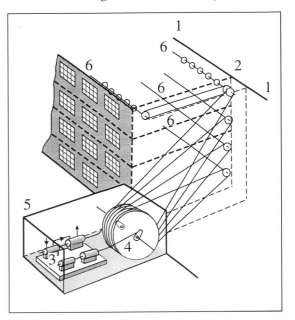

**Figure 23** Diagrammatic representation of a twin tandem compound horizontal steam engine driving a multi-storey double textile mill by means of rope drive. The central engine house is located opposite a full-height rope race between the two sections of the mill (only one shown). A series of annular grooves on the rim of the flywheel carry endless cotton ropes which drive pulleys on line shafts on each floor of the mill. Individual machines are belt-driven from the line shafts. 1 – Rear wall of double mill, 2 – Rope race, 3 – Steam engine, 4 – Rope drum, 5 – Engine house, 6 – Line shafting.

wheel driving one horizontal shaft, which in turn drove several vertical shafts through all floors, did not result in a homologous whole, since the vertical structures of the power transmission system crossed those of social control and space, i.e. the machines and their attendants on each floor. In the more developed cotton mill, on the other hand, a single vertical shaft drove a horizontal shaft on each floor, which in turn powered belts to individual machines (see Figure 22). Rope drives were later substituted for the vertical shaft (see Figure 23), but the logic was the same and the homology now perfect, with power transmission in line with, rather than cutting through, the social and spatial structures of each floor. Commercially, this also made room and power systems possible, whereby the mill-owner could let individual floors to separate firms who utilised the common power source. Markus's methods of analysis have not been pursued by other historians of industrial architecture (e.g. E. Jones 1985), but they are a step towards an understanding of the spatial logic of a mill interior in a novel and challenging way.

Buildings once containing steam engines or, at least, the remains of their foundations, therefore occur in a wide variety of contexts in both extractive and manufacturing industry. From the use of the Newcomen engine for pumping mines in the early part of the eighteenth century to the small horizontal engine which found its way into sawmills, corn mills, foundries and innumerable factories in the second half of the nineteenth century, steam became the dominant power source for industrial production until itself replaced by the more flexible electric motor in

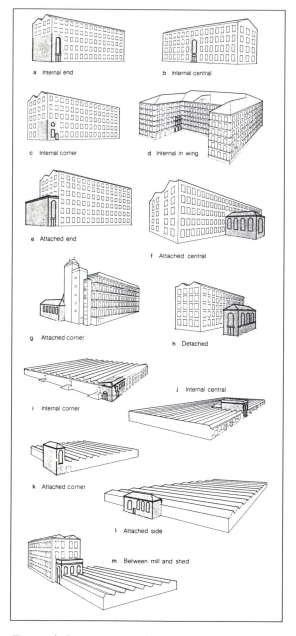

*Figure 24* Common engine house positions in large textile mills in Yorkshire.

RCHME, © Crown Copyright.

the twentieth century. The study of engine houses, however, must proceed beyond functional and typological analysis to a consideration of their context; for example, the effect of power transmission systems on the design of buildings or of their incessant demand for fuel on the local transport network. Although many engine houses in the extractive industries were stark, functional structures, the opportunity was frequently taken in the manufacturing and service industries to make some kind of statement by means of the architectural decoration of these buildings. This could range from ornamental ironwork for the engine supports, often classical in design, to elaborate terracotta or carved brick on the engine houses themselves. In the case of public utilities, the companies or municipal undertakings responsible for them often adopted an elaborate house style as a symbol of ownership, a trend which can be observed on many other Victorian buildings.

This chapter has dealt with a wide variety of industrial buildings and structures, but when the threefold analysis outlined at the beginning – functional, typological and cultural – is undertaken, some common patterns begin to emerge which demonstrate the development of systems of industrial organisation. Functional analysis indicates a group of buildings and structures readily recognisable by their forms, such as bottle kilns, glasshouses, maltings and breweries, and a larger group of mills and factories which could be adapted for a number of purposes as the needs of industry changed. Typological analysis of both groups, however, generally suggests a change from intermittent to continuous working as demand increased. This is most obvious in structures such as kilns and furnaces, but the transition from hand to water or steam power, especially when accompanied by the introduction of gas lighting, made continuous working possible in manufacturing industry. Culturally, then, the workforce, organised on a shift system, became subservient to the incessant demands of the power source. The latter also initiated a change in the gender of the workforce, since women and children could operate powered machines. Company villages like Cromford indicate the break-up of the family unit of production, the women and children working in the mills, the men weaving or knitting in domestic attic workshops, the whole under the control of the entrepreneur. But, as was observed in Chapter Two, the continued existence of mundane types of building such as domestic workshops alongside the more visually striking textile mill or steel rolling mill, shows how many of the workforce clung for as long as possible to their illusory independence, manufacturing finished goods such as cloth or nails and chains from material supplied to them by the entrepreneur who, in reality, controlled their working lives.

# Chapter Four

# Field techniques

Fieldwork is a means of gathering data. This seems a simple enough statement, but it has many implications. What data should be gathered? For what purpose is it being gathered? And how is it to be gathered? The practice of industrial archaeology involves both the recording of upstanding structures and also the survey, and even excavation, of the physical context of those structures. Recording above- and below-ground features are not necessarily similar processes. The process of excavating below-ground features usually destroys the stratigraphy of a site, and therefore some means of recording the data collected as objectively as possible is essential to allow both interpretation and probable reinterpretation at a later date. With upstanding structures, unless demolition is imminent, the recording process is non-destructive and re-evaluation at a later date can often be done by going back to the structure itself rather than to data previously collected. This may mean that the level of detail required, and therefore the amount of data collected, is different for above- and below-ground structures.

There are clearly questions to be answered about the nature of field data before the techniques of collecting it can be described, and so some discussion about the theoretical basis of the recording process is necessary. Recording data obtained from excavation has been dominated by the idea of 'contexts' and 'stratigraphic units' derived from the seminal *Principles of Archaeological Stratigraphy* (E. C. Harris 1979). Harris's theories were based on the geological principles of stratigraphy and therefore firmly rooted in the processual archaeology of the 1960s and 1970s. Given the belief that raw data could be collected objectively, descriptions were drawn in physical terms only, thereby emphasising the role of natural or environmental factors in the shaping of human activity. Several attempts have been made to apply these principles to the recording of standing buildings (Ferris 1989; Davies 1993) which has led to a considerable debate on their validity for upstanding structures. Post-processual archaeologists place much more emphasis on human intervention in the stratigraphic process itself: they argue that what the stratigraphic units actually represent are not natural events but events shaped by human beings. They have also rejected the notion that scientific objectivity is possible in the recording process, since every individual recorder approaches a site or structure with ideas and theories that influence what is actually recorded.

This, of course, can lead to the untenable position that anyone's interpretation of a site or structure is as good as another's, a criticism often levied against post-processual archaeology in general. The way forward is to accept that recording, or the gathering of field data, is subjective, but to make it as objective as possible by ensuring that the recording process is part of an accepted research agenda. Most archaeologists now agree that the purpose of data collection is not to test scientific hypotheses but to illuminate broad historical issues. A research agenda requires that these issues be made explicit so that a recorder can make informed decisions about what to record for a particular site or structure. The agenda itself is derived from the current priorities perceived by whatever organisation has initiated the recording process.

A research agenda, particularly one applied to standing structures, will therefore involve informed decisions about what data is necessary for a particular project, which is in itself a subjective act. But a degree of objectivity can be achieved in the data-gathering process itself by the acceptance of certain techniques. These may involve the use of pro-forma context sheets, even for standing buildings. The design of these, which dictates both the level and type of data to be collected, is part of the research project, and in a sense therefore subjective, but they can, for example, encourage consistency of data collection from one site to another. On the other hand, it is important that a recorder should note differences as well as similarities, and so context sheets need to be used flexibly and to complement rather than replace photographs, drawings and site notes.

Recording, or the collection of field data, is therefore not usually an end in itself, but part of an accepted research agenda, be it for structures or sites. The techniques used in meeting the requirements of such an agenda will be explored in this chapter.

## SITE IDENTIFICATION

The survival of above-ground evidence for the industrial period means that the standard archaeological discovery techniques of field walking, geophysical survey and aerial photography are not always appropriate. None the less, there are sites with no above-ground evidence where such techniques are of value. Aerial photography, for example, can reveal the earthworks of wind-mill mounds and the alterations to water courses for the supply of power to mills and mining sites. Field walking is usually the only means available for locating sites for which there is little documentary evidence, such as pitsteads for the manufacture of charcoal and early bloomery sites, the latter often detected by slag scatters. It is also valuable for the location of features which were either in a ruinous condition, such as lime-kilns or coke ovens, or so ephemeral, like many horse-drawn waggonways, that they escaped the attention of map surveyors. Field walking and aerial photography are particularly appropriate techniques for the upland areas which were rarely surveyed on the large scale applied to populous lowland areas in the mid-nineteenth century.

Ordnance Survey (OS) maps do, however, form the basis of the desk-based surveys for discovery purposes which precede most field projects. For example, Cornwall Archaeological Unit made use of a Tithe Map of 1842 and the first and second editions of the 1:2,500 OS maps of 1877 and 1908 for their historic audit of the town of Hayle. The gazetteer derived from the maps was then evaluated in the field and the surviving monuments classified according to site type (Buck and Smith 1995). The evidence from these early editions can be combined with the information obtained from aerial photographs – a technique being utilised by the RCHME aerial mapping programme and which has revealed large numbers of industrial sites in, for example, the Yorkshire Dales, Dartmoor and Exmoor National Parks. County-based voluntary societies and individuals have produced numbers of gazetteers of sites, as has the Association for Industrial Archaeology in the regional guides produced to accompany its annual conferences. These gazetteers are essentially lists of extant sites which can act as pointers to more detailed analysis of the areas covered. The most intensive use of maps for an area survey has been that carried out in the Ironbridge Gorge (Alfrey and Clark 1993). The authors took as their basis the plots shown on the 1902 edition of the 25-inch OS map, which they argued had an historical significance in representing the way in which the land had been organised in the past. Incorporating evidence from earlier maps and other documentary evidence, each plot was treated as an archaeological site and each feature within it given a context number. This ensured that equal weight was given to all types of feature, and therefore a degree of consistency attained. The plot survey is valuable in ensuring that the *total* landscape is considered and not just the important upstanding structures. It is, however, a time-consuming technique which is probably appropriate only for particularly important landscapes like the Ironbridge Gorge: other areas might not merit such meticulous collection of data. The authors were also fortunate in that many of the plots could still be identified in a landscape which had not, on the whole, undergone intensive redevelopment in the twentieth century.

Maps and documents have played an important part in the identification of water-power sites prior to field investigation. Michael Davies-Shiel has produced an invaluable series of distribution maps of the water-powered industries of the Lake District, ranging from textile mills to corn mills, bobbin mills and paper mills (Davies-Shiel 1978) which give a good idea of the intensity with which water-power resources were exploited. A similar theme was pursued by a research group at Sheffield University, involving the analysis of a wide range of documentary sources to investigate how Sheffield rivers were harnessed for the secondary metal trades (Crossley 1989). The group produced a map of each of the rivers showing the water-power sites in relation to each other: for each site, they researched the uses and changes of ownership and, in most cases, eventual abandonment (Figure 25). Follow-up fieldwork then confirmed any site remains on the ground, including dams, goits and occasional slag scatters. This combination of documentary research followed by field investigation could be applied to other small area surveys.

The most comprehensive thematic survey has been that carried out on textile mills in the north of England by RCHME in association with other local bodies. This again has provided a methodology which can be applied to other categories of buildings. This class of building was under immediate threat, and so the first part of the research agenda was to ascertain the extent of the surviving evidence. For the West Yorkshire survey, the editions of the 25-inch OS maps between 1920 and 1935 were selected for initial study, since they showed the maximum number of mills. Some 1,800 mills were identified in this way: each was then visited and, if extant, recorded using a standard form for speed and consistency. The authors have since recognised the limitations of this method, as the functions of various mill buildings were more complex than previously realised, but it did enable the rapid recording of over 1,400 mill sites with standing remains. From this pilot survey, the investigators were able to finalise their research agenda. They decided to collect further data on mills which met three main criteria: the mills chosen should have contributed to the development of the factory system, to the structural evolution of mill building or to the community of which they formed a part. Some 120 mills were selected on these criteria. As well as normal ground-level photography and building measurement, oblique aerial photography played an important role in the discovery and interpretation of such complex sites (Giles and Goodall 1992). A similar map survey in Greater Manchester revealed 2,400 mill sites of which over 1,000 were actually recorded and a smaller number investigated in greater detail (Williams with Farnie 1992). The East Cheshire survey tackled a more limited area, that of the boroughs of Macclesfield and Congleton, and so was able to produce detailed studies of nearly all the 242 mill sites identified (Calladine and Fricker 1993). This close scrutiny was able to reveal the amount of evidence, both structural and documentary, which survived for the mid- to late eighteenth century and resulted in a greater understanding of the development of the hitherto unresearched silk industry of the region.

English Heritage has been instrumental in the recognition of a large number of industrial sites through its Monuments Protection Programme (MPP). This was designed to review the Schedule of Ancient Monuments, using data derived from Sites and Monuments Records (SMRs) and the NMR. For industrial sites, however, the necessary data did not exist and an industry-by-industry survey was instituted, using the thematic classification of industries devised by Arthur Raistrick (1972). The initial steps of the survey of each industry relied on the collection of published data or that supplied by individuals, culminating in a graded list of known

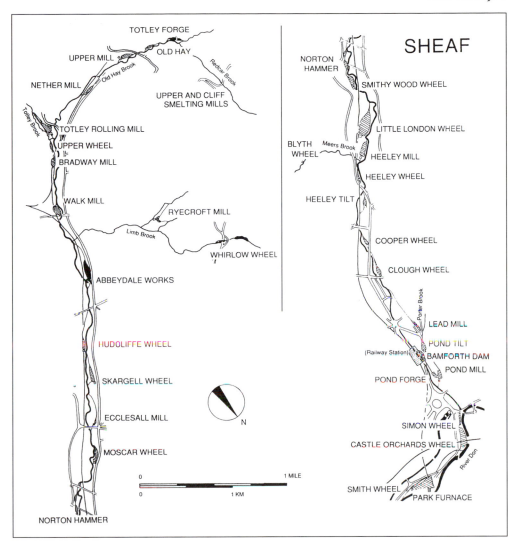

*Figure 25* An example of the maximum use of a small river, the water-powered sites along the River Sheaf in Sheffield, South Yorkshire. These were mostly concerned with metal-working involving rolling mills, tilt hammers and grinding wheels.

Reproduced by courtesy of David Crossley, University of Sheffield.

sites which was then made available for public consultation. MPP then moved from discovery to recording by means of field evaluations of selected sites, which were classified using preferred terms based on the *Thesaurus of Monument Types* (RCHME and English Heritage 1995). Each site description contained a list of components on the site, also defined in preferred terms. Within each industry, a number of key sites are then recommended for scheduling. The programme is a long-term one, which began with the extractive industries in the early 1990s since these were adjudged most at risk (Stocker 1995).

The RCHME textile mill surveys and the English Heritage MPP have been important both in creating a research methodology for selecting buildings and sites which were key elements in the development of a particular industry and for appreciating the relationship between complex site layouts and the processes of production. Recognition of the function of a particular building or feature should in all cases lead to a search for associated features which normally form part of a particular sequence of production. Like the Ironbridge Gorge plot survey, this helps to prevent concentration upon the obvious to the exclusion of the more mundane components, without which the site cannot be fully interpreted. The method of identification of industrial sites in the last decade has attempted to move away from concentration upon the individual monument, as demonstrated in the early lists and gazetteers of industrial sites, to the setting of specific research agendas for the investigation of historical problems in which field data can play an important role.

## RECORDING

Recording sites or structures is the process of obtaining factual information by direct observation in the field. Its purpose is to create an archive, usually both written and illustrative, for permanent storage, a process usually described as 'preservation by record', and in many cases to provide an interpretation of the site or structure. The term 'recording' covers a wide range of techniques from the provision of a written description to a fully measured site plan and researched report. The level of recording, and therefore the techniques, used for a particular site or structure depend on its importance, its above-ground survival and the degree of threat to it.

Several of the identification techniques referred to above include an element of rapid recording by written description only, as, for example, the standard form used in the West Yorkshire Textile Mills Survey. This is the most basic level of recording, perhaps the most 'value-free' and therefore objective gathering of data. The Association for Industrial Archaeology's IRIS (Index Record for Industrial Sites) project is attempting to extend this system to all industrial sites by utilising local voluntary effort. The project involved the construction of a hierarchical wordlist for industrial sites which has attempted to break down the features on a systematic basis, differentiating between the site and the components which comprise it (Association for Industrial Archaeology 1993). This wordlist has now been incorporated into the *Thesaurus of Monument Types*. Unlike the early NRIM record cards, the IRIS recording form has been designed to meet national data standards to enable direct transfer to Sites and Monuments Records and the National Archaeological Record. Figures 26 and 27 illustrate a form compiled for the charcoal-fuelled blast furnace at Duddon in Cumbria (Plate 35). The inclusion of class and site terms selected from the hierarchical wordlist enables computer indexing to assess the relationship of this particular site to other ironworks. The availability of printed reports as well as documentary sources is included, as the form itself is meant to serve as an index to more detailed work already carried out, including measured survey, photography and excavation. Similar rapid recording techniques using photographic and written descriptions have been used by RCHME for their surveys within urban development corporation areas of all buildings of historic or architectural interest dating from before 1945. These covered Bristol, Leeds, Sheffield, Teesside, and Tyne and Wear. Only within the Black Country, for which little previous work existed, did the survey move beyond the basic level and seek to describe the historic forces which had led to the formation of the built environment in the area (RCHME 1991).

RCHME has endeavoured to standardise its recording procedures for all classes of building by the adoption of four levels of recording: these range from Level 1, a simple visual record as described above, to Level 4 which is a fully researched and illustrated record with photographs and measured drawings (RCHME 1996) (Figure 28). Each level incorporates the previous one but amplifies certain aspects such as phasing and national significance and therefore, it could be

## AIA - Index Record for Industrial Sites

*Box 1*

**SITE NAME**
DUDDON IRON FURNACE

Address:  Duddon Bridge,
near Millom

District/~~Borough~~ ....Copeland

Parish/~~Township~~ ...Millom.without....

*Box 2*

**IRIS NUMBER**

| CU | / | AIA | / | MP4 |

Part of: Iron smelting complex

Associated with: ..........

SMR no: ......2704

NMR no: ..........

*Box 3*

**NGR1** [ S . D ][ 1 .9 .6 .6 ][ 8 . 8.3 .0 ]   **NGR2** [ . ][ . . . ][ . . . ]

*Box 4*

Class: Ferr Sme

Site Term: Iron Smelt Works

Site Significance:   L / R / N / I ......1736........< . 1700 . 1750 . 1800 . 1850 . 1900 . 1950 . > ....1867
Charcoal iron furnace with surviving stack, the most complete survival of its type
in England.  The context remains unaltered, with storage barns for ore and
associated woodland charcoal sites.

| At Risk? : In use / Partly in use / Disused ....Scheduled Ancient Monument.... <br> (County Monument No. 402) | Fixtures?   Y/N/U <br> Machinery? Y/N/U |

| Site Details: Stone-built charcoal iron furnace with single blowing <br> arch and single casting arch.  The chimney over the stack is intact. <br> A wheel pit  and bellows floor have been excavated.  Stone-built <br> charging bridge with store rooms under its arches connected to the <br> furnace stack by reconstructed wooden bridge. <br> Adjoining the charging bridge is a two-storey building used as <br> offices and a smithy.  Water-power came from a head-race from <br> the River Duddon. | **PRIME MOTIVE** <br> **POWER** <br><br> Muscle .......... <br> Wind .......... <br> Water .......... <br> Hydraulic .......... <br> Steam .......... <br> Pneumatic .......... <br> Electric .......... <br> Combustion .......... <br> None .......... |

**SITE COMPONENTS**

| No | Component Term | Period | Form | Importance | Status |
|----|----------------|--------|------|------------|--------|
| 1 | Wheel Pit | 1736–1867 | Foundations | H / M / L | L / S / G / N |
| 2 | Bellows Chamber | 1736–1867 | Foundations | H / M / L | L / S / G / N |
| 3 | Casting Floor | 1736–1867 | Foundations | H / M / L | L / S / G / N |
| 4 | Blast Furnace | 1736–1867 | Structure | H / M / L | L / S / G / N |
| 5 | Charging Bridge | 1736–1867 | Structure | H / M / L | L / S / G / N |
| 6 | Stores under bridge | 1736–1867 | Structure | H / M / L | L / S / G / N |
| 7 | Office | 1736–1867 | Structure | H / M / L | L / S / G / N |
| 8 | Smithy | 1736–1867 | Structure | H / M / L | L / S / G / N |
|  |  |  |  | H / M / L | L / S / G / N |
|  |  |  |  | H / M / L | L / S / G / N |

©Association for Industrial Archaeology                    IRIS FORM ver 2

*Figure 26*  Both sections of a completed IRIS form for Duddon Furnace in Cumbria.

## AIA - Index Record for Industrial Sites
(page 2)

*Box 5*

**IRIS NUMBER**

CU / AIA / MP4

*Box 6*

Other Status: ....................................................................................................

Site History: Between 1711 and 1748, eight blast furnaces were constructed in this area to make use of local charcoal and water power. Duddon Furnace was erected in 1736 and worked until 1867 with very little alteration to its original form. The original pair of bellows was replaced in 1785 by two cast-iron blowing cylinders and a new 27' waterwheel was installed. It became a SAM in 1963 but was turned down for Guardianship. Emergency repairs were carried out in 1973, followed by a 21 year lease to Cumberland C. C. in 1974. The site was then leased on a 50 year term by the Lake District Special Planning Board in 1980.

**ASSOCIATED PERSONS/COMPANIES**

| Name | Details |
|---|---|
| Cunsey Co | 1736 |
| Hall, Kendall & Co | |
| Kendall, Latham & Co | |
| Joseph Richard Latham | |
| Harrison, Ainslie & Co | worked site from 1828 |

Site Recording: by Lake District Special Planning Board.

Sources: 1. J.D. Marshall & M. Davies Sheil, Industrial Archaeology of the Lake Counties (1969)
2. Alfred Fell, The Early Iron Industry of Furness & District, (1908)
3. A. Lowe, 'Archaeology & the Lake District National Park' in
4. R. White & R. Iles (eds) Archaeology in the National Parks (1991)
5. P. Riden, A Gazetteer of Charcoal Iron Furnaces in GB in use since 1660 (1993)

Date of Last Visit: September 1993     Reporter: M. Palmer

Compiler: M. Palmer     Date: 18.12.95

Society: Association for Industrial Archaeology

*Box 7*

Continuation Box: Site History continued
Archaeological excavation was carried out between 1981 and 1985, followed by major consolidation work.

IRIS FORM ver 2

argued, moves from the objective to the increasingly subjective. These four levels can usefully be applied to sites as well as structures of the industrial period.

Level 1 surveys require a visual record of exteriors only, supplemented by the minimum of information needed to identify type, location and approximate date where possible. This level is used when the aim is to gather basic information about a large number of buildings, e.g. for statistical sampling or planning purposes. The initial survey used in the textile mills project was a Level 1 survey applied to structures, as was the assessment of engine houses for management purposes carried out by the Cornwall Archaeological Unit (Sharpe *et al.* 1991). Structures identified from documentary sources were visited in the field and graded using the monument appraisal criteria originally developed for MPP. Symbols were devised for categories such as type and function (Figure 29) and the standard entry (Figure 30 and Plate 36) was supplemented by a written description, location map and assessment of condition. This method of recording can clearly be applied to many other classes of industrial structures. Cornwall Archaeological Unit has also made use of what is essentially a Level 1 standard of recording for mining landscapes, using a plot and sketch technique for locating features not recorded on existing maps (Herring 1988). Their surveys were based on 1:2,500 OS maps and involved the setting up of a tight grid of fixed points by means of a plane table, microptic alidade or electronic distance measurement (EDM). Ranging poles were erected at each fixed point

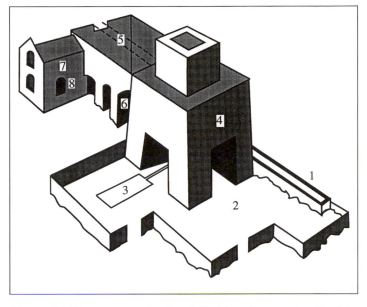

**Figure 27** Diagrammatic sketch of Duddon Furnace in Cumbria. 1 – Waterwheel pit, 2 – Bellows room, 3 – Casting floor, 4 – Blast furnace, 5 – Charging bridge, 6 – Store, 7 – Office, 8 – Smithy.

**Plate 35** The stone-built charcoal iron furnace near Duddon Bridge in Cumbria.

Reproduced by courtesy of Andrew Lowe, Lake District National Park.

and surface features were then pace-sketched along perpendicular offsets within the several triangles formed by the poles. Any errors were thus confined to individual triangles whose average

## RCHME LEVELS OF RECORDING FOR BUILDINGS

| WRITTEN ACCOUNT | DRAWINGS | PHOTOGRAPHY |
|---|---|---|
| 1. Location of buildings, NGR and status | 1. Sketch plan, roughly dimensioned | 1. External view or views |
| 2. Date record made, names of recorders | 2. Plans of principal floors, showing features of historic significance | 2. Overall interiors of principal rooms |
| 3. Statement of building's type, purpose, materials, date | 3. Drawings of other significant structural detail | 3. All exteriors |
| 4. Fuller account of development sequence, plan, form and function | 4. Sections to illustrate vertical relationships | 4. External details, relevant to design, development and use |
| 5. As 4, with evidence for analysis | 5. Drawings of details, eg. doorcases, mullions | 5. Relationship of building to setting |
| 6. Description of past and present uses, including machinery etc | 6. Measured elevations | 6. Interior detail, structural and decorative |
| 7. Evidence for former existence of demolished structures etc. | 7. Site plan relating building to other structures etc | |
| 8. Copies of previous records or information on location | 8. Copies of earlier plans | |
| 9. Relevant information from readily available sources | 9. Three-dimensional projections | |
| 10. Past and present relationship of building to setting | 10. Reconstruction drawings or phased drawings | |
| 11. Potential for existence of below ground evidence | | |
| 12. Significance of building locally, regionally or nationally | | |
| 13. Other historical research, oral information and bibliography | | |

| | Level One | Level Two | Level Three | Level Four |
|---|---|---|---|---|
| Written record | 1-3 | 1-2, 4 | 1-2, 4-9 | 1-2, 4-13 |
| Drawn record | 1 | 1, normally 2 | 2-4 or 5 | 2-10 |
| Photography | 1, perhaps 2 | 2-3 | 3-6 | 3-6 |

*Figure 28* A simplified table showing the four levels of recording for standing structures adopted by the Royal Commission on the Historical Monuments of England

maximum dimension was about 20 metres [22 yards]. Although inevitably there was a small degree of inaccuracy, no archaeological detail was lost. The technique involves only one operator, yet has enabled numerous unmapped features to be located, their extents established, condition assessed and their principal management needs determined.

Level 2 recording applied to buildings involves a full description and photographic record of both the interior and exterior of the building. Roughly dimensioned sketch plans are made, and the written record should include a summary of the building's plan, form, function and phasing but without a full analysis of the evidence on which this summary is based. Most of the building recording undertaken by local voluntary groups is of this level, particularly of buildings under threat of demolition or conversion. Examples include the survey carried out by Somerset Industrial Archaeology Society of a malthouse at Halse before conversion to dwellings (Miles 1989) and that under-

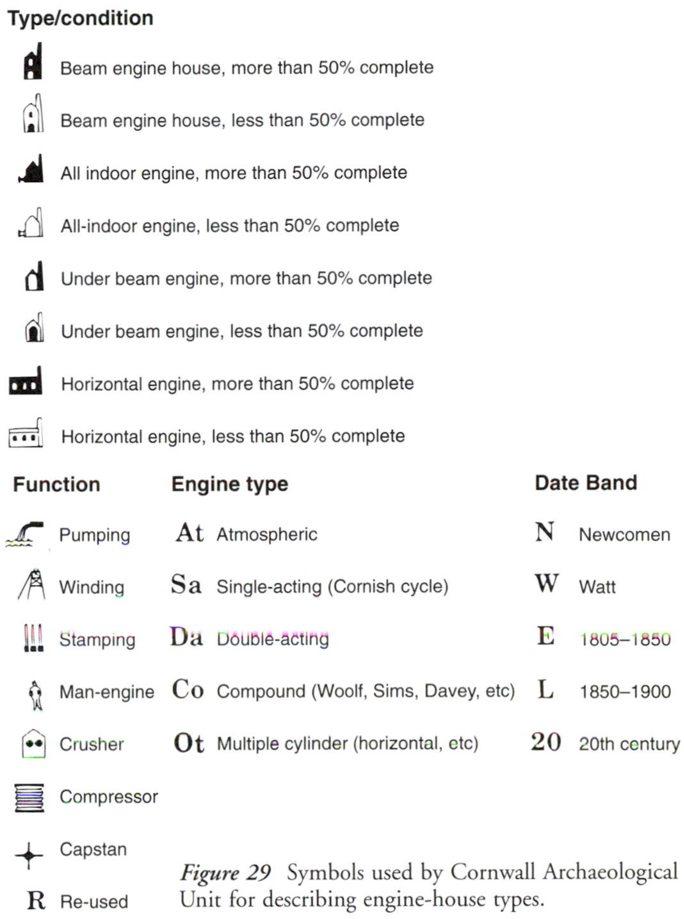

**Type/condition**

Beam engine house, more than 50% complete

Beam engine house, less than 50% complete

All indoor engine, more than 50% complete

All-indoor engine, less than 50% complete

Under beam engine, more than 50% complete

Under beam engine, less than 50% complete

Horizontal engine, more than 50% complete

Horizontal engine, less than 50% complete

| Function | Engine type | | Date Band | |
|---|---|---|---|---|
| Pumping | At | Atmospheric | N | Newcomen |
| Winding | Sa | Single-acting (Cornish cycle) | W | Watt |
| Stamping | Da | Double-acting | E | 1805–1850 |
| Man-engine | Co | Compound (Woolf, Sims, Davey, etc) | L | 1850–1900 |
| Crusher | Ot | Multiple cylinder (horizontal, etc) | 20 | 20th century |
| Compressor | | | | |
| Capstan | | | | |
| Re-used | R | | | |

*Figure 29* Symbols used by Cornwall Archaeological Unit for describing engine-house types.

MINE NAME: **Grenville United**          PRN: **35302.03**
HOUSE NAME: **New Stamps**     CONSTRUCTION DATE: **1891**
FUNCTION: **Stamping (aux. pumping)** ENGINE SIZE: **30" cylinder.** BEDSTONE: **In Situ.**
KB REF NO: **E300**     NGR: **SW 6665 3860**     PROTECTION: **Scheduled, Listed Grade 2.**
OWNER: **Not identified**
FOUNDRY: **Not Known**

| MIV | SMAV | MIV + SMAV | Comments |
|---|---|---|---|
| 42 | 29 | 71 | Also associated structures downslope. |

| Type | Func | Func | Age | Op |
|---|---|---|---|---|
|  |  |  | L | Da |

*Figure 30* Part of a report completed by Cornwall Archaeological Unit for Wheal Grenville New Stamps.
Key:  MIV =  Monument Importance Value, an assessment of the importance of individual structures as examples of their class.
    SMAV = Site Management Appraisal Value, an assessment of the condition of the structures.
Reproduced by permission of the Cornwall Archaeological Unit.

*Plate 36* Wheal Grenville New Stamps, in Cornwall, in 1987.

taken by Leicestershire Industrial History Society of the model farm attached to Carlton Hayes hospital, demolition of which was imminent (Palmer and Neaverson 1990–1). Level 2 surveys can also be applied to sites, again often by local groups, as in the work undertaken by Derbyshire Archaeological Society on the remains of coke ovens (Reedman and Sissons 1985; Battye *et al.* 1991). These sites included ruinous structures once related to both railways and coal mines. The basic plans for these were taken from early editions of large-scale OS maps and supplemented by schematic plans of selected surviving structures.

Level 3 recording includes measured plans and elevations, together with dimensioned sketches of details. It is an analytical record, incorporating an account of the origins and development of the site or structure based on an examination of the building itself together with readily available sources. Many of the surveys carried out by RCHME following the initial survey of textile mills come into this category, such as that of Havelock Mill in Manchester (Williams 1993). This survey paid particular attention to the development of the power transmission system within the mill (Figure 31) and the phasing of the buildings. An example of a Level 3 recording on a site basis is the survey of the Gawton Mine and Arsenic Works near

*Figure 31* A section through Havelock cotton mill, Manchester, showing the remains of the power transmission system.

RCHME, © Crown Copyright

Tavistock, carried out by the Exeter Museums Archaeological Field Unit. The survey team based their work on a wide range of maps and published material and carried out a complete site and building survey. Using documentary sources, as well as field evidence, the unit was able to relate the remains to the largely unrecorded process of arsenic calcining (Pye and Weddell 1992).

The fourth level of recording is employed only for buildings of especial importance and draws on the full range of sources of information. The report will include a discussion of the building's significance in terms of architectural, social, regional or economic history. A good example of Level 4 recording applied to buildings was the survey of the eastern terminus of Britain's first passenger railway from Liverpool to Manchester (Fitzgerald 1980): this report includes drawn plans, elevations and sections of the buildings together with details of interior goods-handling fitments. The survey is set in the context of the development of the railway, particularly its approach to a built-up area involving the construction of numerous bridges. A less ambitious Level 4 survey, undertaken by the authors, was of Glyn Pits Colliery near Pontypool, the only coal mine in Britain to retain steam-powered pumping and winding engines of mid-nineteenth-century origin. Careful analysis of the remaining structures, together with extensive use of documentary sources, has enabled an interpretation of the changes in pumping and winding systems on the mine (Figure 32) which could serve as a model for similar work on other sites (Palmer and Neaverson 1990). Similarly, at the site of the Royal Gunpowder Factory at Waltham Abbey in Essex, RCHME recorded the complex field remains and conducted extensive research into the history of explosives manufac-

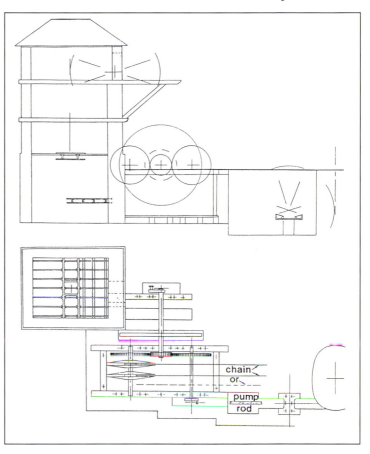

*Figure 32* Simplified elevation and plan of the rotative beam pumping and winding engine at Glyn Pits, near Pontypool, Gwent. The obvious field remains indicated only the pumping function: the previous winding arrangement by means of chain reels in a pit adjacent to the engine house was deduced from fragmentary remains supported by documentary sources.

ture from black powder to tetryl in order to set this important site into its technological context (RCHME 1994a).

These four levels of recording are useful not only in defining what kind of data is to be collected, but also in enabling the resources available to be matched to the task to be undertaken. Clearly, the use of sophisticated equipment reduces the manpower requirement but it is possible for a local group who have sufficient numbers and time available to work to Level 4 standards with basic equipment. The levels need to be flexible since close examination of a structure may reveal important features which demand a higher level of recording than that originally anticipated. Indeed, the authors' work at Glyn Pits began as a Level 2 project, but the anomalies observed during the recording process prompted detailed documentary work which resulted in a Level 4 record.

## SITE-SURVEYING METHODS

Since surveying is a largely field-based operation and the techniques involved cannot easily be learnt from using a text, this section will discuss the survey methods appropriate to a variety of situations but will not deal with the techniques in detail. Industrial archaeologists have a wide range of tools available to them today ranging from the very basic to highly sophisticated electronic instruments incorporating computers. Great flexibility is therefore possible in their adoption and use dependent upon the number of people available, the size and topography of the site and the presence of standing buildings or surface features. A preliminary reconnaissance of the site is essential so that reference points and scales can be agreed upon if several teams are involved in the survey.

Briefly summarised the tools available for site survey are as follows:

- Horizontal distance measurement: rods, chains and tapes; optical tacheometry (theodolite or microptic alidade) and EDM (electronic distance measurement)
- Angle measurement: prismatic compass (horizontal angles) for magnetic bearings; Abney level or clinometer (for vertical angles); theodolite (for horizontal and vertical angles); cross staff and optical square (for setting out right angles); EDM
- Height measurement: folding rods, 5-metre telescopic rods; Abney level or clinometer; theodolite (and use of trigonometry); dumpy, quick-set and automatic levels; total station incorporating EDM and electronic theodolite
- Mapping: plane table with plain or microptic alidade; EDM

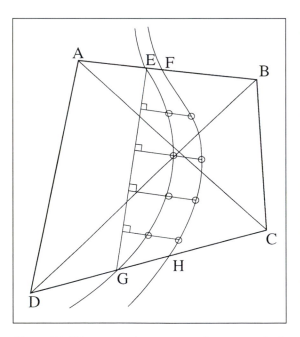

***Figure 33*** Diagram to show a survey by means of tri-angulation and offset measurement. An irregular and level area *ABCD* is crossed by a stream in a curved channel. A plan of area *ABCD* may be made by a chain survey, measuring *AB*, *BC*, *CD* and *DA*, using the diagonals *AC* and *BD* as check measurements. The position of the stream bed may be determined where it crosses *AB* and *CD* by direct measurements. The rest of the stream may be determined within the area by laying out a line *EG* and using the offset method of measurement. At various known points along *EG*, perpendiculars are set and the position of the stream boundary noted in each case.

As noted previously, many sites of the industrial period will appear on the first edition, 25-inch-to-1-mile OS maps or the even larger-scale town plans created in the late nineteenth century, which therefore provide a useful starting-point. However, uncultivated areas of waste and mountain were not mapped on the 25-inch scale, only at 6-inch, and consequently many upland mining sites, for example, have to be surveyed to provide a detailed site plan. Modern large-scale maps can be used as a basis for placing unrecorded features in context, although a copyright fee must be paid if the drawing is published (there is a good account of the use of OS maps in Anthony Brown 1987: 49). The National Grid Reference enables a site to be accurately located and the bench marks provide a means of tying in heights to a national reference point.

To produce a site plan for a more or less level site of limited area, say up to 150 metres [180 yards] in maximum dimension, with no or few upstanding structures, an adequate survey may be made by means of setting up a base line or a grid of lines, visually or by means of a theodolite. The origin of the base line or grid should be at a known position in relation to the OS map if possible. The distances of features from the base line(s) are then recorded by means of measuring offsets or by triangulation from points along the base line(s) (Figure 33). These techniques are described by Brown (1987: 49–54).

For larger, more or less level areas, an adequate plan can be produced by means of a series of base lines as a traverse or grid or by the use of the plane table, or by a combination of both systems (Figure 34). This method is also suitable where there are upstanding buildings. Problems of visibility of points required to be mapped may be overcome by measuring distances by radiation, using tacheometry with a microptic alidade or with a theodolite (see Bettess 1984: 69–77).

Clearly, where the ground is not level there are restrictions on visibility with the above methods, although a telescopic measuring rod is useful for extending the range for plane tabling. With hilly ground it is necessary to use a larger number of base lines from which offsets or sightings are

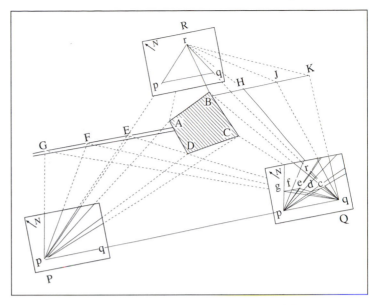

***Figure 34*** Diagram to show site survey using the plane table.
The irregular watermill building *ABCD* is supplied with water by a pipe, supported on uprights at *HJK*, and water discharges through a tailrace *EFG*. It is required to map the building outline and the features *E–K*. Two points *P* and *Q* are selected west and east of the building from which most of the points to be mapped can be seen. The plane table is set up and levelled at point *P* and by means of an alidade, from a point *p* on the drawing sheet a line is drawn aligned with *PQ* and the point *q* is marked at a suitable scale. Without moving the table, rays are drawn on the drawing sheet to intersect points *GFE*, *A*, *D* and *C*. The plane table is then moved to point *Q*, levelled and the ray *qp* aligned with *QP* with point *q* over the *Q* marker. The table is then kept fixed and the alidade used to draw rays to the visible points *BCD* and *E–K*; some of the rays will intersect and these points represent points *C–G*. In order to map the remaining points by means of intersections a third station *R* is selected north of the building from which the rest of the points may be seen. The distance *QR* is measured and scaled off along the ray *qr*. The plane table is then moved to point *R*, levelled and the ray *rq* lined up with *RQ* and a check sight made upon point *P*. Rays are then drawn to produce the intersections *AB* and *H–K*. If a point is visible from only one station, the alidade may be aligned and the distance measured by tacheometry.

taken. In addition a site profile along the base lines must be made or a full contour survey carried out by means of levelling and if possible linked to a bench mark (Figure 35). Levelling may be done using a Sopwith staff and a level (a technique dealt with by Bettess [1984: 40–53]) or by the use of the theodolite (see Leach 1988: 31–5). Site profiles are important in water-power sites and mining landscapes, particularly ore-dressing floors which rely heavily on gravitation for their flow systems (Figure 36).

These relatively simple procedures have in many cases, where financial resources permit, been superseded by the use of the total station EDM and theodolite which will furnish information in three dimensions. This instrument requires careful setting up at each station, preferably one from which a lot of readings can be taken. The EDM produces indirect linear measurements of great accuracy and has a range of over 1 kilometre [0.6 mile] (see Leach 1988: 36–41). The data

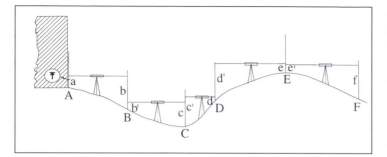

**Figure 35** Diagram showing the use of a simple level.

The difference in heights between the ground levels at points *A* and *B* can be obtained by measuring the heights *a* and *b* by means of a level placed at a station between them and taking a foresight and a backsight to a levelling staff. The building has an Ordnance Survey Bench Mark (OBM) upon it, a distance x above the ground level at *A*, so the actual ground level with respect to Ordnance Datum of *A* can be calculated at *OBM* minus x. In this example, the difference in level between the two points *A* and *F* cannot be found from one station and so it is necessary to repeat the process between points *BC*, *CD*, *DE* and *EF*, taking backsights and foresights between each point and calculating the reduced levels at points *B–E* so that the height of point *F*, relative to point *A*, and the Ordnance Datum can be calculated.

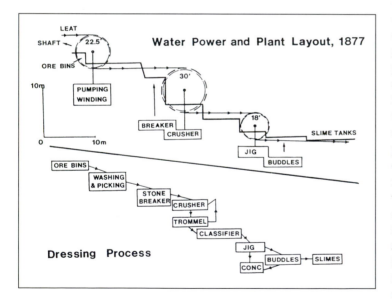

**Figure 36** A schematic diagram of the lead-dressing floor at Ystrad Einion mine in Dyfed, Wales. The water supplied by leat was utilised by three separate wheels, while the lead ore was successively reduced in size. The slope of the land was essential for the gravitational reduction and concentration process.

is down-loaded into a data logger and then plotted through an office computer system.

## BUILDING RECORDING METHODS

The recording of buildings, through the production of drawn plans, elevations and sections, will sometimes form part of a site survey or more commonly be carried out where outline site plans are already available. The techniques of producing measured drawings of industrial buildings using readily obtainable equipment have been fully described by Major (1975). A complete photographic record is also essential for elevations and details of a building or structure (Terry Buchanan 1983). In the case of large sites, oblique aerial photographs which record both block plan and elevation are useful for assessing and planning the recording strategy. In cases of immediate threat or limited manpower, only a photographic record may be possible, although, in suitable cases, elevations can be produced by means of rectified photography. As with site survey, several methods of measurement are possible, including the total station electronic system. If several groups are working on one building it is advisable for one person from each group to make a full reconnaissance of it, as with site survey, so that collectively various points of reference and scales can be agreed. The ground-floor plan of a building, although often indicated on a large-scale map, requires the addition of detail such as door apertures and window frames. In all cases a preliminary sketch of the floor plan should be made to which measured dimensions are subsequently added. Since it cannot be assumed that the walls of a building are regular,

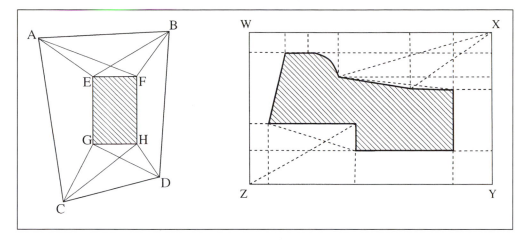

*Figure 37* Methods of determining ground plans of buildings.

LH. A plan of the regular-shaped building *EFGH* within the plot *ABCD* can be prepared by means of triangulation from the corners of the plot *A–D*, and using measured distances *EF*, *FH*, *HG* and *GE* as cross-checks.

RH. If the building to be measured is of an irregular shape, a rectangle *WXYZ* (marked by a measuring tape or string) can be set up around it. The positions of corners of the building and other features can be ascertained by measuring the offset from the side of the rectangle to those points at a known distance along the side of the rectangle. Linear measurements of the straight walls will serve as a cross-check whilst re-entrant angles can be positioned by means of triangulation from the corners of the rectangle *WXYZ*.

the exterior plan is obtained by placing a grid around the building, set visually for small buildings and by optical square or theodolite for larger ones. Measurements are taken from the grid to the walls as offsets or by triangulation (Figure 37). It is usual to show the windows and door apertures on the plan and these verticals should be taken by running measurements along the walls to minimise error. The respective wall thicknesses should be measured at each aperture. Diagonal measurements should be taken within the building as cross-checks and shown on the field sketch in coloured pencil to avoid confusion. The internal walls and any floor-level features are then measured, again using running measurements where possible. For multi-storey buildings, changes in wall thickness in the height of the walls should be measured and separate floor plans made at the same scale for each floor level showing the window and aperture positions.

Preliminary sketches must also be made for each elevation of the building and of any sections which are required, e.g. doors or window-sill and lintel details. As on the ground plan, running dimensions must be taken of the window and door-frame apertures and checks made of the alignment of upper-storey windows in relation to the ground floor (see Hutton 1986: 6–7). Before commencing height measurements, a datum line should be established on the exterior of the building so that account may be taken of changes in ground level. The same datum line should where possible be used for the interior elevations or the distance between the two lines accurately known. Heights are measured either above or below the datum. Measurement of upper-storey apertures may well be possible only from the interior of the building but their vertical positions must still be related to the datum line. Whilst a 5-metre telescopic rod is useful for some height measurements, on tall structures some ingenuity must be employed: for example, where the construction is of uniform-sized ashlar stone or brick, the number of courses can be

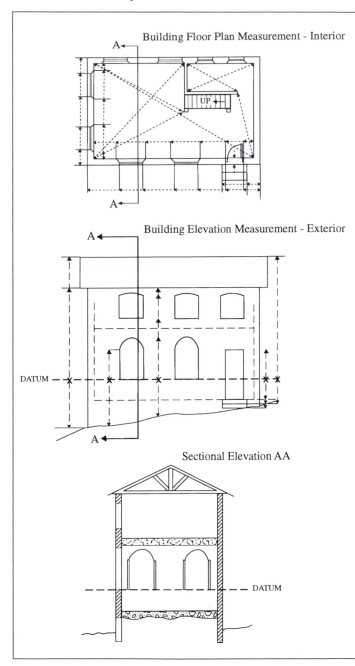

Building Floor Plan Measurement - Interior

A

UP

A

Building Elevation Measurement - Exterior

A

DATUM

A

Sectional Elevation AA

DATUM

*Figure 38* Methods of determining interiors and elevations of buildings.

*Top*: a preliminary sketch is made of the floor plan of a building, noting the features to be shown on the plan. Linear measurements are taken along the walls, noting the positions of door and window apertures, etc. Running measurements are taken from each corner, to minimise possible error. Check diagonal measurements are taken between corners and to position other features to be shown. The wall thicknesses should be measured at door or window apertures to enable the interior and exterior plans to be linked together.

*Centre*: in order to take account of undulating ground surfaces it is necessary to mark out a horizontal datum line around the building: the window-sills may be suitable. If more than one datum is necessary to enable the measurements to be made, it is vital to note the differences in height between them. Once again a detailed sketch should be made showing all the details to be measured. Heights of features on the building are then measured either above or below datum. Horizontal distances and heights of features such as door and window apertures should be made with running measurements to minimise errors. Horizontal distances along the exterior of upper-floor features such as windows may be measured by means of plumb lines hung from them.

This process has to be repeated for all the building elevations. Detailed drawings of window-frames, doors, etc. should be made separately and usually drawn at a larger scale.

*Bottom*: a sectional elevation at a desired vertical transverse plane within the building is often essential to show its construction. This section is through AA of the building shown in the previous example.

counted and the height estimated by calculation. In other cases a theodolite must be used and the height established by calculation (Figure 38).

When preparing the final drawings a suitable scale must be chosen by reference to the largest length dimension. There are accepted conventions for the layout of the respective plans and sections and also for the depiction of details and building materials; these are summarised in the RCHME building recording specification (RCHME 1996).

Another tool available to the industrial archaeologist for the preparation of building elevations is photogrammetry or measurement by photography. There are several methods of an increasing sophistication, the simplest of which is rectified photography. This can produce elevations of reasonable accuracy providing there are no substantial recesses in the building elevation and its height is not excessive. Essentially a photograph of an elevation is taken with the camera film plane vertical and parallel to a wall, or in the case of a long building, a series of photographs is taken from positions along a previously laid-out base line parallel to the wall. Both vertical and horizontal dimensions between features of the elevation must be taken so that a scale may be established. The negatives should be enlarged to a specified scale and for preference printed on transparent film. The series of prints may then be easily overlapped as a photo-montage and a tracing prepared of the whole elevation. Greater accuracy can be achieved by the use of a mono-rail camera with rising front and side movements to the lens or of a 35mm SLR camera with shift lens and grid focusing, particularly in the case of taller buildings. Rectified photography is well described by Dallas (1980b). A more complex but accurate process for producing elevations using stereo photography is stereo-photogrammetry wherein pairs of photographs taken with a metric camera of the required elevation are scanned in a stereo plotter and the scale drawing produced on a plotting table (see Dallas 1980a). More recently computer-aided mono-photogrammetry has been introduced. This process obtains data from a single photographic image, using computer-aided design (CAD) facilities to produce the final drawing; it is described briefly by Swallow *et al.* (1993). In recent years techniques have also been perfected for the recording of building elevations electronically by means of the total station EDM.

## RECORDING MACHINERY AND PROCESSES

The industrial archaeologist is sometimes required to record machinery which may be either part of a building or free-standing. In general, the problems of congestion and complication of components of machinery such as a steam engine, for example, mean that only a limited number of elevations may be possible. If actual physical access to the machine can be obtained then the layout and physical dimensions can be measured. When carrying out measurements, the details which it is desired to show on a sectional elevation must be borne in mind when selecting the plane of section, since many components will be concealed. A series of reference surfaces on the machine must be selected from which dimensions are measured. Many of the details will have to be recorded as annotations to sketches (e.g. numbers and profiles of gear teeth, wall brackets, column profiles) and separate drawings prepared of detail components (Figure 39). Where possible, photographs should be taken of the same plans and elevations for cross-reference. Care must be taken to relate items of machinery and shafting dimensionally to the building structure.

Given that recording machinery is a highly specialised activity for which a training in technical drawing is desirable to produce effective results, a specialist draughtsperson may well have to be employed. Documentary research into machine manufacturers' archives, such as the Boulton and Watt collection in Birmingham Reference Library, may well be productive, offering original or similar drawings of machines and their components. In many cases, however, the position of machinery relative to a building or structure is more important than the details of the machines themselves, and recording this is well within the capacity of most fieldworkers.

This section has been dealing with recording the remains of past industry. But, as Hayman (1997) has said: 'Opportunities to make first-hand records of industry should be grasped whole-heartedly by archaeologists.' It is impossible for field recorders to have a work-ing knowledge of the whole range of industrial processes, but the creation of a film archive of working industry is a

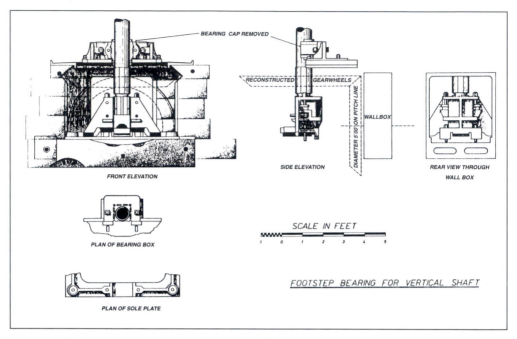

**Figure 39** Elevations and drawings of details of the footstep bearing for the vertical power transmission shaft in Albion Mill, Manchester.

Reproduced by permission of R. S. Fitzgerald.

valuable tool for the future. We already have a valuable resource in the films made, for example, of working canals and railways, textile processes, glass manufacture, etc. (Grant and Ballantyne 1985). This work has been continued through the use of video by, for example, IA Recordings, a group who have concentrated on filming the last days of certain industries, particularly coal-mining. The sudden demise of the latter also prompted the various Royal Commissions on Historical Monuments, Cadw and English Heritage to make visual records, not only of buildings, but also of both surface and underground activity (Thornes 1994; Hughes *et al.* n.d.; Gould and Ayris 1995; Malaws 1997). Much of their work was done as part of emergency record-ing, but these agencies, as well as others, need to be proactive as well as reactive. The problems in recording working processes should not be under-estimated: they can include the dangers of moving machinery, contamination, difficulties of access and the attitudes of a demoralised workforce about to face redundancy. All these problems were encountered by the Scottish Royal Commission on Historical Monuments in their work on the Ardeer explosives works in Ayrshire (Dolan and Oglethorpe 1996). Records of process can therefore be difficult and time-consuming to make, as well as demanding specialist equipment, but they create an archive of past and present industrial activity which is second to none.

## THE WRITTEN REPORT

Every site, building or machine survey should be accompanied by a comprehensive descriptive written report supported by a systematic photographic record (Terry Buchanan 1983). Site reports need to include details of location, and ownership where known, as well as information about soil type, geology and general topography. In the case of a building, the number of bays and storeys should be noted, together with details of the fabric. Changes in building materials, in particular, may help with the phasing of the structure.

It is often useful to treat an elevation of a building in the same way as a section of an archaeological excavation, assigning context numbers to different features. The problem is, what actually is a 'context' on a standing structure? In excavation, 'contexts' are discrete units related stratigraphically to each other and ultimately to unconsolidated natural strata. Generally, below = earlier and above = later. On standing buildings, this does not apply: because one is dealing with a rigid structure, alterations can be made to one area without affecting the rest. Harris's Laws of Original Horizontality and Original Continuity are inapplicable to standing structures. Nevertheless, the technique is a useful one in trying to be as objective as possible in the analysis of a building but a new definition has to be found for a 'context' or 'stratigraphic unit'. Wrathmell (1990: 38) argues that a context is a unit of observation whose identity and significance are widely agreed upon, and therefore a context is defined by the research agenda decided on for recording any particular structure. Only rarely is a stone-by-stone record needed for large industrial structures as it would be for medieval buildings: more often, the 'units of significance' are identifiable objects like windows, numbers of bays, addition of staircase towers on mills, roof-lines, etc. Returning to the discussion at the beginning of this chapter, these units represent deliberate human decisions to alter a building, and therefore assist not only the description of the building but its interpretation in a social as well as structural sense. Separate sequences of numbers can be allocated to each elevation or, in a complex building, to each individual phase of construction. It is then possible to summarise the different features in a schedule of context numbers, each of which is related to the appropriate survey drawing. The use of context numbers in some form does ensure that all features are given equal weight in the description, not just the outstanding features, thereby permitting an archaeological rather than a purely architectural interpretation.

## EXCAVATION

Excavation, unlike the other methods of field recording discussed above, is a destructive act which cannot be repeated: the deposits removed cannot be replaced and the information they might yield can be permanently lost. For pre-industrial-period sites, excavation may be the only method of obtaining information about the function and date of a particular site. But in the industrial period, field survey allied with other forms of evidence such as maps and documents may yield the same information without destroying the stratigraphy. For example, by using a combination of survey and documentary research the authors were able to show that a tin dressing floor at Carnkie in Cornwall had gone through three reconstructions in three decades (Palmer and Neaverson 1987). This is further discussed in Chapter Six.

Excavation is therefore a last resort. If it is undertaken, it must be as part of a defined research agenda. For industrial-period sites, excavation has normally been carried out for one of three reasons: rescue, site display or research. Rescue digs have multiplied in the last decade because of the environmental concern with contaminated and derelict land. The funding which has been made available for this purpose has often included an element for archaeological evaluation, but the conditions under which such evaluation has been carried out have often been far from ideal, the archaeologist barely keeping up with the earth-moving equipment. The information retrieved has often therefore been very fragmentary and has not formed part of a total site record. This kind of rescue excavation has been largely confined to mining sites, which have themselves created the contamination, and considerable information has been recovered concerning mining methods and ore-dressing techniques. Similar rescue digs have taken place in areas of early shaft

*Plate 37* Part of the final phase of the lead-dressing floors at Killhope in County Durham, showing a rectangular buddle of wood and stone construction for separating the ore from the gangue material. This structure has been conserved for display purposes but may well conceal an earlier phase.

By permission of P. Craxford.

mining in conjunction with modern open-cast coal-mining. Careful observation of features in exposed faces has led to limited excavation of old shafts and underground mining features. In Leicestershire, for example, excavations of this kind have exposed timber-lined shafts and systematic pillar and stall working which have been dated by dendrochronology to the fifteenth century (York and Warburton 1991).

It has rarely proved possible for sites revealed by rescue excavation to be conserved *in situ*, but funding has occasionally been made available by local authorities and museums to undertake excavation for the purpose of display. The problem with this kind of excavation is its limited extent, since features which are to be permanently conserved may overlie evidence for earlier periods of working. This was the case with the Killhope lead ore-dressing mill in Weardale, where the final phase of the washing floor was conserved for display purposes (Plate 37), greatly limiting the opportunity to excavate below this level (Cranstone 1989: 44). Only in research excavations can the upper layers be removed to examine the earliest phases, and these have been rare for the industrial period. They have, however, proved invaluable in providing information about processes such as lime-burning and ore-dressing for which little documentary evidence exists.

Few industrial sites are devoid of upstanding structures, and there is always a temptation to carry out the clearance of these without attention to detailed stratigraphy. In some cases, clearance is justified; for example, where the infill is clearly the result of deliberate demolition or tipping – the sort of treatment being received on modern collieries following closure. Thus a test trench may reveal the junction between deliberate infill and stratified deposits. On many industrial sites, there has not always been time for layers to accumulate, and so the careful recording generally carried out on archaeological sites is not always appropriate. Clearance can also be undertaken for specific purposes, as, for example, to reveal the foundations of machinery known to have been present from documentary evidence. At Higher Woodhill Mill, a demolished cotton-spinning factory near Bury in Lancashire, documentary evidence indicated that the original water-power system was supplemented by steam in the 1850s and limited excavation has indicated that this was a house-built engine (Fletcher 1994). In rare cases, the machine itself may survive elsewhere and the excavation is undertaken to examine its previous context. A good example is the 1779 Boulton and Watt beam engine now in the Birmingham Museum of Science and Industry: only in 1982 did the pump-house site at Smethwick, from which the engine was removed in 1897, become available for excavation, the purpose of which was to determine the original layout of the engine and any subsequent modifications (Andrew 1985).

In research excavations, the relationship of one context to another is as important for the industrial period as for earlier periods of archaeology, even though the length of time over which

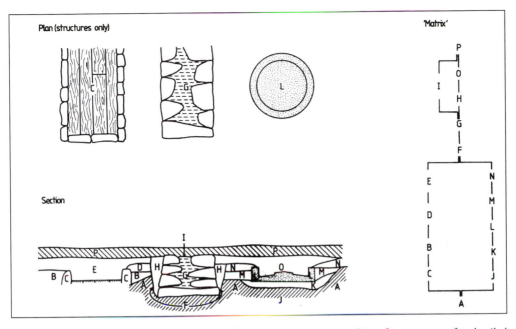

***Figure 40*** Plan, section and matrix of part of a hypothetical mine washing floor: see text for detailed description.

By permission of David Cranstone and Matthew Watson.

the layers were deposited may be very short indeed. Figure 40 shows the plan, section and matrix of part of a hypothetical mine washing floor. The plan shows the stone and timber structures only, as they would be revealed by clearance of soil layers without stratigraphic recording. The impression derived from the plan alone is that the three structures were contemporary. The section, however, indicates that the central wall *G* was built later, at a time when the jigger *C* was disused and infilled, since the infill *H* of its construction trench cuts the infill E of the jigger. The buddle *L* remained open (and perhaps in use) after the construction of the wall *G*, since its infill *O* overlies the top of the construction trench and abuts the face of the wall. The stratigraphic matrix defines the relationship of these structures (after Cranstone 1992). Normally, the excavated sections are first described as objectively as possible without reference to any other evidence, so that the description is separate from any interpretation of the sections.

The stratification of process residues is also important on industrial sites. For example, on the complex site at Aberdulais in West Glamorgan, the existence of mill scale overlying a cobbled floor in part of the working area indicated that the latter was associated with the iron-working rather than the tinplate period of the site (Hayman 1986). The presence of slag and charcoal fragments may be the only evidence for a vanished bloomery or bole hill site. Different grades of residue may also indicate the function of the structures in which they are contained. This is particularly the case on ore-dressing floors where a gradual comminution of particle size took place through a variety of equipment, the ephemeral nature of which makes their remains otherwise difficult to identify (Palmer and Neaverson, 1989).

The post-excavation treatment of finds from industrial sites has been sadly neglected. This is partly because there are no reference collections of ceramics, glassware, etc. for this period against which finds can be matched, with the honourable exceptions of the clay pipe data collated by David Higgins at Liverpool University (1989), that on Scottish brickmarks (Douglas *et al.* 1985) and the data on cutlers' marks being collated at Sheffield University. Valuable information can be derived from slag samples related to specific contexts. The metallurgical report on finds at the Moira blast furnace in Leicestershire indicated that the raw materials had a very high sulphur content which was counteracted by an unusually heavy addition of limestone flux. The furnace was abandoned with its charge intact, showing that the final blowing-out was abrupt and unplanned. The presence of quantities of melted brick in the charge suggested that the furnace chimney had collapsed due to overheating in a final disastrous campaign (Cranstone 1985). This archaeological evidence filled a void in the documentary record, which nowhere accounted for the demise of this short-lived operation. None the less, the analysis of residues is not always conclusive, as has been shown at Bersham in Clwyd. Here, analysis of the residues in a structure identified as a lime-kiln indicated far higher temperatures than those expected for lime-burning, and the structure may well have been used for smelting iron ore (Grenter 1992).

The industrial archaeologist is fortunate in often being able to relate the phases derived from excavation to documentary evidence which allows for absolute rather than relative dates to be assigned. At Aberdulais, for example, the excavation indicated six phases in the working area which were refined from the documentary evidence into eight phases ranging from the earliest copper-smelting period through corn milling, iron-working and tinplate manufacture to abandonment *circa* 1890 (Hayman 1986). At the Clydach ironworks in the Brecon Beacons National Park, the combination of findings from excavation and documentary sources has enabled a chronology of furnace construction to be established (Wilson 1988). It is important, however, that consideration of the archaeological evidence should take precedence in phasing a site, since all changes may not have been recorded in the documentary sources.

## DATING

It is, therefore, sometimes possible to obtain absolute dates for the various features on a site. However, documentary evidence must be treated with caution: on mining sites, for example, where the mine manager's report is often the only available source, the changes he might propose in writing were not always carried out and so need to be verified in the field. Relative dating can be achieved on industrial sites by assigning context numbers to the different features. These can then be organised in a stratigraphic matrix similar to that discussed above for excavated structures, which clarifies their relationship to each other in both space and time. This is a complex operation, but can be useful for multi-phase sites for which little documentary evidence is available. It has been used, for example, to phase the numerous limestone quarries and access routes at Benthall Edge in the Ironbridge Gorge (Alfrey and Clark 1993: 5, 38–9). Construction of stratigraphic matrices for such extensive areas is, however, a lengthy procedure and generally a series of sketch plans showing the different phases of working are more effective.

The construction of a stratigraphic matrix for a standing building is an equally complex operation and depends, as discussed earlier, on what stratigraphic units have been decided on in a particular recording exercise. Understanding their relationship to one another depends on an awareness of how buildings are put together and on what changes the human beings responsible for the building are likely to have made. These are usually physically revealed by anomalies in the structure such as changes in the roof-line, changes in building materials, blocked-in or inserted windows and doors and straight or bonded joints indicating extensions or alterations. The context numbers assigned to each feature can then be organised in the form of a stratigraphic matrix to determine the relative sequence of construction. Figure 41 illustrates this process for the east elevation of a textile mill. The written description assigns context numbers to the elevation from south to north, and notes anomalies such as straight joints

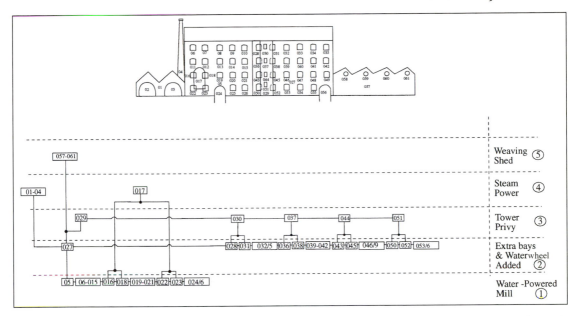

**Figure 41** The use of context numbers and a stratigraphic matrix to determine the phases of one elevation of a textile mill (east wall). *PHASE 1* WATER-POWERED MILL, *PHASE 2* ADDITIONAL WATER-POWERED MILL ADJOINING, *PHASE 3* PRIVY TOWER ADDED, *PHASE 4* STEAM ENGINE AND BOILER HOUSE ADDED, *PHASE 5* WEAVING SHED ADDED.

| CONTEXT NO. | PHASE | DESCRIPTION |
|---|---|---|
| 001 | 4 | BOILER HOUSE EAST WALL |
| 002 | 4 | BOILER HOUSE DOOR |
| 003 | 4 | DITTO |
| 004 | 4 | CHIMNEY STACK |
| 005 | 1 | 1ST MILL EAST WALL |
| 006–016 | 1 | WINDOWS |
| 017 | 4 | ENGINE-HOUSE WINDOW |
| 018–023 | 1 | WINDOWS |
| 024 | 1 | WATERWHEEL APERTURE |
| 025–026 | 1 | WINDOWS |
| 027 | 2 | 2ND MILL EAST WALL |
| 028 | 2 | WINDOW |
| 029 | 3 | PRIVY TOWER EAST WALL |
| 030 | 3 | PRIVY WINDOW |
| 031–036 | 2 | WINDOWS |
| 037 | 3 | PRIVY WINDOW |
| 038–043 | 2 | WINDOWS |
| 044 | 3 | PRIVY WINDOW |
| 045–050 | 2 | WINDOWS |
| 051 | 3 | PRIVY WINDOW |
| 052–055 | 2 | WINDOWS |
| 056 | 2 | WATERWHEEL APERTURE |
| 057 | 5 | WEAVING SHED EAST WALL |
| 058–061 | 5 | VENTILATION GRILLES |

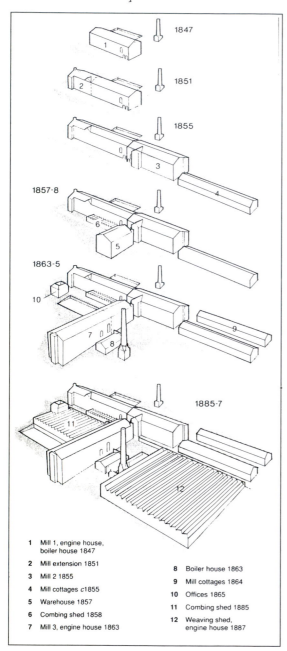

1847

1851

1855

1857-8

1863-5

1885-7

1  Mill 1, engine house,
   boiler house 1847

2  Mill extension 1851

3  Mill 2 1855

4  Mill cottages c1855

5  Warehouse 1857

6  Combing shed 1858

7  Mill 3, engine house 1863

8   Boiler house 1863

9   Mill cottages 1864

10  Offices 1865

11  Combing shed 1885

12  Weaving shed,
    engine house 1887

*Figure 42* Diagram showing the phased development over forty years of Oats Royds Mill, Midgeley, West Yorkshire. RCHME, © Crown Copyright.

between various sections, the addition of a boiler house and chimney and changes in window patterns. The numbers can then be organised as a matrix, which suggests at least five phases of development. The building began as a small water-powered spinning mill which was expanded with the addition of a second mill adjoining, to which a privy tower was added. Water power was then replaced or supplemented by steam power for spinning and finally a single-storey weaving shed was added. The use of a matrix ensures that every observed feature is given equal weight in the interpretation. It might then be possible to confirm these relative phases and assign them absolute dates from map evidence or other documentary sources. The initial phasing, however, as in an excavated section, is arrived at through observation and meticulous recording which must precede any attempt at interpretation, although inevitably prior knowledge of particular types of building affects the observations which are made. Despite the problems of utilising archaeological methods in building recording, it is worth doing because it charts the process of human intervention in building construction to a far greater extent than purely architectural description.

The information gathered for each elevation of a building complex can then be combined to enable three-dimensional reconstructions to be drawn showing the evolution of the complex. This is most efficiently achieved using a CAD system. The value of such phased reconstructions is demonstrated by the work of RCHME on textile mills, as in Figure 42. A refinement, namely the use of a CAD system linked to a database, makes it possible to superimpose a series of matrices, together with the description of each context, on to a three-dimensional reconstruction; this enables all the available information about the building to be interrogated simultaneously. The reconstruction, therefore, remains a tool to be manipulated rather than an image which controls perception. The technique is a complex one which demands considerable familiarity with computer operation and the CAD system (Boast and Chapman 1991; Dobson 1994).

The use of matrices assists in the phasing of individual buildings, but if an absolute date is not known from other sources, the relative position of a building in a sequence of similar types of structure can be achieved by means of typology. This concept has long played an important part in the relative dating of artefacts and is only now being supplanted by more scientific methods. Any type of artefact, such as clay pipes, can be placed in a logical series according to a progression of changes in their shape or differences in their ornamentation. This can provide both a means of classification and a relative dating sequence. Accordingly it is also possible to utilise a typological sequence as a means of classifying examples of a particular type of structure, such as lime-kilns or pottery kilns. Once the general development of a type of structure is understood, the position of a specific example within that sequence can be determined. However, the evolution of most industrial structures took a relatively short period of time compared with the prehistoric artefacts to which the typological method was first applied. As a result, there can be no single chronological sequence for a type of industrial structure because the rate of adoption of new building methods or new technology varied from region to region according to economic circumstances. For example, technical literature reveals that the devices utilised for the gravitational separation of metallic ores from gangue minerals, known as buddles, evolved from the manually worked rectangular type to the water-powered circular type. The field evidence, however, shows that the buddle adopted depended partly on the mineral being treated, but even within the lead industry the Derbyshire miners were using the rectangular type at the same time as those in Cardiganshire had adopted the circular type (Palmer and Neaverson 1989). Typology can therefore be utilised to recognise sequences of structures, and so understand their development, but is not generally valid as a means of dating. Only on a single site or on related sites within a region, which possess a group of structures of the same type, can the method be used for dating with any degree of reliability.

Archaeological fieldwork, whether the recording of buildings or the survey and excavation of sites, demands considerable resources of both manpower and equipment. Since the site remains of the industrial period are more numerous than for earlier periods of archaeology, only selected sites can be accorded full treatment. Determining these priorities has been the stimulus for the various rapid recording methods developed over the last decade, from the RCHME surveys through the AIA IRIS project to the MPP. If we can establish what exists for a particular industry, and make some value judgements about the relative importance of the remains, then limited resources can be deployed to their best advantage.

The first stage, then, is to set the research agenda. This determines what data are necessary for recording particular sites and structures. The four levels of building recording devised by RCHME – which in this chapter have also been applied to sites – provide useful guidelines for the type of fieldwork appropriate to a particular site or structure once its position within the hierarchy has been determined. In many instances, of course, rescue surveys take priority and are generally recorded at Levels 1 and 2: very few sites and structures can be given Level 4 treatment. The recording process, followed by deposition in the public archive, is as important to industrial archaeology as excavation is to other periods of archaeology. Standing structures and site remains disappear all too quickly in a dynamic landscape, and preservation by record is frequently the only option.

The higher levels of recording require some analysis of the development of a building or site. This chapter has suggested that the system of context numbers normally utilised for determining the stratigraphy of an archaeological section can usefully be applied to buildings, once the definition of a stratigraphic unit for a particular recording exercise has been agreed upon. The technique ensures that all features of a building are given equal weight so that it is treated archaeologically rather than architecturally, and therefore the process of human intervention is established. The context numbers can be organised into a matrix to provide a framework for the relative dating of different phases of a building, while the concept of typology has a limited but still important role to play in the relative dating of many industrial structures.

Relative dating can often be transmuted into absolute dating by recourse to documents. But apart from the use of map evidence for the discovery of sites, buildings and sites should normally be considered carefully in the field before much work is undertaken on the documentary sources. This is to ensure that the building or site is recorded as found. Although any recorder will approach a site with prior ideas and theories, some degree of objectivity can be achieved by the use of pro-forma context sheets and other archaeological methods considered in this chapter. Too much prior information carries with it the danger of finding only what one is looking for, ignoring the anomalies which may not appear in the documentary evidence. The relationship between field and documentary evidence is crucial for the methodology of industrial archaeology, and will be further considered in the next chapter.

# Chapter Five

# Documentary research

## THE NATURE OF DOCUMENTARY EVIDENCE

The essence of industrial archaeology is the interrelationship between the field evidence discussed in the previous chapter and the evidence from written sources. The student of the modern period is fortunate in the quantity of written material produced not just for governmental and ecclesiastical purposes, but also in connection with economic activities. Paper was more readily available than it had been in earlier periods and printing was more commonly practised. From the middle of the seventeenth century, Latin ceased to be the language used for official purposes and so working with documents for the modern period does not demand the same specialist skills of palaeography and translation required for students of the medieval period.

This is not to say that documentary research for the industrial period is totally straightforward. Literacy was largely confined to the upper and middle classes until the end of the nineteenth century, so that many of the sources concerning working-class life were written by those not directly involved in it. The surviving records often tell us what employers thought that their workforce experienced; the views of the latter are rarely heard. Government reports about working conditions were often commissioned in response to a particular problem, such as the poverty of the handloom weavers or the employment of women and children in mines, and are not therefore an unbiased account of practices in specific industries. Many accounts were written to reinforce what amounted to foregone conclusions by their authors, who had a particular philosophy to put across. Even technical literature can be misleading, since it tends to concentrate on the innovative and ignores the continuity of tried and tested methods or machines. Consequently, documents of the industrial period, including maps, must be treated with as much caution as those of any other period, establishing reliability, authenticity and intent before their evidence is accepted.

First, the status and capabilities of the author of a particular source must be examined to provide a guide as to the accuracy or otherwise of the evidence. William Cobbett, for example, gives a highly biased account of working-class life because of his political outlook when compared with more objective travellers such as Daniel Defoe or Arthur Young. The latter was the secretary to the newly formed Board of Agriculture, which commissioned a number of 'General Views' of the state of the countryside *circa* 1800. Its reporters understandably concentrated on the new and innovative, as did the industrial spies from Europe who came to discover the secrets of Britain's progress in industry and transport. These spies may not have penetrated everywhere but their reports give considerable technical detail on the sites that they did visit (Henderson 1954; J. R. Harris 1985). Taken in isolation, however, such reports give a misleading impression of the extent of technological innovation in late eighteenth-century Britain and ignore the continuity of established practices.

It is equally important to discover the identity and reliability of early map-makers and their purpose in compiling a particular map. In the second half of the eighteenth century, the Society of Arts awarded premiums for developments in cartography which encouraged the production of many county maps. A map of Leicestershire, for example, published in 1777, was compiled by John Prior and dedicated to the Earl of Huntingdon (Figure 43). Research has shown that Prior himself was a schoolmaster and clergyman with antiquarian interests, who employed a professional surveyor, Joseph Whyman, to make the map which bears his own name. Whyman had served an apprenticeship with P. P. Burdett, whose Derbyshire map had been the recipient of a society premium in 1767 (Welding 1984). Both these maps give considerable detail of the locations of coal-pits, limestone quarries, water- and windmills, etc. but cannot be relied upon for complete coverage. The same limitation applies to special classes of map, such as tithe, lease, enclosure and mining maps, which were compiled for particular purposes.

The historian or archaeologist also needs to understand the original intent of any piece of written evidence. For example, the regularly published reports of metalliferous mining companies were intended to impress and possibly to elicit further financial support from shareholders. They may well refer to new discoveries or to new installations of plant that more objective sources, such as financial records, together with the archaeological evidence, often show were never made. Equally, documents not obviously relevant to a site may well reveal incidental information of interest to the archaeologist. Nineteenth-century geological surveys may include descriptions of the plant used by extractive industries, while official reports on accidents in collieries and gunpowder mills often contain considerable detail of their working methods. The industrial archaeologist is therefore making use of a wide range of sources for purposes other than those for which they were originally intended and cannot expect consistency of information. The inclusion of an item within a document may be entirely coincidental to its original purpose and it must not therefore be assumed that all such items would be included in every document of the same type. For example, some fire insurance policies, such as those for early textile mills, provide considerable detail not only about the buildings but also about the working practices carried on within them, whereas others have only minimal value as a source.

Large collections of documents, like fire insurance policies and local authority building control plans, pose another problem to the researcher, that of locating those concerned with a specific name or site. Although registers may exist, they are often chronologically arranged and not indexed, therefore requiring considerable searching. There was also little consistency in the way in which buildings were referred to; some may have to be tracked down by means of the names of owners, tenants, architects or builders rather than by site name. A particular problem arises with collections of technical drawings, such as those made by the suppliers of steam engines to mills and mines. The same component drawing may have been utilised for several customers and annotated accordingly, making it difficult to relate to a particular site or name. Documentary research is analogous to archaeological excavation in the patience required to piece the evidence together.

Although the survival rate of written sources for the industrial period is clearly far better than that for earlier periods, it is by no means complete. There has been no consistent policy towards the preservation of company archives, which may often have been destroyed through mergers or relocation. The most likely category of documents to survive is those which were required for legal purposes following moves towards limited liability in the middle of the nineteenth century: once put aside, they were frequently overlooked and escaped destruction. Documents relating to the day-to-day operation of a manufacturing concern had a limited life and were often destroyed once their immediate commercial value had passed. These have potentially greater value for interpreting a particular site or structure than the company reports issued for public consumption

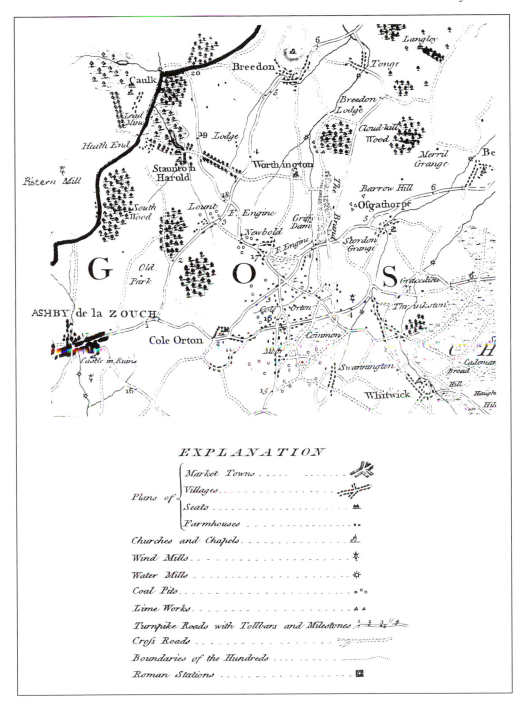

*Figure 43* An example of one of the privately produced 1 inch to 1 mile maps of the late eighteenth century. John Prior's map of north-west Leicestershire, published in 1777, gives considerable detail of industrial activity in the area.

Leicestershire Record Office.

and therefore subject to bias. The records of undertakings which required official sanction, such as canals, railways and public utilities, had a better chance of survival since they had to be deposited with either Parliament or the local authority. The process of nationalisation in the mid-twentieth century brought together the records of many previously privately owned companies: the National Coal Board, for example, took over archives relating to small mining concerns which could date back several centuries. Industrial decline, combined with recent privatisation, threatens the survival of this class of document and once again only those records with legal significance are likely to be retained.

## LOCATING WRITTEN SOURCES

The obvious starting-point for any documentary research is the local library. This may well have a local studies section containing some of the numerous pamphlets and books which are published locally and often difficult to track down. The material in the local studies collection may be indexed by personal or place names, although seldom under subject, which can make researching a specific industry rather difficult. The central reference library for a particular area usually has an extensive local studies section including a range of trade directories, illustrated town and county guides and other standard local publications. It may also contain a collection of local newspapers, occasionally going back to the eighteenth century and now often on microfiche.

Once the local printed material has been searched, the next port of call is the county or city record office. There are several publications listing these, giving their locations, opening hours and telephone numbers (Royal Commission on Historical Manuscripts 1992; Gibson and Peskett 1988). *A Guide to Archive Sources in the United Kingdom* (Foster and Sheppard 1995) is an invaluable directory of archive repositories and archive-holding bodies. Although its stated policy is to exclude businesses, in practice it contains much information on business records. Collections of documents may also exist elsewhere in a locality, such as the archives of landed families and those remaining in museums, private businesses, transport undertakings, etc. In the case of record offices, it is always wise to telephone in advance of a visit, since many have limited space and operate an appointment system, particularly for the use of maps and microfiche readers. Proof of identity is usually required before a reader's ticket is issued, although some offices operate jointly within the County Archive Research Network. Because county record offices have evolved independently of each other, there is no common indexing system to the material they contain. Most operate a card index of place and personal names, together with a limited subject index, which refer to more detailed schedules of individual collections of records. In some instances, however, collections may not have been calendared and are not yet on public access: details of these and new additions to the record offices can be found in their annual reports. Some papers may have been deposited with limited access and the permission of the donor has to be sought before research can take place. Most offices contain records of local government, parish affairs, municipal undertakings and population: some are also diocesan repositories and include tithe material, wills and inventories. Their collections of family and business papers vary enormously, some being of more than local significance. For example, West Glamorgan Record Office houses the extensive collection from the Neath Abbey Ironworks whose heavy engineering products had a world-wide market.

The most reliable means of locating these important collections of documents is through the National Register of Archives, which is housed in the London search room of the Royal Commission on Historical Manuscripts (RCHM). This was established in 1869 to identify documentary sources in private hands and to make these accessible through its *Reports and*

*Calendars* series. From 1945 onwards, the scope of the Commission was widened to include many important business and industrial collections as well as those in the newly established county record offices. The National Register of Archives includes name and place indices which can be invaluable for tracking down information in a wide variety of repositories. The *Reports and Calendars* series has been succeeded by *Guides to Sources for British History*, which is being extended to cover *Records of British Business and Industry, 1760–1914*: published volumes include those on textiles and leather, metal processing and engineering (Royal Commission on Historical Manuscripts 1990; 1994). RCHM also published until recently annual *Accessions to Repositories and Reports added to the National Register of Archives*, which have enabled the searcher to identify new material. A visit to the Commission's offices at Quality House, Quality Court, Chancery Lane, London WC2A 1HP can save hours of travelling time (James 1992). A similar facility exists for Scotland in West Register House, Edinburgh. Both England and Scotland also have Business Archives Councils, organisations which seek to encourage the preservation of business records. *Business Archives*, the journal of the English Business Archives Council, has published many relevant articles for those seeking to familiarise themselves with such records. The councils undertake surveys and produce thematic lists, such as those on brewing and shipbuilding published by the English Council. Their *Directory of Corporate Archives* describes the formal archive facilities provided by many of the corporate members of the council and its use can again save time. The University of Warwick houses the Modern Records Centre, which contains much of interest relating to trade union activities and social conditions within industry.

The Public Record Office (PRO) was founded in 1838 to conserve the archives of state departments and the central courts of law for both England and Wales. The increase in the number of government departments and the transfer of important collections of records such as those of the British Transport Commission resulted in overcrowding in the Chancery Lane premises and the construction of a purpose-built repository at Kew. The three-volume *Guide to the contents of the Public Record Office* was compiled before the move to Kew, but is still valuable for understanding the structure of the public records. The *Public Record Office Current Guide* is a regularly updated microfiche. There are also numerous finding aids published by the List and Index Society which was founded by the readers themselves. Similar national collections exist in the Scottish Record Office, founded in 1787 and based in Register House in Edinburgh, and the Public Record Office of Northern Ireland founded in 1923 in Belfast. For the industrial archaeologist, the Public Record Office at Kew is particularly useful for early transport records and, in some cases, records of nationalised industries.

The national libraries in London, Edinburgh and Aberystwyth all have departments of manuscripts as well as comprehensive book collections. The British Library is responsible for the national newspaper collection housed at Colindale which also contains runs of periodicals, including important sources for industrial history such as the *Mining Journal, The Engineer* and *The Illustrated London News* (Figure 44). The Official Publications Department of the British Library contains a comprehensive collection of Ordnance Survey (OS) maps, together with abandoned mine plans, etc. The national technical museums have specialist libraries and archive collections related to their subject: these include the National Railway Museum in York, the National Maritime Museum at Greenwich and the National Museum of Science and Industry in London. Many learned societies in both London and the provinces were founded in the nineteenth century and have collections of specialist material. The London-based societies include the Institutions of Civil, Mechanical and Electrical Engineers, the Royal Institute of British Architects and the Institution of Mining and Metallurgy, together with a whole range of specialist institutes established from the 1880s onwards. Many county towns had their own learned societies which still maintain collections, a good example being the Royal Institution of Cornwall in Truro. The Guildhall Library in London holds the major collection of fire insurance registers, since these were generally City companies. Many provincial libraries also have major specialist holdings as a result of their location; for example, the Boulton and Watt collection in Birmingham Reference Library. Some university libraries also maintain an archive collection; for example, Nottingham, Birmingham and the John Rylands Library attached to Manchester University.

The three Royal Commissions on Historical Monuments have built up considerable photographic collections, including aerial surveys: the English Commission at Swindon, for example, curates the important Watkins Collection of photographs of stationary steam engines. Their archives also include plans, architectural drawings and reports on sites recorded: these should be checked before research or recording is commenced to avoid duplication of effort. English Heritage's ongoing Monuments Protection Programme is generating a considerable archive on industrial sites in England, full copies of which have been deposited with RCHME in Swindon, the Council for British Archaeology in York and the Association for Industrial Archaeology in the library of the Ironbridge Gorge Museum Trust. This material may eventually find its way into county Sites and Monuments Records, whose coverage of industrial sites varies considerably but which should be consulted.

The British Isles therefore have rich collections of documentary sources at both the national and local level, but discovering the location and content of a particular set of records requires both time and patience. The primary task of an archivist is the preservation of records, not making them available to the public, and there have been increasing restrictions on both the use and reproduction of documents in recent years. On the other hand, the finding aids have widened in their scope and more material, particularly OS maps, is available on microfiche with facilities for its reproduction. For all original research the recommended route is to begin with the local library and record office, followed by a visit to the National Register of Archives which will open doors to national avenues of research. It is, however, a time-consumingalthough rewarding process.

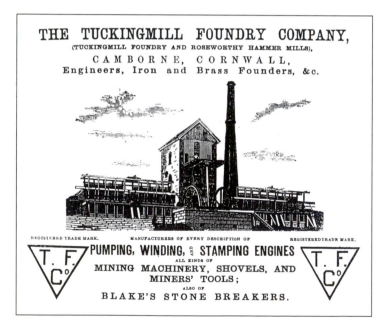

*Figure 44* An advertisement for a Cornish foundry company, published in the *Mining Journal* in 1880. It gives considerable detail of a steam-driven stamps battery, probably that at West Basset New Stamps installed in 1875 by that company. (See Chapter 6.) On that site, only the engine house and the supports for the stamps axles survive, and consequently the illustration allows a fuller interpretation of the more ephemeral structures in wood and iron.

## SECONDARY SOURCES

The starting-point for local research is still probably the relevant volumes of the *Victoria County History* series, which has not yet been completed for some counties of England and Wales. The introductory volumes give general accounts of the development of industry and transport, together with invaluable tabulations of population statistics. Their footnotes provide an introduction to local documentary and newspaper sources. For many counties, a multi-volume history was compiled in the late eighteenth or early nineteenth centuries. The bias of these is understandably towards landed estates and ecclesiastical matters, but they often include transcriptions of original documents and detailed accounts of individual parishes. Nichols's four-volume *The History and Antiquities of the County of Leicester*, for example, published between 1795 and 1811, describes the industries being carried on in various villages, including framework-knitting and coal-mining, and cites population figures from the first census.

Industrial topics receive some treatment within modern county history series. Inspired by the work of W. G. Hoskins, the *Making of the English Landscape* series usually includes chapters on the industrial landscape and the pattern of communications, although the amount of space devoted to these topics depends on the interests of the author. The first volume was *Cornwall: an Illustrated Essay on the History of the Landscape* published in 1955 and later reissued in revised form with a picture of an engine house on the dust jacket (Balchin 1983). The *West Riding of Yorkshire* volume was written by Arthur Raistrick, who contributed so much to the early development of industrial archaeology (Raistrick 1970). The *Darwen County History* series, published by Phillimore, now covers most counties, but their industrial references are again dependent on the authors' specialisms. The meetings of the British Association for the Advancement of Science often result in a comprehensive volume on the county in which they were held, usually including sections on the economic structure of the county. Longman are contributing their *Regional History of England* series, producing two volumes for each region, one pre- and the other post- AD 1000. A particularly good volume in this series for the industrial archaeologist is that on *The West Midlands from AD 1000*, with the Gladstone Pottery Museum on the dust jacket (Rowlands 1987). Finally, many collections of old photographs have been published, notably by Alan Sutton, which include many of industrial interest.

The CBA's Industrial Monuments Survey inspired some publishers to initiate county gazetteers of industrial sites. In the 1960s, David & Charles began publishing their invaluable series of regional industrial archaeology studies, which regrettably never covered the entire country. Each volume contains an analysis of the industrial development of a region, followed by a detailed gazetteer which is still a useful starting-point. Batsford were later into the field with a series of *Guides to the Industrial Archaeology of the British Isles*, which achieved only six volumes and a useful introductory volume (Falconer 1980). Examples of all these are included in the Bibliography.

Local research on industrial history and archaeology has resulted in a plethora of articles in a great variety of journals which are often very difficult to track down. A series of invaluable bibliographies has been produced by John Greenwood, the Liaison Librarian at the Open University, covering northern England, the Midlands and south-eastern England (Greenwood 1985, 1987, 1990). The University of Exeter has published a useful bibliography on British metal-mining jointly with the National Association of Mining History Organisations (Burt and Waite 1988), while an annual bibliography, *British Mining History*, on a similar theme is produced by the Peak District Mines Historical Society based in Matlock Bath. National and regional journals, such as *The Local Historian, East Midland Historian* and *Northern History*, include bibliographies of recently published work on a regular basis. Regular series of abstracts of articles of industrial archaeological interest are included in *Industrial Archaeology Review* and *British and Irish Archaeological Bibliography*, the latter published by the CBA.

## PRINTED PRIMARY SOURCES

The publication of newspapers grew apace in the course of the eighteenth century, few major provincial towns lacking a weekly newspaper by the time of the War of American Independence (1775–83). These report, for example, on new transport developments, such as the letting of toll gates and the meetings of proprietors of canals, together with new mines and quarries being opened. Their advertisements often reveal the products of manufacturing industry, while invaluable detail concerning buildings and plant can be gleaned from notices of sale. The *Macclesfield Courier and Herald* for 20 April 1811, for example, advertised Little Street Mill for sale:

> The factory is three storeys high, thirty yards long and nine yards wide, or thereabouts, and full of silk machinery, the most part whereof is new and which the tenant may be accommodated with. . . . The machinery has hitherto been turned by horses, but a steam engine may be erected at a trifling expense.

> (Calladine and Fricker 1993: 57)

Magazines also came into existence in this period, notably the *Gentleman's Magazine*, which ran from 1731 to 1922, and the *Penny Magazine*, started in 1832, both of which can be surprising sources of industrial information and illustration. The following century saw the growth of the specialist technical journals, such as the *Mechanic's Magazine* from 1823, the *Mining Journal* from 1835, *The Builder* from 1843, *The Engineer* from 1856 and the *Colliery Guardian* from 1860. Several major technical encyclopaedias were published in the first half of the nineteenth century, following on from Diderot's great *Encyclopédie* published between 1751 and 1765, which is in itself an important source for industrial developments. The British publications include W. H. Pyne's *Microcosm*, Rees's *Cyclopaedia, or Universal Dictionary of Arts and Sciences*, Tomlinson's *Cyclopaedia of Useful Arts*, Andrew Ure's *Dictionary of Arts, Manufactures and Mines* and J. Loudon's *Encyclopaedia of Cottage, Farm and Villa Architecture and Furniture etc.*; many of these appeared in parts or volumes over a number of years. They furnish not only technical descriptions of processes but also engravings of buildings and machines and useful information on building materials. Contemporary developments and new inventions were also described in the transactions of learned societies, beginning with the *Philosophical Transactions* of the Royal Society in 1665. It must not, however, be assumed that the new technology described in these publications was immediately and universally adopted.

The records of the proceedings and debates of Parliament were published as *Parliamentary Papers*; these can be useful, for example, in tracing the progress of a canal or railway proposal through the committee stages in Parliament. *A Guide to Parliamentary Papers* gives some preliminary guidance to the use of this vast source (Ford and Ford 1972). Even more valuable are the reports of Royal Commissions on various industries, particularly those with labour problems such as handloom-weaving, framework-knitting and coal-mining. These include not only the reports of the commissioners but also transcripts of the oral evidence provided by both employers and workers. For example, one of the commissioners looking into the declining handloom-weaving industry in 1840 reported that:

> I have seen them working in cellars dug out of an undrained swamp: the streets formed by their houses without sewers, and flooded with rain: the water therefore running down the bare walls of the cellars and rendering them unfit for the abode of dogs or rats

but he also found

> streets of small, modern-built houses, in which the cellars occupied by the cotton weavers

were light and convenient apartments, and in many towns the cotton weavers worked not in cellars but in an unboarded room on the ground floor.

(Report of the Commissioners on the Hand-Loom Weavers of the United Kingdom, 1840 [Irish University Press, *Industrial Revolution: Textiles*, Vol. 10, Shannon: IUP, 1970: 657])

These descriptions accord well with fieldwork carried out on cotton-weaving workshops in central Lancashire (Timmins 1977).

The reports of commissioners' enquiries into Children's Employment, the Condition of Framework Knitters and the routine Factories and Mines Inspectors' reports also are valuable sources of information on workshop and factory layouts and their contents. In the 1870s, for example, the statistical returns of the factory inspectorate enable the researcher to assess the impact of steam power on manufacturing industry. These Commission Reports can be located in Parliamentary Papers, but have been collected together by the Irish University Press in a series of thematic volumes such as *Children's Employment, Textiles, Industrial Relations, Factories, Transport, Water Supply, Sanitation* and *Agriculture*.

The growth of trade and industry in the second half of the eighteenth century prompted the publication of provincial as well as London trade directories. These are invaluable for assessing the range of industries in particular towns and the firms operating therein. Most of the directories give a short account of the history, industries and communications of towns and villages, followed by a list of gentry, manufacturers and tradesmen although this may not be complete as a charge was often levied for inclusion. The earlier directories often provide classified lists of manufacturers, Bailey's and *The Universal British Directory* being the only country-wide volumes. From the early nineteenth century, the Post Office produced directories which included full address information to ensure the delivery of mail, a service later undertaken by Kelly. These directories enable particular premises to be identified and can usefully be compared with large-scale OS maps and town plans. A sequence of directories can be used to construct a chronological development of industry for a specific locality, often revealing the decline of some classes of manufacture and the rise of others. This can be invaluable in identifying the use and re-use of particular buildings. The Royal Historical Society has published a guide to the directories for England and Wales issued before 1856, which discusses their limitations as a source as well as listing those available (Norton 1984).

Improved roads led to increasing mobility during the eighteenth century, and travellers' diaries are another important contemporary source. The earliest traveller to comment on industry was the intrepid horsewoman Celia Fiennes who traversed the land in the last decades of the seventeenth century. A more detailed account was given by Daniel Defoe in his *A Tour Through the Whole Island of Great Britain*, 1724–6, which indicates how much of the country was already sending manufactured goods to London for the domestic market or for export. Later in the eighteenth century, the Romantic movement inspired a generation of travellers who lamented the desecration wrought on the landscape by industrial development, but provided useful information at the same time. Among these were Viscount Torrington, William Cobbett and several antiquarian clergymen, notably Richard Warner and James Plumptre (Moir 1964). More objective information was provided by the so-called industrial spies from Europe, who came to discover the secrets of Britain's early industrialisation. Their numbers included men with specialist knowledge of the metallurgical industries, like the Swedish travellers Svedenstierna, Schröderstierna and Triewald and the Frenchmen Gabriel Jars and Moissenet (J. R. Harris 1985): the latter two made meticulous drawings of the machinery they saw (Figure 45). A fascinating account of the landscape of the Black Country was provided in 1868 by the American diplomat

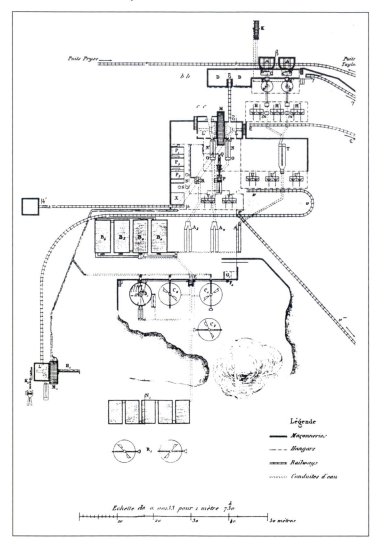

*Figure 45* An example of the meticulous drawings made by Leon-Vivant Moissenet, in this case the washing floors of Frongoch mine in Cardiganshire.

Plate II from 'Préparation Mecanique du Minerai de Plomb aux Mines de Lisburne, Cardiganshire, Pays de Galles', *Annales de Mines*, sér. 6, tôme ix [1866]: 1–137.

Elihu Burritt who, unlike the earlier industrial spies, was well aware of the persistence of hand technology in this seemingly industrialised area (Burritt 1868).

The foundation of the Board of Agriculture in 1793 led, as has been seen, to a valuable series of reports on the British landscape in a period of transition. These so-called *General Views* were published for most counties between 1800 and 1822. Although their remit was to consider the state of agriculture, the reporters took note of related occupations such as lime-burning and extractive industries which were often carried on as an adjunct to farming. In Leicestershire, for example, William Pitt noted that 'the Earl of Moira has erected an iron foundry at great expense, by the side of the Ashby Canal, where the ore has been smelted and cast into pigs, as well as utensils for various purposes' (Pitt 1809: 8). The most valuable of the *General Views* for industrial content is that for Derbyshire by John Farey, who was commissioned at the same time by the Royal Society to examine the mineral wealth of the county (Farey 1811–13). Arthur Young, the first Secretary of the Board of Agriculture, who wrote six of the county volumes, was himself an inveterate traveller and has left published accounts of his journeys through the regions of England: although largely concerned with innovations in farming, he noted the existence of manufacturing industry such as stocking-weaving in Kendal and lace manufacture in Bedfordshire (Young 1771).

The increasing interest in the landscape at the time of the Romantic movement led to the publication of topographical works, such as Britton and Brayley's eighteen-volume *The Beauties of England and Wales* which appeared between 1801 and 1815 and Samuel Lewis's *Topographical Dictionary* (fifth edition 1844). As a source, these include town plans and, surprisingly, much information on contemporary economic conditions. The growth of the tourist industry, promoted by railway development, initiated a new range of guide books; for example, Black's

*Picturesque Tourist and Road and Railway Guide through England and Wales* (1850). The railway companies themselves produced illustrated commentaries for those who travelled on their routes, describing not only the engineering marvels on the line but also the views from it, including those of industrial landscapes. Numerous local guidebooks were also published, directing people to beauty spots in the vicinity but often also including engravings and descriptions of buildings which have since vanished. For example, Robinson, Son & Pike produced *Loughborough: its History, Manufactures, Trade* in 1892, detailing the history of individual firms in the town and providing engravings of their premises and products (Figure 46).

*Figure 46* An engraving of the Taylor's Bell foundry in Loughborough, Leicestershire. On the left is the new foundry block of 1875; the right-hand frontage had been destroyed by fire in 1891 and was being rebuilt at date of publication.

From *Loughborough: its History, Manufactures, Trade* (Robinson, Son & Pike, 1892).

## PICTORIAL SOURCES

Much of the printed matter referred to above is also a rich source of illustrative material, both deliberately included in the text and incidentally derived from the advertisements therein. These engravings often enable subsequent alterations and additions to buildings to be identified but they need to be treated with caution since the artist frequently exaggerated the scale of individual buildings to make them appear more impressive, particularly in advertisements and letterheads (Figure 47). Early technical illustrations are often highly stylised but those in Agricola's *De Re Metallica* (1556), for example, assist in the interpretation of mining landscapes since the basic technology survived in many areas well into the nineteenth century (Figure 48). These illustrations enable the archaeologist to interpret the often enigmatic remains of wooden structures which were the foundations of very primitive water-powered technology; they also indicate the extent of manual labour required on such sites. Illustrations of machines in later technical magazines and

*Figure 47* Letter and document headings, calendars and other publicity material were often used to show the extent of business premises. Raven's factory, which is still extant, is typical of the multi-storey hosiery mills which came to dominate the streets of Leicester in the last quarter of the nineteenth century.

Leicestershire Record Office.

makers' catalogues can also assist in field identification. Greens of Aberystwyth, for example, provided lead-dressing apparatus whose foundations can frequently be traced on late nineteenth-century sites such as Frongoch and Killhope, while illustrations of Blake's stone crushers in the *Mining Journal* can be linked to site evidence on numerous mine and quarry sites.

Processes involved in industrial production were also the subject of engravings. Many of those for the textile industry are well known; for example, the depiction of a child piecer underneath a spinning mule, the introduction of Cartwright's power loom and William Hincks's portrayal of the Irish linen industry. Other engravings show, for example, the processes of gun-powder production, the working of a large iron foundry or the interior of a glass-house (see Chaloner and Musson 1963). These illustrations are valuable not only in determining the processes of production in a particular complex of buildings but in understanding the gender and spatial distribution of the work-force within them. Such sources do, however, have to be looked at critically since they may be highly selective in their treatment of the human aspect of past industry.

The novelty of industrial land-scapes attracted the attention of artists, whose paintings need to be treated as images of industry rather than as factual statements. Joseph Wright's painting of Cromford Mill at night and de Loutherbourg's richly coloured impression of the Bedlam and Madeley furnaces in the Ironbridge Gorge re-create the impact of new industrial processes on the contemporary conscious-ness, which is difficult for us to imagine from the empty shells of the buildings which remain in the twentieth-century landscape. The drawings of Thomas Hair are now often the only source for

A—Box laid flat on the ground.  B—Its bottom which is made of iron wire.
C—Box inverted.    D—Iron rods.    E—Box suspended from a beam, the inside being visible.  F—Box suspended from a beam, the outside being visible.

*Figure 48* Agricola's illustration of a battery of water-powered ore stamps. He shows that the broken ore is passed through a series of sieves and the coarser material returned to the stamps for further reduction. The remains of similar boxes and sieves have been found on excavations of nineteenth-century metallic ore-processing sites, showing their continued use long after his sixteenth-century drawing.

understanding the landscapes of the north-east coalfield in the nineteenth century (1844), while J. C. Bourne's sketches of railway construction demonstrate the human effort required for these massive undertakings (1839). A surprising number of industrial structures were included in paintings, ranging from lime-kilns to glass cones and iron forges as well as the better-known river navigation features which appear in several of Constable's paintings, such as Dedham Lock. There is no comprehensive thematic index for industrial scenes, although the Elton Collection of the Ironbridge Gorge Museum Trust has brought many of these together, as has Francis D. Klingender's *Art and the Industrial Revolution* (1947).

By the last quarter of the nineteenth century, it became possible to record in photographic form the kind of scenes which Bourne had captured in pen and wash. S. W. A. Newton travelled the length of the Great Central Railway during its construction in the 1890s and his photographs depict not only the railway structures but the towns in which many of them were built. These are now housed in the Leicestershire Record Office, while many other record offices, libraries and institutions have accessioned similar collections, such as the photographs of Cornish mining taken by J. C. Burrow. Those of national importance have generally found their way into the National Monuments Records, like the Rev. Denis Rokeby's photographs of railway stations, many of which have now been altered beyond recognition or demolished, or George Watkins's invaluable record of stationary steam engines. The photographs taken by the three Commissions as part of their own recording programmes since 1908 are in themselves an invaluable resource, although their interest in industrial buildings is comparatively recent (see RCHME 1985). The Commissions' work has also included aerial surveys of industrial landscapes and building complexes, whilst historic collections of aerial photographs are also held by the Cambridge Committee for Aerial Photography (see Hudson 1984) and by the commercial company Aerofilms Ltd which was established in 1919.

Pictorial sources, therefore, put the flesh on the bare bones of the archaeological evidence: they reveal long-vanished superstructures and often provide some indication of the nature of the labour force. They do, however, need to be treated with caution. Paintings and engravings are often selective in content and need careful analysis, as has been shown by comparing a sequence of artists' impressions of the industrial complex at Aberdulais Falls in the Vale of Neath (Hayman 1987). The industrial content of photographs was often incidental, and so illustrations of specific sites or structures can be difficult to track down from indexes. Nevertheless, these sources bring alive past landscapes in a way peculiar to the industrial period, since it is rarely possible for earlier archaeology.

## MAPS AND PLANS

Maps and plans are the richest source of information generally available to the industrial archae-ologist, and a thorough search should be made for them before fieldwork is commenced. As a rule of thumb, the topographical information shown on plans is usually all to scale, whereas on the smaller-scale maps features such as roads and railways are generally exaggerated for clarity. Large-scale OS maps can be used as base plans for field surveys, whereas the other classes of map dealt with below furnish only historical information.

Estate maps are the largest category of unpublished cartographic material and tend to be scattered throughout collections of family papers, which can make them difficult to locate. Some date back to the sixteenth century (Fowkes 1992), but the majority are seventeenth- to nineteenth-century in date. Many estates were sold or leased for urban development and so the maps are not purely rural in scope. Since landowners in Britain had the right to exploit the mineral resources on their estates, such maps frequently record industrial as well as agricultural features. As industrial activity increased in the eighteenth century, areas not previously surveyed were often covered for the first time. In central Wales, for example, the Pryce family of Gogerddan extended their mining interests and their archives include 160 late eighteenth- and nineteenth-century maps of Cardiganshire. Estate maps indicate the attempts by landowners to be self-sufficient in activities such as lime-burning and brick-making.

By the nineteenth century, many landowners had abandoned working their own minerals because of the capital costs involved and leased their holdings in return for a royalty on production. The leases, renewable at regular intervals, usually survive among their papers but the attached maps depicting the landholdings are often missing. Where they do exist, they can provide useful evidence concerning the chronological development of a site if a series can be found. However, lease maps were intended to delineate boundaries, not usually to portray surface features, and it cannot be assumed that because a particular feature is not marked, it did not exist when the map was drawn. In cases of change of leaseholder, it is possible that plant abandoned by the original lessee is indicated on the new lease map since it had reverted to the lessor.

Open fields and common lands were enclosed first by agreement and then from the mid-eighteenth century until the middle of the nineteenth century by Act of Parliament. In England after 1760 some 5,100 Enclosure Acts covered over 6.5 million acres [over 2.6 million hectares] of land, although the maps do not necessarily survive for all of them. Deposited enclosure plans and their books of reference depict the boundaries of the new land allotments in both urban and rural areas. Buildings and other features are not often shown on the maps, although the field names can provide valuable clues to their past or current usage, e.g. 'brick-kiln close', 'slitting mill pasture', 'furnace field' and 'lime yard'. Similar maps, usually depicting boundaries only, and schedules with field names resulted from the Tithe Commutation Act of 1836 which abolished the tithes which were then still payable to the Church of England in some two-thirds of the parishes in England and Wales. By 1886, some 11,800 tithe apportionments had been made under the 1836 Act. The tithe surveys have to be sought in the original church diocesan record offices which may not necessarily be those of the county in which the land is located. Since tithes were usually commuted at the time of Parliamentary Enclosure, it is rare to find both types of map for one parish and therefore changes in land usage cannot be traced.

Many of the original enclosure or tithe apportionment boundaries can usually be related to those on the later large-scale OS maps. The Board of Ordnance began the Primary Triangulation of Britain in 1791, which formed the basis not only for its own maps but also for several privately published county maps which therefore have a greater degree of accuracy than those pre-dating official triangulation. Most of England and Wales was covered at scales of 1 inch or 1.5 inch to the mile in the 1820s and 1830s by the maps of Christopher Greenwood and Andrew Bryant. These have to be treated with caution since they were often reissued without revision and the information shown may relate to the original date of the survey, not that of publication. They do, however, record an important period of industrial development (Smith 1990). The OS 1-inch series was much slower appearing and was not completed until 1870 for England. The David & Charles reprints of the first editions of the 1-inch OS are valuable because they pre-date the later large-scale maps, but many include information from subsequent revisions, such as railways, which can be very misleading if the detailed commentaries are not studied carefully. Surveys at 6 inches to 1 mile commenced in Ireland in 1825 and were extended to the northern counties of England and Scotland by the 1840s. However, projects such as railway construction needed even larger-scale maps and from 1858 the 25 inch to 1 mile scale was adopted as a standard except for uncultivated areas which continued to be mapped on the 6-inch scale. Early large-scale maps for upland mining districts may not therefore exist. The researcher is directed towards several useful guides to early Ordnance Survey maps (Harley and Phillips 1964; Oliver 1991, 1993). An ever-increasing number of 25 inch to 1 mile OS maps, usually editions *circa* 1900–20, are being reproduced in a reduced size format for sale by Alan Godfrey. A sequence of editions of the large-scale 6-inch and 25-inch maps can be used to advantage in determining site development over a period of years and their evidence can be used to confirm other sources.

Whereas the Ordnance Survey is comprehensive in its coverage, many selective maps were produced for specialist purposes. These fall into three main categories: maps for geological and mineralogical purposes, which include details of mines and quarries; transport maps, including horse-drawn tramways, roads, river navigations, canals and railways; and urban plans dealing with water supply, drainage and public utilities.

The foundation of the Geological Survey coincided with an upturn in the metalliferous mining industry in the 1830s. Its progenitor was Henry de la Beche, who was personally responsible for the surveys of Devon and Cornwall and had considerable expertise in mining. The survey also produced mineral statistics in conjunction with the Mining Record Office, whose first Keeper, Robert Hunt, was himself a cartographer. His maps of Cardiganshire mines, for example, include details of surface features such as wheel pits and pumping systems (Figure 49). In the 1920s, the Geological Survey produced a series of memoirs on the mineral resources of Great Britain which include useful maps showing the major lodes and sites of mines. These are available in the Official Publications Section of the British Library, but many have been republished under the auspices of the Northern Mine Research Society (e.g. O. T. Jones 1922). There are also many mining maps produced by the mining adventurers themselves, often for the mineral lords, which depict surface features as well as underground sections. These need to be treated with caution; first, since they may depict intent rather than actuality, as discussed earlier, and, second, since features were often added to them over a period of years without the original survey date being amended. The same is true of many of the early colliery maps, some of which remain in the possession of British Coal while others have found their way into county record offices since the demise of the Mining Record Office. Abandoned mine plans were an official requirement because of the dangers of flooding and subsidence, and many survive in the British Library.

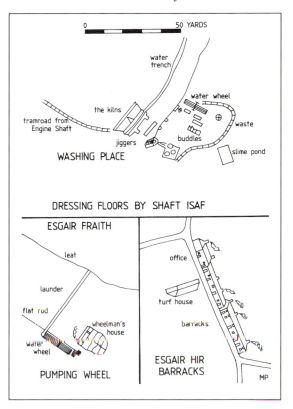

**Figure 49** These sketches were drawn in ink on a coloured base map of the Esgair Hir and Esgair Fraith mines in Cardiganshire, signed by Robert Hunt and dated 1837. They were probably added at intervals to show developments on the mining sett and proved invaluable in interpreting fragmentary field remains.

Redrawn from a map in the former Mining Record Office.

The main purpose of many early maps was to indicate roads to assist the traveller. The first road atlas is probably John Ogilby's *Britannia*, first published in 1675 and reprinted several times until 1698. The book contains 100 plates, each with six or seven strip maps showing the road and features alongside. For the industrial archaeologist, windmills, watermills, coal pits and, in some cases, types of bridges are often indicated. For example: 'a Moore with a great many Colepitts' is shown off the Oakham to Richmond road to the north of Mansfield in Nottinghamshire, but in other areas where one might expect to find these shown, as in the Newcastle area, they do not appear: Ogilby was clearly selective about what he recorded. The later county maps nevertheless made use of his information on roads. Eighteenth- and nineteenth-century road development can be traced from enclosure maps, since roads were often replanned in the enclosure process. The records of turnpike trusts have usually found their way into county record offices. These include plans showing the locations of toll houses and bars, together with side roads joining the turnpike whose destination was usually recorded: in industrial areas, these were often coal mines or limestone quarries, for example, whose traffic was a valuable source of income to the trusts.

Surveyors of river navigations were required to produce large-scale plans of cuts around obstructions such as mills and weirs. These are often the clearest documentary evidence to survive for the layout of leats and mill ponds. It cannot, however, be assumed that what the surveyor intended was always carried out and the documentary evidence needs to be checked in the field. For example, in 1790 William Jessop produced a plan of 'The Intended Navigation in the Rivers Wreake and Eye from the proposed Leicester Navigation to Melton Mowbray'. His papers also include drawings for locks, all of which were to be positioned at the upstream end of the cuts. In the event, however, they were placed at the downstream end of the cuts (Miller and Fletcher 1984: 10). The Syston to Peterborough Railway was built close to the navigation in 1846 and the survey maps for that are in fact the best documentary source for the river navigation as it was actually built. Canal promoters were obliged to provide plans for the entire length of their undertaking, since land had to be purchased for the route. Pre-1795 canal maps are usually on a fairly small scale, but nevertheless usually record the positions of features such as windmills and limestone quarries. Later maps were produced on a scale of at least half an inch to the mile and indicate a strip of land a field wide each side of the proposed route. Since industrial cargoes would be a valuable source of revenue to the company, all potential users such as brickyards, coal-pits and manufacturing concerns are usually shown. The diversity of information which may be gathered from maps and plans of waterways makes these an invaluable source for the industrial archaeologist as well as the transport historian.

Maps also depict the horse-drawn tramroads and waggonways that were constructed in large numbers to connect mines and quarries to navigable waterways. The earliest concentration of these, in north-east England, was shown on Casson's 'Plan of the Rivers Tyne and Wear' of 1804, which also depicts the riverside staithes to which they ran. The waggonways required wayleaves and so the plans usually depict both the fields alongside and the industrial concerns to be served by them. For example, Christopher Staveley's map of 'An Intended Navigation from Loughborough to Leicester' of 1790 shows a network of waggonways at the western end of the Charnwood Forest branch of this, which was intended to open up new coal mines on Swannington Common. For locomotive railways, plans were generally prepared on a much larger scale, particularly when the railway was to penetrate a built-up area, and they usually depict existing developments for some distance on either side of the proposed route. Many of these plans pre-date any available large-scale OS maps and, with the associated books of reference, are valuable sources for urban industrial archaeology even though the actual railway was never built (see Simmons 1953–4, 1957–8, 1961 for lists of deposited plans). The railway mania of the 1840s exhausted the supply of competent surveyors, and the plans of this period cannot always be relied upon for accuracy.

Urban improvements in the late eighteenth and early nineteenth centuries generated a series of town plans which also pre-date the large-scale OS maps. The first were those undertaken by various Improvement Commissions for paving, cleaning and lighting the streets, which resulted in some early town plans, such as that for Rochdale in 1809 on a scale of 24 inches to 1 mile. In the 1840s, the creation of Boards of Health led to numerous town surveys which were necessary to design adequate sewerage and drainage systems as well as clean water supplies. Some of these were undertaken by the Ordnance Survey, which was beginning its own, unfortunately uncompleted, series of town plans, some at the very large scale of 1:500. The existence of these plans has been detailed by Harley and Phillips (1964). Schemes for the provision of public utilities such as gas, electricity and tramways were required by Parliament to include large-scale plans, many of which have now found their way into county record offices. Finally, the plans prepared for fire insurance purposes by firms such as Chas E. Goad Ltd give an unrivalled amount of information concerning the urban environment. These were to enable insurance underwriters to determine the degree of fire risk, and hence the premiums for a particular building. The plans therefore detail the building materials, power supplies, fire hydrants, and means of access to premises as well as the function of the buildings shown (Figure 50). Since the plans

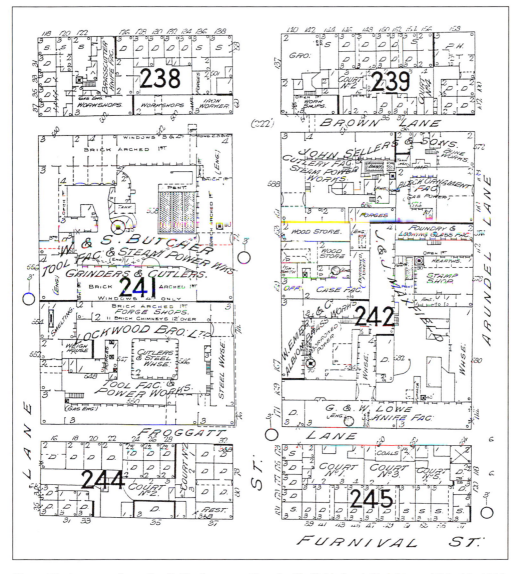

***Figure 50*** An extract from Goad's Fire Insurance Plans for Sheffield, South Yorkshire, published in 1896. The plan shows the variety of industrial premises each side of Arundel Street, typical of the small-scale cutlery and edge tool works common in the town. It also indicates the provision of both gas and steam power, sometimes shared between production units. The numbers 1, 2, 3, etc. in each block indicate the number of storeys whilst cramped court and back-to-back housing filled available space. A photograph of the premises of W. & S. Butcher is reproduced as Plate 15.

were restricted to commercial and industrial areas of towns, they are of immense value to the industrial archaeologist, especially as they were normally updated at frequent intervals until the 1960s. Goads paid particular attention to warehousing districts in both towns and ports because of the high fire risk of goods in storage, and their plans occasionally incorporated sectioned elevations of warehouses and granaries, etc. (Rowley 1984). Taken altogether, these various urban plans can be used to compile a sequence of site development from the late eighteenth to the mid-twentieth century, which is particularly valuable where archaeological data cannot be obtained.

Plans and elevations of individual buildings were generally restricted to the more prestigious structures until the second half of the nineteenth century, when concern for public health led to the creation of local by-laws for urban development. It became compulsory to submit plans to the new local authorities both for alterations to existing structures and for new buildings to ensure compliance with their regulations. Many hundreds of these building plans survive in record offices, together with the registers which enable particular plans to be traced. This is not always easy as the plans were sometimes submitted in the names of the builder or architect and the exact location of the premises can be found only by reference to map sources, using the dimensions given on the plans. The collections include both plans and elevations of new factories, many of which have disappeared in twentieth-century redevelopment but whose foundations may survive in the archaeological record. Working-class housing, undertaken both by private speculators and the local authorities themselves, can be studied and the plans often reveal the survival of domestic industry at surprisingly late dates. Industrial archaeologists are therefore remarkably fortunate in the variety of maps and plans for their period but, as can be seen, their use is not always as straightforward as might be imagined.

## MANUSCRIPT SOURCES

The plethora of manuscript sources available to the industrial archaeologist is such that only a small proportion can be considered here. The reader is referred to various aids to using documentary sources (Camp 1963; West 1982; Riden 1987; Porter 1990) together with the useful series of *Short Guides to Records* issued by the Historical Association (Munby n.d.; K. M. Thompson 1994). The first category which will be discussed is that of documents which enable occupations to be identified and therefore the spatial distribution of particular industries to be established. The second category is that of sources identifying and describing particular industrial enterprises, including buildings and their contents.

The detailed inventories which formed part of the probate process from the late sixteenth until the early nineteenth century are invaluable sources for ascertaining occupations. These accompanied wills and listed the contents of a testator's house shortly after death. Not every will had an inventory attached to it, and not all survive, but locating those which do exist means understanding the probate process. In England and Wales, the wills of those of yeoman or artisan status, for example, were proved in archdeaconry courts and found their way into diocesan record offices, which are now generally combined with county record offices. Wills of the wealthy, particularly those with possessions in more than one diocese, or of people conscious of their status, were proved in the Prerogative Courts of York and Canterbury. On 1 January 1858, the ecclesiastical courts lost their jurisdiction over the probate process and since then wills have been proved in the Principal Probate Registry. Inventories are rare after this date, but the wills themselves can indicate occupations, land ownership, family connections, etc. Pre-1858 wills proved in York are now in the Borthwick Institute at York and those proved in Canterbury are in the Public Record Office. Fewer inventories survive from the prerogative courts than the archdeaconry courts, so county record offices are the best source for them. The complications of the probate process have been made easier through the extensive work of family historians, who have often calendared wills and inventories, which makes individuals simpler to track down. However, the value of inventories to the industrial archaeologist lies in the possibility of analysing the occupational structure of a particular area. The occupation of the deceased is frequently stated, and it is often possible to identify crafts from the equipment listed. For example, in 1756, William Bentley of Shepshed in Leicestershire is identified as a hosier: his house contained a Shop and Warehouse Chamber and eighteen stocking frames were listed among his possessions. The total value of his goods and chattels was £1,281 6s 7d, and he was clearly an employer of framework knitters. The latter would be unlikely to leave inventories, their estates falling below the normal threshold of 50 shillings in value. This illustrates the limitations of probate inventories as a means of establishing a true occupational structure, but they can give an idea of the spatial distribution of particular crafts and industries. Inventories can also be useful in identifying artefacts associated with particular crafts, although the terms used are often difficult to interpret (Trinder and Cox 1980; Thornes 1981).

Probate inventories can be used in conjunction with other records to amplify the information on the occupational structure of a particular area. Registers of baptisms, marriages and burials frequently record occupations, especially once standard forms of register were introduced after 1812, but exclude Nonconformists who usually made up a substantial proportion of the working population. The latter were included once civil registration was introduced in 1837. Poll books listing the qualifications of those entitled to vote were introduced after the General Election of 1695 and continued until the introduction of the secret ballot in 1872. The lists generally include occupations of the voters, but the use of these is limited as not all elections were contested anyway and the franchise varied from borough to borough. They are, however, particularly useful for the eighteenth century before the widespread introduction of trade directories. Another series of lists which include occupations are those of men liable for militia service, which were required by the Militia Act of 1757. These also have their shortcomings, but can be a valuable source for the occupational structure of the late eighteenth and early nineteenth centuries. The most complete record of occupations is that of the census, begun in 1801 and taken decennially, except for 1941. Detailed census information is embargoed for 100 years but comprehensive details of names and occupations, including women as well as men, are available from 1841 onwards. Since the place of birth is given from 1851, it is possible to identify immigration into a particular locality, which can indicate the growth of new industry there and its decline elsewhere. Depending on the diligence of the enumerator, the place of work of individuals can also be ascertained and the labour force in a particular enterprise estimated. None of these sources is adequate on its own to establish the occupational structure of a specific area, but collectively they can provide the basis for a working hypothesis.

The second category of documents, those identifying industrial enterprises, buildings and their contents, is both more diverse and also difficult to interpret. A source frequently used by historians to study land ownership is the Land Tax returns, which date from 1692 but whose survival is patchy until 1780, from which date until 1832 duplicate returns had to be lodged with the Clerk of the Peace. It is possible to identify land exploited for industrial purposes from these returns, especially where mineral rights for metalliferous or coal-mining were concerned (Unwin 1986). Whereas the Land Tax returns are of most value in rural areas, the rate books giving details of those assessed for various forms of local rates can assist in the identification of property in an urban environment. The comparison of successive rate books can establish building or demolition dates of both houses and commercial buildings, change of use and new developments.

One of the largest classes of document in county record offices is the Quarter Sessions papers. These quarterly meetings of local Justices of the Peace were originally concerned with cases of law and order, but they gradually became the main organ of local government until the Municipal Corporations Act of 1835 and the Local Government Act of 1888 put in place new administrative bodies for towns and counties respectively. Quarter Sessions were therefore in receipt of all acts of central government affecting the localities, such as enclosure, turnpike road, canal and railway proposals, and the plans associated with these, along with explanatory books of reference, had to be deposited with the Clerk of the Peace who maintained the records of Quarter Sessions. It must be borne in mind that abortive as well as successful projects are included in these records and can thus provide incidental information about other aspects of the economy. The importance of these papers was partly responsible for the creation of county record offices, and a search through the schedules will usually prove rewarding. The successors, corporation and council proceedings, provide similar information to the papers of Quarter Sessions but, especially in the case of towns, yield details of municipal schemes concerned with urban development and public utilities. The latter assumed considerable importance following the creation of Boards of Health in 1848, the reports to which provide considerable information on local topography since they are usually well illustrated by maps and plans.

Whilst the Quarter Sessions deposits contain maps and books of reference for canals and railways, the full records of the companies that built and operated them were brought together by the British Transport Commission at the time of nationalisation in 1947. This invaluable collection of material dating back to the eighteenth century was transferred to the Public Record Office at Kew and classified as RAIL (see Hadfield 1955–6; L. C. Johnson 1953–4). The minute books of canal and railway companies provide a detailed account of the motivation behind a particular undertaking, the methods of construction, the problems encountered and modifications adopted, together with requests from potential users for branches to collieries, quarries and brickworks, etc. For example, the Ashby Canal committee ordered that their engineer

> do procure in the cheapest manner, either by canal or land carriage, or partly by one and partly by the other, a boat load of blocks from Little Eaton on the Derby Canal not to exceed 100lbs weight each, to be drilled 1¼in. diameter and 5in. deep, to be not less than 7in. thick or more than 8in. – such blocks to be laid on the [tram] road between Ashby and Willesley.
>
> (PRO RAIL 803/4 7 June 1814)

As the original tram road was laid in 1802, this extract suggests that the stone blocks supporting the plateway had proved unsatisfactory. Benjamin Outram's original specification, of which a copy is also included in PRO RAIL 803, had stated that the blocks were not to be less than 150 lb in weight and that each block was to have

> a hole drilled near the centre one inch and a half wide and six inches deep to receive an octagonal plug of oak five inches long in which a spike or large nail is to be driven to fasten the ends of the two rails which are to be bedded on the blocks.

The blocks were to rest on ground to be 'well stamped so that each block may be firmly bedded and the spaces between and round the blocks to be filled up with small stones or gravel'. This was necessary to prevent the track going out of gauge and the surviving field evidence indicates that Outram's instructions were adhered to.

The huge collections of family papers in county record offices are another important source for illuminating the industrial development of large areas of the country. They have been extensively used by economic historians (see Ward and Wilson 1971) but, because of the lack of a systematic index, have not been sufficiently utilised by industrial archaeologists. It is necessary to have a good idea of the date and development of a particular site being researched before tackling family papers. They can, however, provide details which can be obtained nowhere else. For example, the extensive archive of Pryce of Gogerddan in the National Library of Wales contains the bargain books detailing the contracts for the construction of an ore-dressing floor and its water supply at Esgair Hir in Cardiganshire. The massive 40-feet [12.1 metres] diameter pumping wheel was constructed in 1840 and its underground tailrace driven by a team of five men on a bargain of 5 shillings a yard, while another team were paid 40 shillings 'to make a pool for the washing place' and 20 shillings 'for making a water course and fixing the launders'. All these features can still be identified on the site (Palmer 1983: 25–7). British landowners did not attempt to hide their interest in their industrial undertakings, and their letters often help in dating sites and structures. On 3 June 1810, the Earl of Moira wrote to his wife: 'We were at the Woulds yesterday to see castings made with the new iron. I saw it taken from the furnace without any intermediate process and cast into articles of the greatest nicety.' He was referring to his new blast furnace, now a scheduled ancient monument in north-west Leicestershire (Cranstone 1985).

The family papers of the Earl of Moira demonstrate the problems of using this type of record. They are split between the collections in the private possession of the Marquis of Bute, the Huntington Library in California and Leicestershire Record Office, where they can be found both in the Hastings family archives and among papers deposited by a local firm of solicitors. The latter class of record represents a huge and largely untapped reserve of information, ranging from legal papers concerning landownership to the formation and activities of industrial concerns. Many solicitors' collections are so vast that they have not been catalogued and are therefore not always on public access; others require permission before use.

Business records are another very diverse source, which either may remain with the original firm or its successor, or may have found their way into various record repositories. Much of the information they contain is of economic interest but material of interest to industrial archaeologists may occasionally be found. As was suggested earlier, it is the larger firms with national or international interests who safeguarded their records. For example, the archives of the Gregs of Quarry Bank Mill in Styal contain maps and plans, together with memoranda which have proved valuable in dating the phases of the mill building. The important textile machine manufacturers Platt Brothers of Oldham have left a considerable archive which includes not only plans of their premises but also drawings of the vast range of machines they produced, together with details of their installation. Such collections also often contain other valuable illustrative material in the form of photographs, catalogues and publicity material. Business records can also provide details of obsolete processes which help with the interpretation of archaeological evidence. For example, the firm of Walkers, Parker & Company of Elswick in Northumberland became the largest lead manufacturer in Britain and managed the shot towers which were once a feature of towns such as Bristol, Chester, Elswick and London. Their records include inventories and valuations of their various premises, together with technical notes on production processes. Smaller firms have, on the whole, not retained such a complete range of records and often only individual account books and ledgers have found their way into public repositories.

The lack of information in business records about the premises in which firms operated can to some extent be compensated for by looking at records specifically concerned with buildings, such as fire insurance policies. Early textile mills, especially those processing cotton, were a particular fire risk and most were therefore insured. The entries in fire insurance policy registers usually refer to the building materials, the source of power and the processes carried out in various sections of the mill. For example, a Royal Exchange policy of 1778 describes the first cotton mill built by the Robinsons in Nottinghamshire as: 'stone built and slated, turn'd by water'. A sequence of policies can be used to trace the building additions and changes as an enterprise expanded: by 1782, the Robinsons had added another cotton mill and a cotton and worsted mill, together with workers' housing, to their original mill building. Five years later, a further insurance policy records the addition of a steam engine in one of the mills (Greatrex 1986–7). Stanley Chapman has demonstrated the value of fire insurance policies for the study of early Arkwright-type mills (Chapman 1981). These policies can also be used to demonstrate the continuity of domestic production after the introduction of powered spinning. A firm of merchants in Kendal insured their premises as follows in 1802:

> On a house, situate on the West side of Stricklandgate, in Kendal aforesaid £600
> On a warehouse, 2 cottages, stable and outbuildings all adjacent behind £400
> Utensils etc. £400
> On a weaving shop situate at the South end of the croft nearby £100
> Utensils and trade therein £100
> On a weaving shop north of the last, in the same croft £200
> Utensils and trade therein £400
> Memo – there are stoves in the weaving shops for the purpose of heating their irons. Warranted that no parts of the cotton manufacture, except warping, weaving or cutting, be carried out in the premises.
>
> (Guildhall Library, City of London, Royal Exchange 194326, 1802)

Cotton-spinning was clearly regarded as the major fire risk.

Whereas the normal routine of business often creates information of value to the economic historian, it was usually only when things went wrong that descriptions of assets or buildings were drawn up. Such occurrences could be a legal dispute, an arbitration between owner and tenant, disposal of assets by sale, or, at the worst, bankruptcy. The records of the Court of Bankruptcy are held at the Public Record Office, but manuscript copies may well be found in deposits in local record offices. The assets of a company or an individual were also listed when the industrial concern was either sold or let to a new tenant. When the lead mine at Cyffty, near Llanwrst, was sold to a new company in 1899, the plant was as follows:

> No.1 Engine Shaft: One large Cornish Engine with Boiler, 10 to 11 tons in weight, ready to work;
> Wooden Rod with Bob attached; Winding Drum; Pit Head and Pulley with Dividing down the Shaft; Ladders to bottom of Shaft;
> Tramrails and Waggons underground;
> One large Iron Kibble & 18yds. of 9in. lift complete; Dressing Floors with Zinc Roof;
> One Hand Jigger; Round Buddle;
> Crushing Iron Waterwheel 20ft. by 3ft. breast in working condition with 1ft. Crusher Rolls attached in good building with wooden floors, and some dressing tackle inside;
> Smithy & Storeroom with Bellows, Anvil, Steel Tools, Chain & Iron and Office;
> One large Pumping Wheel 35ft. by 3ft. breast with Iron Rods, Travelling Bob Pulleys and Bob on top of Shaft with Rods connected to the Pump;
> Horse Whim with Capstan and Chain;
> Three Iron Kibbles and Lift of 10ins. Pumps complete;
> The bottom Lift of 8ins. Pumps complete;
> Rails & Waggons in the bottom of the Mine.

This description can be related to a water-colour of the mine by H. E. Tidmarsh in 1884 (Plate 38) which shows the steam engine, head gear, crushing house and waterwheel and the single

**Plate 38** Cyffty mine, then known as the Pencraig mine, as painted by H. E. Tidmarsh in 1884. This view shows the steam winder, the waterwheel which powered crushing rolls in the adjacent square building and the round buddle in the foreground. This water-colour is an important source of evidence as the engine house was needlessly demolished in 1966: the site has since been consolidated and interpreted by Snowdonia National Park.

Reproduced by permission of the National Library of Wales.

round buddle. Together, they enable the industrial archaeologist to reconstruct the site of a small mine which was largely reduced to rubble in the 1960s (Bennett and Vernon 1993: 77).

The last example exemplifies what is perhaps the ultimate use of documentary sources, the re-creation of past landscapes and sites for which the physical evidence has disappeared. This process of re-creation has become increasingly necessary to understand the development not only of previously mined landscapes, but also of whole areas of towns where former industrial concerns have been totally obliterated. Maps provide the basic framework for these reconstructions, supplemented by many other types of evidence including aerial photographs. In order, however, to trace the spatial distribution of earlier industrial premises, the industrial archaeologist needs to understand from surviving examples, or photographic evidence, the physical characteristics of a particular type of building so that it can be recognised on early maps. For example, in Northamptonshire the stitching of leather uppers for boots and shoes was carried out in small workshops set against the back garden or yard walls separating rows of terraced houses, which were themselves spatially related to the small factories which cut out the leather and finished the boot or shoe (Palmer 1994a). These workshops can be recognised on maps because of their location, whereas the workshops of the textile industries, characterised by long windows rather than distinctive ground plans or locations, are not so easily picked out. John Prest traced the previous existence of many of the cottage factories for ribbon-weaving built in Coventry in the 1850s by the appearance on maps of groups of houses in triangles or squares around a central steam engine (Prest 1960): similar spatial relationships have been observed in the Sheffield cutlery industry. Away from towns, many industrial structures such as lime-, pottery- and brick-kilns, engine houses, arsenic calciners and buddles are also recognisable on maps by their distinctive shapes or positions so long as they are not housed in a roofed building. Once the existence of these buildings or structures is indicated by map evidence, the hypothesis can be checked against the many other kinds of documentary sources available.

The relationship between the two major kinds of evidence available to the industrial archaeologist, field and documentary, is therefore highly complex. Neither kind tells a complete story and their relative importance varies from site to site. The aim of the industrial archaeologist is not the writing of a piece of economic history but the understanding of a landscape. An example of industrial archaeology in practice is the subject of the next chapter.

*Chapter Six*

# Industrial archaeology in practice

The previous two chapters have defined first a set of field methods and second a set of techniques for handling documents for use by the industrial archaeologist. In practice, a combination of these has to be employed and whether the study of field evidence comes before a documentary search or vice versa depends on circumstances. It has been seen in previous chapters that large-scale surveys of industrial archaeology usually begin with a desk-based study. These can be either area surveys, such as those carried out by RCHME in the Yorkshire Dales and the Midlands Forest, or thematic surveys, like those of textile mills. In both cases, field enhancement is required as a second stage, followed by more detailed recording of sites selected as a result of the initial survey. A similar methodology has been applied to thematic surveys in more restricted areas, such as the county surveys of wind- and watermills in Hampshire, Lincolnshire and south Shropshire (Ellis 1978; Dolman 1986; Tucker 1991), surveys of beam engine houses in Wales (Bick 1989) or of cellar workshops for cotton weavers in Lancashire (Timmins 1977).

At the other end of the scale are the single-site surveys, often carried out as rescue measures under threat of demolition or clearance. In this instance, field survey inevitably precedes documentary research. The ideal situation when studying single sites is to begin in the field, investigate the potential of documentary resources and then allow each type of evidence to enhance work carried out on the other. Single-site surveys, however, must be set in a wider cultural context, taking into account topography, settlement patterns, communication networks, etc., if the interpretation is to be meaningful. An example of the methodology used by the authors on a single-site survey is discussed in detail below.

## THE BASSET MINES OF CORNWALL

The landscape of the Camborne–Redruth area of Cornwall has been proposed for World Heritage Site status because of the quality of the remains of the tin- and copper-mining industries. Yet only a decade ago, the study of these had, with the exception of several steam engines which remained *in situ* (Cornish Engines Preservation Society 1943), been largely confined to purely historical research (Barton 1965, 1967; Morrison 1980, 1983). Some excellent studies of individual mines had been published in the 1970s (Noall 1970, 1972, 1973; Harris 1974) and the landscape impact of the engine houses recognised in several collections of archive and contemporary photographs (Ordish 1967, 1968; Trounson 1968, 1980–1). Little attention had, however, been paid to standing buildings, other than engine houses, or to the archaeological context of the mine setts. These had already, in some cases, been ravaged by reworking of waste tips and were increasingly being subjected to new land reclamation schemes involving demolition and site reuse. It was for this reason that the authors, together with a voluntary group, undertook a survey in 1985 of one of the most complete of these setts, Basset Mines, to the

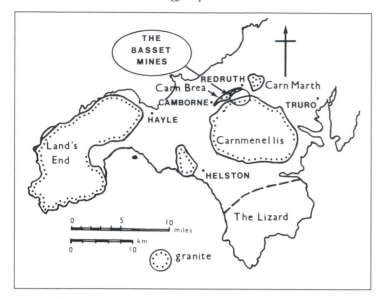

*Figure 51* Location map of the Basset Mines, situated between the granite outcrops of Carn Brea and Carnmenellis near Camborne and Redruth in Cornwall.

*Plate 39* The pumping engine house at Marriott's shaft, Bassett Mines, Cornwall, with the fenced shaft in the foreground. There is clearly no conventional bob-wall to support a rocking beam. The foundations within the engine house indicated the use of an inverted beam engine which was supported by loadings at first-floor level. Subsequent research showed that the house had been intended for two Davey compound engines, only one of which was installed in 1898.

south of Camborne in the parish of Illogan (Figure 51), which was selected on the advice of the Trevithick Society of Cornwall (Palmer and Neaverson 1987). The research agenda was therefore to make as detailed a site survey as possible, to evaluate the techno-logical and historical importance of the mine sett and to investigate its cultural context. This agenda was slightly modified when it became clear that the dressing floors were a particularly significant survival and so their interpretation assumed a more dominant role in the project.

The secondary sources indicated that Basset Mines Ltd had been formed in 1896 by the amalga-mation of six separate mining setts, which had been operative since the 1830s. The combined operations failed in 1919, and there had been some subsequent reworking and clearance. The period of working meant that the setts had been mapped on three editions at the 25-inch scale by the Ordnance Survey, and so a complete site survey was unnecessary. Detailed surveys of important areas such as the dressing floors were undertaken using sim-ple equipment. Plans and eleva-tions of the majority of the upstanding buildings were drawn, since some were thought to be in danger from the renewal of mining operations. A contour survey was also undertaken at the dressing floors to enable a cross-section to be drawn, since differences in level were important to the dressing process.

## Field evidence

The close attention afforded to buildings during the survey revealed their diversity and scale. There were substantial engine-house remains at the five most recently worked mining shafts, showing both different layouts and changes in technology. These included the conventional pairs of pumping and winding houses at Pascoe's and Lyle's shafts, the larger pumping engine house close to the shaft and the winding engine set up to 100 yards [91.4 metres] away. At the Daubuz shaft, the measured plan indicated an engine which both pumped and wound (Figure 52). The surface remains at Marriott's shaft presented a complete contrast to the others, since the pumping engine house was not of the conventional Cornish type, having no bob-wall, and appeared to have been built to house an inverted compound engine with the beam pivoted at ground level (Plate 39). The winding engine house was equally unconventional, the loadings indicating a horizontal cross-compound engine with a recess for the central winding drum. The group of buildings around Marriott's shaft also included a compressor house, a stone breaker, boiler house and chimney, and a heated building for drying the miners' clothing. The survey of the pit-head buildings suggested a chronology of development, with the conventional engine houses surviving from the earlier individual mine setts whereas Marriott's shaft had clearly been re-equipped on a single occasion, probably after the amalgamation of the separate setts.

There were two substantial dressing floors surviving at the eastern end of the combined sett, although a vast amount of re-grading and removal of mine waste would indicate the previous existence of dressing floors at each separate sett. At West Basset stamps, a series of buildings occupied the sloping ground below the stamps engine, culminating in the ruins of a large building which contained sixteen circular buddles (Figure 53).

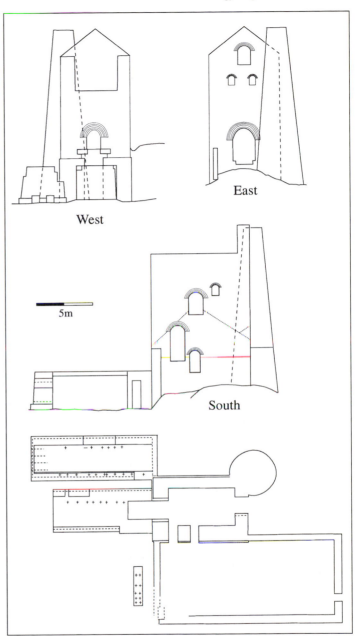

**Figure 52** Elevations and plan of the Daubuz engine house on the Basset Mines sett of South Wheal Frances. The house was set well back from the mine shaft with extensive loadings in front of the bob-wall. The position of holding-down bolts and recesses in these loadings indicated an engine driving both a winding drum and flat rods which pumped from the distant shaft.

These were a mixture of convex and concave buddles, which were cleared together with their interconnecting channels and settling pits (Figure 54). Alongside the buddle house were the remains

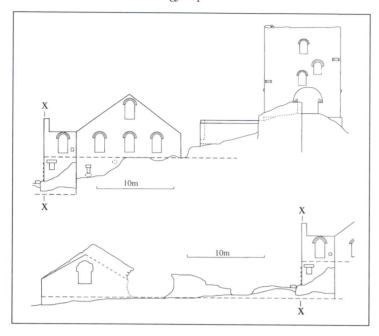

*Figure 53* The east elevation of the buildings on the West Basset dressing floors, showing how the ground slope enabled gravity flow in the tin ore-dressing process. On the top right is the stamps engine and loadings, succeeded by the vanner house and finally the ruined buddle house.

of a double Brunton calciner with a flue connecting to a surviving chimney. At East Basset, on the opposite side of the valley, the dressing mill had clearly been altered during its working life and now contains the concrete foundations of twentieth-century separation machines. The twin stamps engine houses had been modified to act as ore storage hoppers. The two dressing floors were linked by an inclined railway, the remains of which could still be traced across the valley. Both floors were also connected by railway to the western end of the combined sett, suggesting that once amalgamation had taken place the entire ore output was processed at them. The two sites appeared to demonstrate changes in the practice of dressing ores. At West Basset, the large building immediately below the stamps had been superimposed

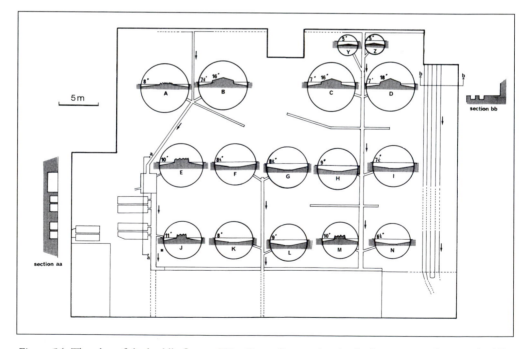

*Figure 54* The plan of the buddle floor at West Basset Stamps showing both concave and convex buddles linked by channels. Various settling strips and tanks are also shown.

on an earlier buddle floor, since one buddle remained outside the wall. There were no obvious foundations in this building to indicate the type of machinery housed there but the stamps engine had continued in use until closure. The East Basset dressing floor, on the other hand, had clearly been adapted for reworking waste tips in the twentieth century.

Water supply for dressing and boiler use was always a problem in Cornwall, and the field evidence indicated that careful provision had been made on the Basset sett. Reservoirs were situated behind the stamps engines, those at West Basset being supplied by an aqueduct which ran alongside the railway. The form of the stamps engine house at the latter, with its two thick bob-walls, suggested that water was recirculated by means of a pump connected to a secondary beam driven from the stamps engine.

Compared with other mining sites in Cornwall, the Basset Mines complex contained an impressive series of buildings, particularly the surviving dressing floors. Evidence of capital expenditure at a comparatively late date in the nineteenth century, or even early twentieth, was provided by the atypical surface buildings at Marriott's shaft and the modifications to the dressing floors. The completeness of the range of surviving buildings merited documentary investigation to understand both the chronology of their development and the apparent anomalies which they presented. The West Basset dressing floor, in particular, indicates the sequence of processes necessary for the concentration of tin ore.

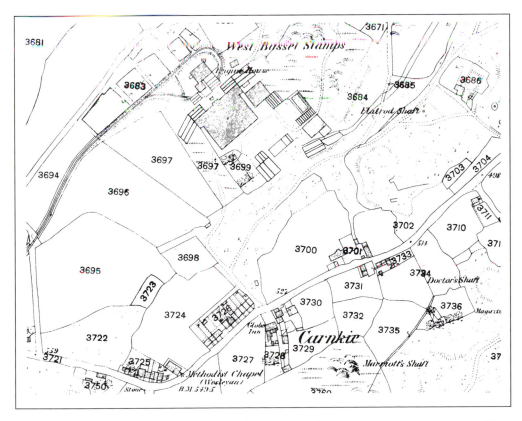

*Figure 55* This section of the first edition 25-inch-to-1-mile Ordnance Survey map was already out of date when it was published in 1880. The West Basset Stamps are depicted but the area around Lyle's shaft (between plots 3699 and 3700) is shown as clear. In fact, this shaft was in the process of being re-equipped when the survey took place in 1878 and was in use by 1880. (Sheet LXIII.11)

## Documentary evidence

Fortunately, the Basset Mines sett was surveyed at the 25 inch to 1 mile scale in 1878 and 1906, which provides two detailed maps showing the changes in surface development between the two surveys. Close study of the 1878 edition for the Carnkie area (Figure 55) in conjunction with other documents, however, reveals one of the problems of mapping in a period of rapid development. Lyle's shaft, on the former North Wheal Basset sett, had been first sunk in the 1840s and a mining map in the Tehidy estate papers, dated 1852, portrays the surface plant on the mine. This included a pumping engine and capstan on Lyle's shaft, together with a water-powered winder and crusher near an adjacent shaft, indicating that the mine was then producing copper ores. Yet, on the 1878 OS map, the whole site is shown as cleared. In fact, by the time the map was published in 1880, following a change of leaseholder for this portion of the sett, Lyle's shaft had been re-equipped with steam pumping and winding engines. The new layout is shown on a mine plan of 1889 and it is the remains of these buildings that can still be seen. It is always essential to note the dates of survey, rather than publication dates, of OS maps when studying a rapidly changing environment. As well as filling in the gaps between Ordnance Surveys, the sequence of mining maps in the Tehidy estate papers was also invaluable for tracing the earlier development of the setts which eventually became part of Basset Mines Ltd. The elaborate West Basset Stamps shown on the 1878 OS map had in fact been in use for only three years, replacing extensive dressing floors near the mine shafts at the western end of the combined setts.

Other useful collections of papers were those of the consulting engineers who were responsible for buildings and plant design. For example, Nicholas Trestrail acted in this capacity for many of the Camborne–Redruth mines and his papers have been deposited in the Cornwall County Record Office. Among them are draft contracts for building the pumping engine house on Lyle's shaft, mentioned above, which was to be constructed out of stone from two nearby disused engine houses within a span of twelve weeks! Trestrail also prepared inventories for the mine company at various dates including the closure in 1918: these provide a valuable resource for interpreting surface evidence, as was seen in Chapter 5. His papers also contain drawings for steam engines as well as dressing plant. These, together with illustrations in contemporary publications, can help make sense of foundations and engine bases recorded in the field. For example, the 1918 inventory indicated that vanners were then being used for dressing the tin ores: these were continuous flow tables introduced in America in the 1870s which reduced the intensive labour required for tending round buddles.

Cornwall is particularly fortunate in its collections of archive photographs of mining scenes, many of which were collected together by the late J. H. Trounson, a former president of the Trevithick Society. Although many are undated, their dates can often be inferred by cross-reference to other records such as maps and mines reports. Plate 40 shows the West Basset New Stamps with the vanner house below the stamps, which other sources indicate was built 1901–2. In the foreground is the flue and chimney stack for the double Brunton calciner for removing arsenic from the black tin, which was added to the dressing floors in 1905. The original stamps engine can be seen in the background with its two rocking beams, one driving the stamps axles and the other recirculating water for the dressing process: this confirmed the hypothesis arrived at during fieldwork to account for the presence of two thick engine-house bob-walls instead of the usual one.

The chronology of development on the mining sett could be pieced together from the pages of various technical journals, especially *The Mining Journal*, and, as mining was the life-blood of west Cornwall, local publications such as the *Proceedings of the Mining Institute of Cornwall*, the *Cornish Post and Mining News* and the *Cornubian and Redruth Times*. These were supplemented

*Plate 40* The west elevation of West Basset Stamps, photographed *circa* 1906. The beam at the rear of the stamps engine house indicates that the engine also served to pump water for dressing purposes. The vanner house on the right had been built 1901–2. The chimney and flue in the foreground served the Brunton calciners, which had been added to the dressing floors in 1905 for removing arsenic from the black tin. (Compare with Figure 53.)

C. Johns, Carnkie, Cornwall.

by the frequent reports of the various mine captains deposited in the Tehidy Estate papers. For example, the report for October 1868 stated:

> we have during the last two months fixed the two new stamping engines and boilers with 35 fathoms of 15 inch plunger lifts, also two balance bobs with three 16 heads stamps axles and erected 12 round buddles with the necessary driving gear. The whole is now working satisfactorily.
>
> (Cornwall Record Office, Tehidy Estate Papers, TEM 286, Wheal Basset Report, 6 October 1868)

This clearly referred to the Wheal Basset sett, where there were remains of a double stamps engine house, but also showed that buddles had preceded the existing vanner house on this site.

A combination of site survey, photographic evidence, documentary sources and contemporary comment in the technical literature enabled the reconstruction of the phases of the dressing floors at West Basset New Stamps. The first dates from the layout of the new floors in 1876, which is as shown on the first edition of the 25-inch OS map surveyed in 1878 (see Figure 55). The dressing process followed earlier Cornish practice, the slurry from the stamps grates being allowed to settle in pits or strips before being dug out in sequence, mixed in dumb buddles and fed to the convex and concave buddles. Final concentration took place in kieves and any fine slime tin which remained in suspension in the waste water from the buddles was retrieved in settling pits further down the slope. Ways of preventing the loss of slime tin led to considerable

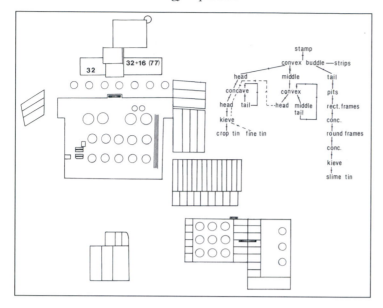

*Figure 56* The ore reduction and concentration process at the West Basset Stamps site in 1893, derived from documentary and field evidence. This was the second phase of the dressing process, using round buddles below the stamps instead of the settling strips shown on the 1880 OS map (see Figure 55).

debate among mine captains in Cornwall during the 1880s, since the mines themselves were losing profit to numerous tin streamers on the local rivers below the mines. One solution was the adoption of round buddles immediately below the stamps grates, and this appears to have been implemented at West Basset: the mine captain's reports refer to the erection of additional buddles and Cornish frames in 1892 and a photograph of the stamps shows the round buddles in position as indicated in Figure 56. Only eight years later, however, the manager for Basset Mines Ltd complained that he could not get sufficient skilled labour for working the buddles and proposed the use of vanners instead. These were installed in the new building immediately below the stamps, which was erected over six of the buddles built in 1892: the seventh still survived to the east of the building. This layout is shown on the 1906 OS map together with the extensive rag frames in the valley to the east which were designed to remove the last vestiges of black tin (Figure 57). This reconstruction of the chronology of development illustrates the wide variety of sources which are available to the industrial archaeologist but also indicates the relationship between field and documentary evidence. Anomalies in the field prompt the industrial archaeologist to investigate the documentary sources, and the anomaly here was the single buddle remaining to the east of the vanner house. This suggested that the vanner house had been built on top of an earlier row of buddles, a hypothesis confirmed by an early photograph, while the initial layout preceding the buddles was shown on the first edition 25-inch OS map. The two major types of evidence illuminate each other.

The documentary evidence also put the field evidence into perspective in another way. It became clear that the physical remains on the site, despite their complexity, were in fact the evidence of major re-organisation on the Basset Mines sett in the last two decades of the nineteenth century and the first two of the twentieth. What the documentary evidence showed was that the most profitable years on these setts had in fact been the 1850s and 1860s, when the mines were producing copper rather than black tin. Copper production declined in the late 1860s, when at the same time the price of copper fell because of changes in the world market. Some of the mines bottomed their copper lodes to find tin, but its exploitation demanded considerable capital investment both because of the depth at which the tin ore was found and the difficulty, compared with copper, of dressing the ores to extract black tin. The physical evidence remaining, therefore, reflected a final attempt by a mining company to win a living from the ground rather than the most profitable years of the mining setts. Such an interpretation is not uncommon in industrial archaeology, and can be arrived at only by use

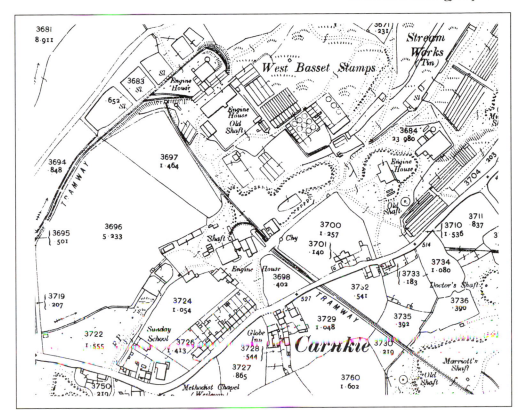

**Figure 57** This section of the second edition 25 inch to 1 mile Ordnance Survey map was published in 1906. The West Basset Stamps are depicted in their final form, together with rag frames in the valley to the east. Lyle's shaft (between plots 3696 and 3700) has been re-equipped and connected by tramway to the East Basset Stamps on the south side of the valley. (Sheet LXIII.11)

of the documentary evidence. The speed at which technology changed in the nineteenth century meant that mining sites in particular were cleared before being re-equipped, as had been the case on the West Basset sett, and so earlier phases cannot be ascertained from the field evidence alone. The establishment of the chronology of development can be achieved only by using all the sources available.

## THE CULTURAL CONTEXT

Our study of the Basset Mines complex indicated human intervention in the landscape on a considerable scale in the second half of the nineteenth century. The documentary sources provide a good deal of information about the owners of the sett, the Bassets, Lords de Dunstanville, who received mining royalties; the engineers who installed the mining equipment; and mine managers who reported progress. More faceless, however, are the men and women who provided the labour. They left few written records of their own, and can be discovered only through field remains such as housing, churches and chapels, tombstones, etc.; occasional photographs; and official records of population, mining disasters and so on. What do these tell us?

The landscape around Basset Mines is one of small villages and scattered settlement, despite the nearness of the two towns of Camborne and Redruth. It is poor agricultural land, yet many of the houses appear to have large gardens, almost smallholdings, which may be testimony to the part-time nature of mining before the advent of the steam engine. In fact, the Bassets of Tehidy had encouraged the development of this landscape in their efforts to attract labour to the area. In the first half of the nineteenth century, Francis Basset had offered 3 acres [1.2 hectares] of wasteland to anyone prepared to cultivate and build a house on it: if successful, the tenant would be given a further 3 acres. Basset therefore built up a group of tenants who were both small-holders and miners, a useful dual occupation given the uncertain nature of mining activity. Some 400 acres [160 hectares] of wasteland were brought into cultivation in this way between 1798 and 1842, and 2,000 people added to the population of the parish of Illogan (Tangye 1984: 48). The ephemeral buildings put up by these tenants have now been altered out of recognition, but the settlement pattern has survived. Other buildings were added in the later nineteenth century, notably rows of brick-built terraces and semi-detached houses which are alien to the Cornish landscape, but suggest the growth of population in the period.

The official population records indicate that growth had taken place in the Basset Mines area in the first half of the nineteenth century, but was even greater between 1841 and 1881 and then followed by a considerable decline. This helps to account for the addition of houses in the later nineteenth century, but suggests that the massive development of the mining sett from the 1880s, as shown by the field evidence, did not lead to any great influx of miners compared with the earlier periods. These 'incomers' had been mainly Cornishmen, with very few from outside the county, suggesting a mobile population which followed the prosperity of mining concerns. The parish records also give some idea about the development of mining in the area, the 'tinners' listed at the beginning of the century being replaced by copper and tin 'miners' by the middle of the century: part-time activity working the tin streams had been replaced by more full-time activity on heavily capitalised mines.

The gender balance is more difficult to ascertain, as the census records do not give this kind of detailed information until 1841 and after. In the second half of the nineteenth century, comparatively few women are listed as working at the mines: in Carnkie, the nearest village to West Basset, in 1861 there were 160 males but only 34 females at the mines. One would expect significantly more men, but photographs like Plate 41 indicate the work that women did on the tin-dressing floors, although the notorious bal-maidens, strong-armed women who broke up the ore with hammers, had by then been largely replaced by mechanical stone breakers. Possibly female employment on the mines was more erratic than that of men, and so was not necessarily recorded in the census returns. Plate 41 also shows a young boy, and both boys and girls under 14 were employed on the mines in a proportion similar to that of women. The 1842 Mines Act had forbidden the employment of all three categories of people underground, hence their

*Plate 41* A group of tin dressers at Basset Mines. The exact site and date are unknown.

C. Johns, Carnkie, Cornwall.

surface activity. Plate 42 shows the normal surface clothing of male workers: a collarless shirt, jacket, waistcoat and trousers. Hats were used to determine status, the trilby of the man on the right signifying his higher rank compared with the workmen with their flat caps on the left. Underground, miners wore similar, although rougher, clothes, without the waistcoat and with a leather cap to which was attached a candle to provide light.

The risks attached to mining naturally led both to superstition and to religious activity in the mining communities. The landscape of the Basset Mines shows that they were, however, little touched by Anglicanism, the nearest churches being in the towns along the main road to the north. But every settlement in the area boasts its own chapel, often more than one of different denominations and frequently rebuilt in the later nineteenth century. Methodism took hold of Cornwall, and its disciplined way of life seemed to accord well with that perforce experienced by miners in large mines such as Basset. The practice of hard work, thrift and temperance preached by Methodist ministers must certainly have been welcomed by mine managers, and there is little evidence of industrial or political activity among miners in the area.

The study of the Basset Mines sett was originally undertaken as a single-site survey, but the importance of certain aspects of the site, notably its well-preserved dressing floors, led to a typological study of these throughout south-west England and eventually comparison with lead ore-dressing processes in the rest of Great Britain (Palmer and Neaverson 1989). In addition, Cornwall Archaeological Unit has since carried out a survey of surviving engine houses and other buildings in the Mineral Tramways Project area which has shown the importance of the Basset Mines complex (Sharpe 1991). Considerable consolidation work has taken place, and the sites

*Plate 42* Lyle's shaft at Basset Mines after re-equipment showing the pumping engine house, a capstan engine in the foreground whilst the gantries in the distance carried the main winding ropes from a remote winder further down the valley. Some of the miners are carefully posed in the foreground.
Royal Institution of Cornwall.

either are scheduled or await scheduling. Not all surveys of industrial archaeological sites merit this final stage of resource management, but where the monument is sufficiently important and funding permits, it is the preferred option.

It was the excellent survival of a wide range of buildings and structures which attracted us to the site in the first place, and the process of recording these led to greater understanding of the rapid development of Cornish mining technology in the later years of the nineteenth century. Yet the documentary evidence indicated that this massive capital expenditure was not followed by very rich returns, and that the mining sett had been far more profitable in the mid-nineteenth century, from which period very little field evidence survives. The cultural context also indicates that the mining heyday of the southern part of the parish of Illogan was past when the present buildings were put up. The meaning of these buildings, in an archaeological sense, is therefore rather different from that which would be accorded them from visual appreciation only, and the study shows how important it is that the industrial archaeologist should make use of the widest possible range of sources.

# Chapter Seven

# Cultural resource management of the industrial heritage in Britain

Industrial archaeology, as has been seen, is concerned with the material culture of the last 250 years or so. In so far as elements of that culture have survived into the present, they comprise a resource by means of which the past can be better comprehended. The survivals may be landscapes, buildings, archaeological sites or artefacts: their transformation into a cultural resource depends on the use which is made of them in the present.

The acceptability of elements of past culture in the contemporary landscape is a matter of public perception. Whereas medieval monasteries were, in many cases, razed to the ground in the sixteenth century, those which did survive are now cherished as precious monuments: the concept of monasticism, abhorrent in sixteenth-century England, is now better understood and vested with an aura of past idealism. Industrial monuments, on the other hand, have only just ceased to be treated in the same way as sixteenth-century monasteries. In the mid-twentieth century they were regarded as relics of sweated labour and unacceptable working practices, consequently being swept away in urban development or land clearance schemes. Only in the last quarter of the twentieth century has the international significance of Britain's industrial heritage been understood and its value as a cultural resource appreciated.

As Lipe has pointed out, value is not necessarily inherent in any item of material culture received from the past, but is given to it by contemporary society: it thus depends on the cultural, intellectual, historical and psychological frames of reference held by the particular individuals or groups involved (Lipe 1984: 2). One kind of value, he suggests, is the associative or symbolic, in which cultural resources serve as tangible links to the past from which they have survived. This has always had a role in industrial archaeology, care being taken to preserve structures associated with inventors and pioneering engineers such as Abraham Darby or Thomas Telford. However, this concentration on the innovative and spectacular has detracted from another kind of value, the informational, since all the survivals in the whole range from the industrial past are sources of information about it. The greater the amount of evidence, the more reliance can be placed upon information derived from it. But, in a dynamic environment, cultural resources must have an economic value and justify their existence in monetary terms as a 'heritage attraction' or, in the case of buildings, a viable adaptive reuse. The selection of past structures for retention in these ways is often dependent on a fourth kind of value, the aesthetic, which can conflict with the other values discussed above. For example, the conversion of the aesthetically pleasing New Mills at Kingswood (Plate 43) to an office complex has given the late nineteenth-century structure a viable future, yet it is atypical of the buildings of the woollen industry in general and consequently has little informational value as a cultural resource.

The problem with the industrial period is the quantity of the resource compared with earlier archaeological periods and the consequent need to be selective. At the national level, the criteria for retention have only recently been clearly defined by English Heritage through the Monuments

*Plate 43* At Kingswood, near Wotton-under-Edge in Gloucestershire, a high-tech company converted the romantically sited red-brick New Mills into a prestigious headquarters to impress overseas clients.

Protection Programme and the re-listing surveys (Stocker 1995; Cherry 1995). Hitherto, retention often rested with local initiative rather than proper consideration of the value of a site or structure in symbolic, informational, economic or aesthetic terms. Prime movers attracted local enthusiasts, who took over steam railways and the stationary engines of public utilities but have found difficulty in raising the recurrent costs of maintaining them. Many projects have foundered once the initial enthusiasm of the participants waned, especially if they had not been integrated into local government strategic plans (see Alfrey and Putnam 1992). Too many sites have been turned into industrial museums of various types, which have difficulty in maintaining visitor levels despite their value as an educational resource. This is not only a British problem: in Europe, financial resources intended for industrial heritage projects have often been diverted to other purposes, as in the proposed regeneration and interpretation of the vast copper-mining complex at Rio Tinto in Spain (Willies 1989). Only perhaps in the USA has the combination of federal and state resources ensured adequate funding provision, both capital and recurrent, for the management of the industrial heritage. In Britain, piecemeal and unstructured management hitherto has resulted not only in the loss of important industrial monuments and sites but also in a considerable wastage of limited financial resources.

Effective cultural resource management of the industrial heritage therefore depends first on defining the criteria for selection and second on informed management of the sites and monuments chosen for retention. The selection process is based upon academic research to increase knowledge of the context of the industrial heritage, followed by an assessment of the resource in relation to any threats posed to its continued existence. The management of the selected sites or monuments then needs to be reviewed in the light of available funding, making the best use of the volunteer labour which has always been a characteristic of heritage preservation in Britain.

## ARTEFACTS

The movement for the preservation of industrial artefacts and structures pre-dates the development of the discipline of industrial archaeology. It began with the Great Exhibition of 1851, which was a proud display of Britain's industrial pre-eminence but also paid tribute to her industrial past. Many of the exhibits were retained as the nucleus of the collections in what was later to become the Science Museum in South Kensington, which included examples of pioneering developments in stationary steam engines and locomotives. The centenary celebrations of Britain's earliest locomotive railway, the Stockton and Darlington, in 1925 resulted in the formation of the original York Railway Museum and another exhibition in Newcastle upon

Tyne led to the opening of its Museum of Science and Engineering in 1934. In the USA, exhibits from the 1876 Centennial Exposition in Philadelphia were housed in the Arts and Industries building of the Smithsonian Institution in Washington. This collecting tradition was continued by individuals, notably Henry Ford, who built up at Dearborn, near Detroit, an international collection of steam engines and transport artefacts (Plate 44). The majority of the objects in these early museums were collected for their technological interest, but were not necessarily representative of their type and have symbolic rather than informational value.

*Plate 44* A steam engine devoid of context: a Newcomen engine for pumping and winding which was collected by Henry Ford from Reservoir Colliery in Leicestershire and displayed with many others in his museum at Dearborn, USA.

The second half of the twentieth century has seen unprecedented changes in both the design and range of consumer products. This has prompted an increasing interest in the preservation of domestic artefacts associated with recently vanished ways of living, beginning with the Victorian era but recently including pre-Second World War examples, like the intriguing Museum of Advertising and Packaging in Gloucester Docks. Folk museums have sprung up in many parts of the world, containing usually random collections of such artefacts although they are occasionally displayed in re-created settings. There has been no systematic collecting policy on a national basis, resulting in a total lack of reference collections for further study, except for isolated examples like the collection of shoes in Northampton Central Museum. This is equally true of pottery, usually regarded as a yardstick of social development in the archaeological record. While many museums and country houses have excellent displays of the superior chinaware produced for the elite by firms such as Wedgwood and Spode, there are no reference collections of the ordinary domestic ware of the industrial period except for that maintained by the Society for Post-Medieval Archaeology in Stoke-on-Trent. Modern consumer trends make the maintenance of such collections an impossible task, although individual manufacturers may retain samples as well as catalogues. This is equally true of glassware, museums such as the Broadfield House Glass Museum near Stourbridge inevitably displaying individual specimens rather than examples of glass in everyday use. It is therefore very difficult to determine typological sequences in the domestic artefacts of the industrial era.

Larger items of technological interest are, however, usually displayed with some attention to their historical development, as can be seen, for example, in the many steam engine galleries in large industrial museums. Although these have an informational value, this is limited by the lack of any context: a visitor to the Science Museums in London or Birmingham would not appreciate that most large steam engines were structurally related to standing buildings. *In situ* preservation retains the context but is often the result of local enthusiasm rather than any systematic cultural resource management. What eventually became the Sheffield Trades Historical Society was founded in 1918 to conserve both the tools and skills of the Sheffield metal-working trades and was influential in preserving the Abbeydale crucible steel and edge tool works, the Shepherd's Wheel knife-grinding shop and the Wortley Top water-powered forge, which dated back to the mid-seventeenth century but ended its life making railway axles. In Cornwall, a group of enthusiasts formed the Cornish Engines Preservation Committee in 1935 which ensured the preservation in their original houses of some of the steam pumping and winding engines from the declining metal-mining industry. Now renamed the Trevithick Society, only in 1992 did it bring at last to fruition, with the support of the National Trust, its initial project of steaming the 1840 winding engine at Levant mine (Plate 45). There are several Victorian water- and sewage-pumping stations maintained and run by voluntary groups, such as Kew Bridge in London and Ryhope in Tyne and Wear. In all, there are more preserved pumping engines than mine winding engines, although the latter were originally equally numerous: the surviving cultural resource therefore gives a misleading impression of the application of steam technology in the past.

Modern museum display techniques have gone to the other extreme, emphasising the cultural context at the expense of the artefact. At the newly furbished Museum of Iron in Coalbrookdale, the typological sequences of cast-iron objects which used to form the nucleus of the display have been largely discarded. Those remaining are dispersed between interpretative panels and audio-visuals, the latter now an obligatory element of museum display. The result is probably more attractive and comprehensible to the average visitor, but of less value to the industrial archaeologist seeking to identify or date an object. In order to attract visitors, industrial museums now have to include interactive exhibits of various kinds, ranging from models which can be

***Plate 45*** The Levant mine near St Just in Cornwall, *circa* 1900 when the mine was still operating. In the left foreground is the 1840 winding engine house, containing the engine which has been restored to working order by the Trevithick Society.

made to work through hands-on science and engineering demonstrations to the experience of virtual reality. The artefacts themselves now take second place, often being presented not in physical form but in graphics or computer models. While this has probably resulted in greater understanding on the part of the general public, the industrial archaeologists are obliged to seek their artefacts in museum out-stores or reserve collections, assuming that funding has been available to maintain them.

The artefacts of the industrial period are difficult to manage because of their size and quantity. While recognising the value of the small folk museum in its local context, there is an urgent need for a more formal collection policy to ensure the survival of a representative collection of artefacts. This may result from the collection and disposal policies adopted by the Museums and Galleries Commission as part of museum registration. The maintenance of large, working artefacts such as steam engines is still largely in the hands of volunteer groups, who need some public funding in return for management agreements to ensure the proper curation of the artefacts. Within industrial museums, the use of graphics has enabled artefacts to be set within their topographical and cultural contexts but the artefact itself has often become a secondary consideration.

## BUILDINGS

The criteria for the evaluation of industrial buildings have changed considerably over the past century during which an increasing proportion of the historic environment has been brought under statutory protection. This has been demonstrated by the increasing chronological span which the Royal Commission on the Historical Monuments of England (RCHME) has been prepared to accept for the inclusion of buildings on its inventories. When RCHME was established in 1908, the terminal date was 1700. In 1921 the end date was brought forward to 1714, in 1946 it was extended again to 1850 and then a final closing date was removed altogether in 1963. The Survey of London, founded even earlier in 1894 on the personal initiative of the architect C. R. Ashbee and now the responsibilty of RCHME, has also extended its remit to include industrial buildings, which figure largely in the most recent volumes on the dockland areas in Poplar and the Isle of Dogs (RCHME 1994b).

There are two forms of legislation intended to provide statutory protection to the historic environment: scheduling and listing. Scheduling is the older concept, dating back to the Ancient Monuments Protection Act of 1882, and intended to preserve unoccupied sites and structures that had no further practical use. Some were taken into state ownership or guardianship. It was a considerable time before any industrial structures were scheduled and very few have ever been taken into guardianship. Although the Iron Bridge in Shropshire was scheduled in 1934, the Coalbrookdale furnace was not scheduled until 1976 and the bridge taken into guardianship only in 1975. Listing, on the other hand, was intended to protect the historic fabric of a building while it continued in use. The concept was first introduced in the Town and Country Planning Act of 1932, when local authorities were first allowed to impose building preservation orders on buildings of special architectural or historic interest. The intervention of war led to the foundation of the National Building Record under RCHME. It was not until after the war that the concept of listing was strengthened by further Acts of 1944 and 1947, by which the compilation of lists of historic buildings became compulsory. The latter Act provided a listed building with protection against demolition or radical alteration: it was the first to interfere with an individual's property rights and has remained the basis for heritage conservation legislation ever since.

The first national survey of historic buildings, begun in 1947, took some twenty-two years to complete. Rapid urban change during this period, together with a growing realisation of the value of the built environment of the Victorian period, meant that the lists were recognised as inadequate well before their completion. In 1969 a national re-survey was commenced, during which the economic, social or technological significance of a building or its importance as an example of a building type were among the factors considered by the re-survey teams, resulting in the inclusion of many industrial buildings for the first time. The re-survey was not completed until 1990, by which time an estimated total of 450,000 buildings had been listed, representing over 2 per cent of the nation's building stock (Ross 1991). The lists were further extended after 1987, when the cut-off date of 1939 was amended to permit the listing of buildings up to ten years old.

The legislation considered above dealt with individual buildings and structures, often designating a monument while ignoring its context. The protection of whole urban areas of special interest, including collections of buildings, was not considered until the mid-1960s when the government commissioned four reports on the towns of Bath, Chester, Chichester and York. The problems facing such communities, from economic pressures, through traffic, to general decay of buildings and finding new uses for old ones, were addressed. One outcome was the creation of Conservation Areas, areas of special architectural and historic interest, which were to be preserved or enhanced in their entirety; by 1991 some 6,300 areas had been so designated. This concept has proved useful for the protection of industrial buildings which individually did not merit listing but collectively were worthy of preservation. The model communities established in the early days of the cotton industry have benefited from Conservation Area status, such as Belper and Cromford in Derbyshire, Styal in Cheshire and New Lanark in Scotland. Some important urban complexes have also been treated in this way, notably the Lace Market in Nottingham and the warehouse area of Little Germany in Bradford. New 'villages' grafted on to to settlements by railway companies such as Derby and Swindon (Plate 46) have been successfully revitalised by this procedure. This legislation was instrumental in highlighting the landscape importance of industrial buildings, often in advance of the re-listing procedure mentioned above. Not until 1990 with the Planning (Listed Buildings and Conservation Areas) Act was all the legislation consolidated.

The 1983 National Heritage Act established the Historic Buildings and Monuments Commission for England, or English Heritage, which became responsible for advice on listing and for the management of 400 properties in care. Parallel measures in Scotland had established the Historic Buildings Directorate of the Scottish Development Department (now Historic Scotland) and in Wales, Cadw (the

**Plate 46** Cottages in the western half of the new village at Swindon in Wiltshire, begun in the 1840s by the Great Western Railway. The quality and vernacular style of these and others in adjacent streets made the area acceptable for Conservation Area status.

Welsh verb 'to keep') was responsible as part of the Welsh Office. In Northern Ireland the Department of the Environment (Northern Ireland) is responsible for listing and built heritage matters, while Manx National Heritage occupies a similar role in the Isle of Man. However, of the properties in care managed by the five heritage bodies, only thirteen are industrial monuments, of which four are windmills and four are iron or steel furnaces; the remainder are a corn mill, a water-powered bobbin mill, a distillery, the Laxey wheel and the Iron Bridge.

Industrial structures and buildings, as well as landscapes, are affected by both scheduling and listing but the distinction between the two is not always very clear. For example, Bestwood Colliery winding house and headstocks in Nottinghamshire are scheduled because of the survival of its steam engine *in situ*, but the winding house is also listed Grade II* (Plate 47). Recent legislation has attempted to remove some of the anomalies, although the flexibility of being able to apply either type of protection to industrial structures can be very useful. The Ancient Monuments and Archaeological Areas Act of 1979 consolidated previous legislation and introduced more stringent controls to prevent their destruction. It led to a scrutiny of the existing schedules, and the Monuments Protection Programme (MPP) was introduced in England to update them. It had been recognised that industrial monuments are severely under-represented in the schedules and a comprehensive research programme, industry by industry, has been instituted (Stocker 1995). Equally, the deficiencies of the listing system as applied to industrial buildings have been brought home by such projects as the thematic textile mills surveys by RCHME and the rapid surveys, also by RCHME, in the designated Urban Development Areas. These have led to the establishment of new criteria for listing industrial buildings, which now recognise their informational and associative value as well as their aesthetic appeal. The criteria include the degree of completeness of a site, which enables the context of buildings to be considered; the extent to which evidence exists for evolutionary change; and buildings which signal key stages in the development of forms of industrial architecture. These have been worked out in response to the need to list a representative selection of cotton mills in Greater Manchester, but should have equal application to other types of industrial buildings (Cherry 1995; English Heritage 1995a). However, English Heritage and its sister bodies can only tender advice to the Secretaries of State, who can and do disregard it. In addition, in England, the recommendations for listing have now been opened to public consultation, which could have a negative effect on the conservation of the historic environment unless greater sympathy for it is engendered by growing awareness of its value.

The statutory bodies can, however, consider only industrial buildings of national significance and local initiatives are necessary to ensure the identification and protection of a wider sample of

*Plate 47* The now isolated vertical steam winding engine house and headstocks of the former Bestwood Colliery in Nottinghamshire. RCHME © Crown Copyright.

industrial buildings. Local planning authorities can also recommend buildings to English Heritage for listing and are responsible for the development control process through which applications to alter or demolish listed buildings are first made. Guidance to planners on listing criteria has been set out in *Planning and the Historic Environment* (PPG 15 1994). However, local commissioned surveys such as that for the town of Hayle, surveyed by the Cornwall Archaeological Unit (Buck and Smith 1995), and the routine operation of the planning processes in the Black Country have stressed the continued vulnerability of industrial buildings (Boland 1995). Although the statutory bodies give considerable grant aid to repair protected industrial buildings, these grants have to be matched from the public or private sector and the funding is often not forthcoming. The limitations placed on development by the listing process can, in fact, prevent the future viable use of industrial buildings when it is considered that adaptation would materially alter their integrity. This has often resulted in the loss of unoccupied listed buildings through the ravages of weather, fire and vandalism. Designation, whether by listing or scheduling, of industrial buildings is not an end in itself and is only the start of a management process to ensure their survival.

If the development pressures are too great for the retention of an important historical building on site, the alternatives are preservation by record before demolition or the careful dismantling and rebuilding on a new site or in a suitable museum context. The rebuilding option can be suitable only for small structures on account of the logistical problems and, of course, the expense. The idea of an open air museum where a number of buildings under threat were

*Plate 48*  A reconstructed village street at the Blists Hill Open Air Museum in the Ironbridge Gorge. On the right is the doctor's surgery, which originally stood at Donnington on the Duke of Sutherland's Lilleshall estate. Down the slope is the ironworks, housed in an iron-framed building designed by Sir John Rennie for Woolwich Dockyard in 1815 and moved to this site in 1974. The plant of the ironworks came mainly from Messrs Walmsleys' Atlas Forge in Bolton, which closed in 1976.

collected together originated with Skansen in Sweden in 1891, followed by the Netherlands Open Air Museum at Arnhem in 1912, and Henry Ford's Greenfield Village at Dearborn in the USA in 1929. In Britain, the collection of buildings from various regions was implemented considerably later, with industrial structures being moved and re-erected in museums such as the North of England Open Air Museum at Beamish in County Durham, the Blists Hill Museum at Ironbridge in Shropshire, the Black Country Museum at Dudley and the Ulster Folk Museum at Cultra. At Blists Hill, the existing landscape of canal, railway, clay- and coal-mining and the foundations of blast furnaces has been utilised to provide the context for additional buildings and artefacts, including an iron rolling mill and an industrial village (Plate 48). These collections are important for what they have preserved but the context of the original structures cannot be entirely replicated and the groupings of buildings are inevitably artificial. Their informational value may be enhanced by their preservation within a museum context, but their associative value is lost.

*In situ* preservation of industrial structures may seem a better alternative, but often statutory protection has been afforded only to a single item and ancillary structures are consequently destroyed. The industrial monument may therefore survive totally devoid of context, like the colliery winder at Washington in Tyne and Wear. The horizontal steam engine of 1888 has been retained in its engine house, complete with lattice steel headstocks, but the rest of the surface buildings have been cleared and the area landscaped. The glass cone at Catcliffe in Sheffield, one of only four such survivals in Britain, now forms a feature in a housing estate and is a complete contrast to the cone at Stourbridge, complete with workshops and in its original canalside setting (Plate 49). Associative value is not always ensured by *in situ* preservation.

This is, however, an important means of retaining and demonstrating historic processes and skills, which is no better seen than in the many working wind- and watermills. These have considerable aesthetic value, and Rex Wailes had begun photographing windmills in the 1920s. In 1931 the Society for the Protection of Ancient Buildings (SPAB) set up a windmills section, to which it later added watermills. SPAB lobbied Norfolk County Council to take the lead in protecting some of the hundred or so windmills then remaining in the county, but it was not until 1963 that the Norfolk Windmills Trust was formed and the successful restoration of many mills is still progressing. Lincolnshire and Essex County Councils have taken similar initiatives. The National Trust has successfully preserved processes at the linen beetling mill at Wellbrook and at Patterson's spade mill at Templepatrick in Northern Ireland. The Sheffield Museums service has maintained the water-power installations at Abbeydale Forge and the Shepherd's Wheel cutlery grinding shops so that processes can still be demonstrated (Plate 50). Textile production

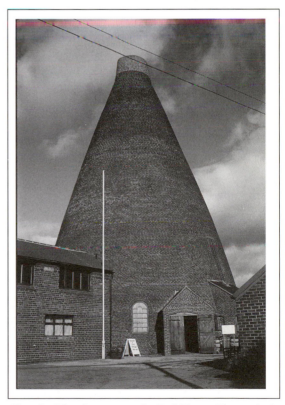

*Plate 49*  The glass cone at the Red House Glassworks in Stourbridge, West Midlands is not operative but preserved as part of a working site. Built *circa* 1790, it is the most complete of the surviving glass cones in Britain.

*Plate 50* The edge tool works at Abbeydale in Sheffield, South Yorkshire, part of an industrial hamlet. The production of scythes ceased here in 1933, but crucible steel production was reinstated during the Second World War. The site was acquired by Sheffield Corporation and opened to the public in 1970.

using hand- or water-powered technology has been revived recently, including commercial production for restoration projects at the Working Silk Museum at Braintree in Essex and the demonstration of both spinning and weaving of cotton at Quarry Bank Mill in Cheshire. Several voluntary groups still carry out hand-spinning and -weaving, together with the production of socks and shawls on knitting frames, as at Ruddington in Nottinghamshire. Working steam engines are preserved at several pumping stations with volunteers working for charitable trusts such as that at Papplewick Pumping Station in Nottinghamshire. The informational value of such projects is undoubted but their economic viability is often precarious. This form of preservation requires considerable resolve and manpower, needing a continuous supply of new recruits willing to learn the skills. Volunteer preservation groups also face the problem of the lack of recurrent funding after the initial grants for the preservation project itself; their dependency on visitor income makes their long-term outlook perilous.

All *in situ* preservation projects of this kind are inevitably part of the tourist industry, dependent for the majority of their income on visitors, and their long-term funding is the responsibility not just of the heritage bodies but also of local and regional tourist initiatives. Marketing the industrial heritage has become an important element in cultural resource management in recent years, exploiting the public's nostalgia for escapism into the recent past. Robert Hewison has argued that the heritage industry is an attempt to dispel a climate of decline in Britain by exploiting the economic potential of our culture and that its products are replacing the real industry upon which this country's economy depends (Hewison 1987: 9). He pillories the Wigan heritage centre, which took advantage of the literary and even music-hall connotations of Wigan Pier to create a major tourist attraction housed in redundant buildings alongside the Leeds and Liverpool Canal. The theme of the centre is 'experience the way we were', exploiting the element of nostalgia – 'hear, see and touch life as it was in 1900' – through living history. Whatever the criticisms aimed at it, the long-term benefits of this enterprise are surely the re-vitalisation of a derelict area, the restoration and reuse of derelict canal warehouses, and the preservation of skills through the working cotton-spinning mill driven by the world's largest operative steam mill engine. Wigan Pier is not the only industrial heritage centre which uses costumed performers to help the static exhibits come alive. This is done with considerable success at Morwellham Quay in Devon, previously a derelict copper ore shipment quay, and also in industrial museums such as Beamish and Blists Hill. However, not all such projects are guaranteed success nor do all of them have nostalgic elements on which to base their visitor interest. Wigan Pier had considerable financial help from Greater Manchester Council, but other items of industrial heritage, intrinsically every bit as valuable as those at Wigan, are mainly dependent on visitor income. These are always at risk, as illustrated by the closure of the major coal-mining museum at the Chatterley Whitfield Colliery, near Stoke-on-Trent, once funding by a local authority was withdrawn (Plate 51). Yet the value of this colliery site as a cultural resource has been confirmed by its scheduling and listing by English Heritage.

Intrinsic importance does not, therefore, guarantee visitor interest when preservation is not accompanied by the creation of a lively heritage centre, but tourist attractions cannot be the entire salvation of the industrial heritage. By far the most cost-effective means of preserving historic industrial buildings is by means of suitable adaptive reuse, preferably within their context where possible. None has argued more vociferously for this option than SAVE Britain's Heritage, founded by Marcus Binney in 1975. Although concerned with all kinds of buildings, SAVE has mounted campaigns for the retention of railway buildings and the reuse of redundant textile mills. Its efforts have been spearheaded by evocative photographic exhibitions and publications to draw public attention to the quality of many industrial structures (Binney *et al.* 1979). More

*Plate 51* Three of the shaft head gears on the Chatterley Whitfield coal mine near Stoke-on-Trent in Staffordshire, only a fraction of a complex site whose conservation has posed major problems. The largest pit on the Staffordshire coalfield, it employed over 4,000 men at its peak. Unusually, it retains many of the ancillary structures such as a washery and heapsteads, which have been removed at other disused coal mines.

recently, SAVE has looked at the whole spectrum of industrial and transport buildings and put forward creative schemes for their reuse. This solution has been widely adopted for industrial buildings with aesthetic value, particularly those in attractive rural environments, such as water-powered corn mills. Many have been adapted to residential or commercial use with their machinery preserved as attractive features within them, although the latter is not always a feasible option. Former industrial buildings in waterside situations also lend themselves to residential or office conversions (Binney *et al.* 1990). However, not all environments are conducive to such adaptations and many projects have foundered due to continuing economic stringencies.

Reuse of industrial buildings is more difficult in an urban setting with difficulties of access and parking for modern transport. The wholesale rundown of some industries, due to foreign competition or obsolescence, has meant that large numbers of similar buildings have been vacated simultaneously as, for example, the textile mills of Lancashire and Yorkshire which were highlighted in a report commissioned by various local authorities in 1984 (Greater Manchester Council and West Yorkshire County Council 1984). Government directives have not always encouraged the retention of redundant industrial buildings. The creation of Urban Development Corporations, with exemptions from some planning regulations, and City Challenge schemes can lead to the demolition of potentially valuable buildings, hence the rapid surveys carried out by RCHME. In general, however, the tendency is now towards the preservation of historic buildings unless a substantial case can be made for demolition and this should benefit the survival rate of industrial buildings (Plate 52). Some fine multi-storey factory buildings in late nineteenth-century industrial quarters of cities have been successfully retained by a process of selective demolition, provision of car parking, refurbishment or renewal of housing and the sub-division of large factories as, for example, in the Industrial Improvement Area of New Basford in Nottingham. Generally less adaptable are the huge workshops of the Sheffield steel industry in the Lower Don Valley, but a flagship project here is the conversion of the former Firth's West Gun Works into a light engineering works for Gripple Ltd, which received an award from the Royal Institute of Chartered Surveyors. Retail supermarkets have been encouraged to adapt existing important buildings, or their façades, as, for example, the former Green Park station in Bath, the office block of the Hoover factory on the Great West Road in London and the former Kayser-Bondor hosiery factory at Baldock in Hertfordshire. The route towards adaptive reuse is not always easy; the financial outlays are enormous and locations are not always suitable for residential or commercial conversions, whose viability fluctuates with the economic climate. Multi-storey maltings, now almost entirely redundant, find ready reuse for flats within easy commuter travel of London, as for example, at Long

*Plate 52* The fortress-like structure of Chubb's former works in Wolverhampton, West Midlands, whose appearance reflected the security provided by their products, namely safes and locks. Built in 1899, it has now been refurbished as a media centre.

Melford, Ware and Sawbridge-worth, but the same buildings in, for example, Burton-on-Trent or Newark are not so attractive for conversion. Aesthetic value has to take second place to economic value in adaptive reuse projects (Plate 53).

The examples discussed above relate to complexes or single buildings rather than whole towns. In the USA, a holistic approach was adopted at Lowell, which in the 1970s was a rundown textile town but which was designated a National Historical Park in 1978. Through a combination of public ($21.5m) and private finance, a programme was launched which has culminated in a showpiece city, with one million visitors a year to a network of

*Plate 53* Disused oasts and adjacent stowages, such as these at Lamberhurst in Kent, provide attractive residential conversions within easy commuter distance of London.

museums. Some of the former mills have been converted to residential use while others have provided a base for a new thriving electronics industry (Plate 54). In Britain, some City Challenge projects have adopted this approach to whole areas in cities, using public funding to improve the

*Plate 54* Some of the densely packed cotton mills in Lowell, Massachusetts, USA, converted to residential and office use and suitably landscaped.

environment which then attracts large sums of developer funding, often for adaptive reuse projects. Canal basins have lent themselves to such schemes in Sheffield and Manchester, where warehouses have been successfully adapted to both commercial and leisure use (Plate 55). Such schemes can, however, revitalise a city centre while leaving the suburbs in a state of dereliction.

**Plate 55** Middle Warehouse at Castlefield in Manchester. The former Bridgewater Transport Services building has been converted into offices, retail units and luxury apartments. The two central unloading arches have been retained and glazed from floor to ceiling to form an attractive space.

The means of statutory protection for buildings has, then, evolved over the past century but industrial buildings still form only a small percentage of those so treated. Compared with many buildings in rural settings or in planned urban streets and squares, industrial buildings often lack aesthetic value, are located in unfavourable surroundings and present major conservation problems because of their sheer size. Changing public perceptions have, however, resulted in statutory protection being afforded to some industrial buildings, particularly those with symbolic value, or their inclusion within Conservation Areas. Non-statutory protection has also been achieved by movement to museum sites, *in situ* preservation by means of voluntary effort or re-investing redundant industrial buildings with an economic value by means of the increasingly adopted alternative of adaptive reuse.

## LANDSCAPES

The extensive surveys carried out in the past decade by means of aerial photography, followed by field enhancement, have resulted in the identification of important industrial landscapes, particularly in the upland regions of Britain. Once identified, however, their protection and management are not so straightforward as for buildings since the statutory protection of landscapes is in its infancy. At the Royal Gunpowder Factory site at Waltham Abbey, for example, a combination of listing and scheduling has been used to protect the roofed buildings on the one hand and the canal network and archaeological deposits on the other (Cherry 1995). This flexible application of statutory measures clearly has great potential for industrial landscapes.

The Waltham Abbey site introduces a further problem in the management of landscapes previously used for industrial production, that of contamination. The Environmental Protection Act of 1990 empowered the Secretary of State to require local authorities to maintain registers of potentially contaminated land and, in some cases, to take drastic action to neutralise the contamination. Landscapes of metalliferous mining have been deemed a particular hazard and the removal or burial of waste heaps has been instrumental in the destruction of much archaeological evidence. The lead-mining landscapes around Minera in Clwyd (Bennett 1995), Van in Dyfed and Snailbeach in Shropshire have been transformed by land reclamation work, although archaeological evaluations were carried out in advance of the work and some isolated features retained (Palmer 1994b). Other threatened sites include those of arsenic production in Cornwall, especially in West Penwith (Plate 56). Cornwall has also been particularly vulnerable to another offshoot of the Green Movement, the rehabilitation of derelict land, much of it funded from European sources and therefore welcome in an area of high unemployment. Reclamation has involved the capping of shafts for safety reasons, which can involve the destruction of surface

*Plate 56* The derelict remains of Brunton calciners at Levant mine in Cornwall, once used for the production of arsenic on many tin mines. The consolidation of such structures has to encompass decontamination procedures.

archaeology (Sharpe 1995). Both these initiatives have attracted short-term funding for archaeological work and the consolidation of industrial structures but the long-term result has been the sudden transformation of a historic landscape which had evolved over a long period.

The management of historic industrial landscapes is therefore fraught with problems. Although many have been identified and often scheduled, their actual management as a cultural resource usually depends upon whether their environment is already subject to other forms of protection. It is fortunate, therefore, that many important industrial landscapes lie within National Parks. The park authorities have demonstrated an enlightened approach towards their management, utilising the protection afforded by Environmentally Sensitive Areas or Sites of Special Scientific Interest to cover areas of archaeological importance as well as natural habitats (White 1991). Where this is not possible, management agreements have frequently been reached with landowners which have enabled measures to be taken to ensure the survival of archaeological sites. The policy adopted has been that of 'consolidate as found', preventing further deterioration by the stabilisation of standing structures but not attempting to re-create their original appearance. These measures have been successfully applied, for example, to important lead-smelting mills in the Yorkshire Dales National Park such as Surrender and Old Gang (see Plate 24) and the water-powered pumping and winding engine at Cwm Cipwrth in Snowdonia. The priority of the National Park authorities is the conservation of the landscape rather than the encouragement of visitor access, which can result in further erosion, and so they do not normally provide specific industrial trails. However, the interested visitor who reaches a site is often provided with low-key interpretation such as information boards as can, for example, be seen at Hafna mine in the Gwydyr Forest in Snowdonia (Plate 57). The Brecon Beacons National Park, however, as early as 1979 published a booklet of industrial archaeology trails in the Clydach Gorge which included some panoramic sketches interpreting features in the landscape. It also funded the consolidation of structures including the Clydach ironworks (Wilson 1988) and various batteries of lime-kilns. Further south in Wales, the Pembrokeshire Coast National Park has also consolidated and interpreted the lime-kilns which were a feature of numerous inlets and provides 'site cards' for the interested visitor (see Briggs 1992).

Land acquisition by the National Trust, particularly coastline as a result of Enterprise Neptune, has brought many industrial landscapes under its protective umbrella. These incorporate monuments ranging from early nineteenth-century engine houses in Cornwall to post-Second World War weapons-testing structures at Orford Ness in Suffolk. The trust's policy, like that of the National Parks, has been to create an inventory of archaeological structures in its care and, in selected cases, to consolidate rather than rebuild them. In recent years, attention has been paid to the total context of industrial structures rather than simply maintaining them as monuments in the landscape. A good example is the site of the Ravenscar alum works in North Yorkshire, where not only have the remains of the processing plant been carefully recorded and

*Plate 57* The Hafna lead and zinc ore-dressing mill in the Gwydyr Forest near Llanwrst in North Wales. The site illustrates the development of ore-dressing techniques over 150 years. It has been cleared and consolidated, like several other mine sites in the vicinity.

consolidated (Figure 58) but care has been taken to incorporate within the interpretative scheme both the quarries, which were the source of alum shale, and the incline down to the shore where ships bringing coal were beached (Marshall 1995). On its more traditional landholdings, the country estates, the trust is beginning to appreciate the importance of using the archaeological evidence to demonstrate their economic base. Landowners made considerable use of water power for milling corn and sawing wood, and on many estates the mills are retained as working entities together with their ponds and leats. In Northern Ireland, for example, a sawmill has been preserved at Florence Court in the west of the province and a corn mill and its ancillary buildings at Castle Ward in the east. Erddig, on the Welsh borders, retains its steam-powered sawmill and mortar yard, while various brick-kilns together with small buildings housing water and sewage pumps still exist on the Blickling estate in Norfolk (see Thackray 1995). While these have all been archaeologically evaluated, their management presents problems of interpretation and visitor safety as well as maintenance costs, a problem echoed on other National Trust properties throughout the country.

Industrial landscapes outside the protection of National Parks and the National Trust depend for their survival on the attitude of local authorities. Many of these, however, have come to realise the cultural significance of industrial landscapes, especially in areas where industrial activity is now little more than a memory. A classic example is the Ironbridge Gorge in Shropshire, where the creation of a new town to revitalise the economy of the rundown East Shropshire coalfield threatened a landscape often described as 'the cradle of the industrial revolution' and later recognised as a World Heritage Site. Through the efforts of pioneers of industrial archaeology such as Arthur Raistrick and Michael Rix, the area of the gorge was included within the new town of Dawley (later Telford) in recognition of its historical importance and amenity potential. In 1959, the Coalbrookdale Company had opened its museum of iron founding to celebrate its 250th anniversary and revealed the continued existence of Abraham Darby's original coke smelting blast furnace, first erected *circa* 1638. Following problems with the conservation of the Iron Bridge itself, the Ironbridge Gorge Museum Trust was established in 1968 'to conserve for posterity the monuments of the Industrial Revolution in the Ironbridge gorge'. This was heavily subsidised in its early years by the Telford Development Corporation (see *Industrial Archaeology Review* 1979). Abraham Darby's iron bridge of 1779 across the River Severn has become an icon of the industrial revolution and the symbol of the new town, its tangible link with the past (Plate 58). The area has now become a series of museums within a landscape, preserving the infrastructure of settlements, water-supply systems and transport links which were the context of its iron, coal and clay industries. The historical development of the landscape has been extensively studied in the Nuffield Survey previously referred to (Alfrey and Clark 1993). On a far smaller scale, other industrial landscapes have been contained within a museum context, notably at the Black Country Museum in Dudley where local buildings have been re-erected on a derelict landscape which included the remains of coal mines, lime-kilns and a canal system.

Undoubtedly, preservation within a museum environment maximises the educational value of an industrial landscape but limited resources prevent this solution from being widely adopted. Other derelict landscapes have been made freely accessible by local authorities as country parks, preserving major features of past industry but without elaborate interpretation or curatorial input. This strategy has been utilised on several of the ironstone quarries in Northamptonshire, where the characteristic working faces and the hill-and-dale landscape created by the stripping of overburden have been retained. In the West Midlands, Sandwell Metropolitan Borough Council has created Warrens Hall Park around a canal interchange at Windmill End. One canal branch disappears into Netherton Tunnel, while attractive cast-iron towpath bridges mark other branches which once fed the numerous iron- and brickworks nearby. The whole is dominated

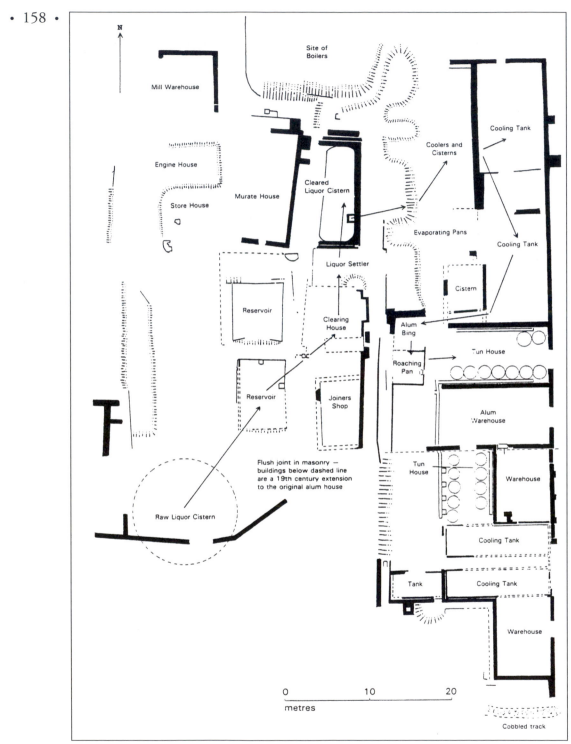

*Figure 58* A plan of the central part of the Peak alum works at Ravenscar in North Yorkshire. It was acquired by the National Trust along with other alum works along this coastline and has been carefully consolidated and interpreted.

Reproduced by permission of Gary Marshall (The National Trust).

*Plate 58* The Iron Bridge across the Severn Gorge in Shropshire, the world's first iron bridge, cast in Abraham Darby's Coalbrookdale foundry in 1777 and erected in 1779. Now in the care of English Heritage, the bridge was originally saved by the Ironbridge Gorge Museum Trust and is the centrepiece of an industrial landscape accorded World Heritage status.
By permission of the Ironbridge Gorge Museum Trust.

by the empty shell of Cobb's engine house as a symbol of the area's industrial heritage (Palmer and Neaverson 1994: 187–92). The repeated use of a river for the generation of power is illustrated in the Roe Valley Country Park near Limavady in County Londonderry. Most of the stages in processing flax into linen were carried out here and there are remains of scutching, weaving and beetling mills, together with the watch-towers which protected the linen spread out on the ground to bleach. There is also a corn mill and a hydro-electric generating station. Bury MBC was not so fortunate in possessing upstanding buildings to symbolise the industrial past of the upper Irwell valley, once the location of several cotton mills. The transformation of this valley into the Burrs Countryside Park has included the excavation of Higher Woodhill Mill and its associated water courses, the foundations of which are now contained behind railings as points of interest (Fletcher 1994). Reconstruction drawings such as Figure 59 enable the public to envisage vanished superstructures and machinery.

Many of the local authority initiatives discussed above were able to utilise industrial landscapes as a cultural resource because they were within easy reach of large centres of population, thereby investing them with an economic value. The lack of incentive for similar initiatives in remote areas which are not National Parks, such as the lead-mining landscapes of central Wales or the

*Figure 59* Reconstruction drawing of the suspension wheel and gearing at Higher Woodhill Mill, Bury, in Lancashire. This was undertaken to enable visitors to the Burrs Countryside Park to understand the consolidated remains of the water-power installation.

By permission of Mark Fletcher.

Pennines, places them at risk. A Register of Historic Landscapes can only draw attention to their importance, not provide the resources to manage them, and their long-term survival hangs in the balance.

Less vulnerable are the derelict railways and canals, which lend themselves to the creation of linear recreational areas where modern leisure activities take place in the confines of past industrial corridors. These areas therefore have both an educational and an economic value, while many of the features associated with their past transport use add an aesthetic dimension. Trails have been established along much of the Birmingham Canal Navigation system, but the outstanding section is undoubtedly that of the Galton valley, crossed by Telford's magnificent cast-iron bridge of 1829 (Plate 59) and revealing the successive engineering solutions to crossing the high ground at Smethwick (Andrew 1995). Plans to re-open the Montgomery Canal have ensured the survival of many features along this rural waterway, particularly the many lime-kilns along its length, which have been consolidated and interpreted. In Derbyshire, the Cromford and High Peak Railway closed in the 1960s but was immediately transformed into a walking and cycling trail, ensuring the preservation of its unique engine houses and inclines. These are but a few examples of probably the most successful area of resource management in the industrial heritage, since past methods of transport have nostalgia value, continuing use for leisure purposes and few associations with the hardship and squalor which characterised so much of the industrial past.

The volunteer input which has been so significant in British industrial archaeology has been instrumental in ascribing an informational value to many locally important landscapes which do not merit national consideration. The activities of local societies and further education groups have ensured the availability of a wide range of local guides, both to urban and rural areas. In 1978, the Wales Tourist Board published a guide to industrial trails and preserved industrial structures which was the forerunner of many others (Wales Tourist Board 1978). Some of the trails were created by local authorities, such as that at Bersham in Clwyd around the sites associated with the ironmaster John Wilkinson. Others were produced by local groups such as the South West Wales Industrial Archaeology Society, mainly for the Lower Swansea Valley whose industrial heritage was fast disappearing. By contrast, the Greater London Industrial Archaeology Society has created a number of walks in London, many of them along the Regent's Canal pointing out the industrial structures which clustered on its banks (Plate 60). In north-west Leicestershire, local groups have provided trail leaflets and information boards for both the Leicester and Swannington Railway and the landscape around the coke-fired blast furnace at Moira. In many instances these efforts have focused attention on important sites and structures, leading to their protection and consolidation.

It is therefore apparent that the management of industrial landscapes is a patchwork of different initiatives, ranging from the very local to the wide expanses in the care of the National Trust and the National Parks. In the latter, these landscapes are increasingly regarded as

**Plate 59** Telford's improvements to the line of the Birmingham Canal in the Galton Valley near Smethwick, West Midlands, resulted in a deep cutting which presented problems in bridging it. His solution was this magnificent cast-iron bridge of 1829.

**Plate 60** An urban industrial landscape: St Pancras lock on the Regent's Canal in London with St Pancras station framed between a series of gas holders which are currently under threat from the developments associated with the Channel Tunnel terminus.

an important cultural resource and protected accordingly. The greatest threat, however, is the current concern not just to treat contaminated land, which is justifiable, but also to use short-term funds to 'prettify' what is classed as derelict land, thereby destroying the historic evolution of the landscape and detracting from its cultural value.

## DOCUMENTS

The long-standing establishment in Great Britain of both national and local repositories for documentary sources would not suggest that there could be a problem in this aspect of the management of the cultural resource. However, the very factors which have created large numbers of redundant buildings, such as industrial decline and the privatisation of previously nationalised industries, have equally led to vast numbers of documents becoming liable to destruction. Many business records, as discussed earlier, are very large in size, such as building plans and engineering drawings, or repetitive, like the details of machinery components. Record repositories, themselves underfunded and with an uncertain future as a result of local government re-organisation, have been understandably reluctant to burden themselves further by taking all these resources into their care. In many cases, they have not even had the opportunity as the documents have been destroyed by the firms involved, who see no economic value in them as a resource and ignore their informational value (Atterbury 1995).

The problem is really twofold. In the first place, firms which are closing or being taken over need to be persuaded of the historical value of the resource they possess in their archives and to allow interested parties access to them. This has been tackled to some extent by the three Royal Commissions on Historical Monuments and the Public Record Office, but there is still a large credibility gap. In the second place, archivists – who cannot be experts in every field – need assistance in selecting from among the often vast range of documentary material those records which are likely to have the most informational value. This is a process entirely analogous to that presented by large categories of suddenly redundant buildings, but has not been dealt with in so systematic a manner. It is once again a task which needs to be undertaken by the professional and the volunteer in tandem, both giving of their expertise. It is also a task of equal importance to that of assessing the value of the physical remains of the industrial heritage since, as has been discussed, their interpretation is partly dependent on the use of documentary sources, especially the large maps and plans which are the very documents archivists find so difficult to curate.

Since industrial archaeology in Britain arose out of the need to preserve sites and structures of early industrial activity, it has always been more concerned with cultural resource management than other areas of archaeology. It is only recently, however, that the world significance of Britain's industrial heritage has been recognised and professional bodies have come to play a major role in its management. This has led to a wide-ranging re-assessment of the whole stock of industrial remains and the formulation of policies concerned with their recording and conservation. Previously, aesthetic or associative values were generally the criteria for preservation, with windmills, watermills and prime movers taking precedence. Management of the industrial heritage was a patchwork of different initiatives, with volunteers shouldering most of the burden. The growing involvement of professional bodies at both the national and the local level has coincided with the decline in the enthusiasm of volunteers: the two elements are probably connected but there is not enough data available to be categorical about this. Undoubtedly, the two ends of the spectrum are equally essential in managing the industrial heritage: there are insufficient resources in the public purse to meet the costs if volunteer activity should be largely withdrawn. There is also an immense fund of knowledge in the voluntary sector, which the AIA's

IRIS project is trying to make available in the public domain for development control purposes, while recognising that the information remains the intellectual property of those who have carried out the research. It has never been more necessary for the professional and voluntary sectors to work together, a key element in the policy of both the AIA and the CBA.

The change in public perception of the value of the industrial heritage in the last decade has led to many industrial buildings being adapted to other uses rather than being demolished. This in itself is not new, since substantial mills and factories have always lent themselves to conversion for other industrial processes. The earliest surviving cast-iron-framed building at Ditherington near Shrewsbury began life in 1797 as a flax mill and then became a floor maltings, although a further adaptive reuse is still under discussion. What has transformed the process of cultural resource management in the last two decades has been the adaptation of former industrial buildings for non-industrial purposes, such as apartments, offices, shops, hotels and leisure centres. This is not, of course, universal practice, as some types of industrial monuments are not suitable for conversion, hence the rapid demolition of ironworks and the surface remains of coal mines. But redundant docks and wharves, often reduced to wastelands, have now become attractive locations for residential development by the combination of reuse of warehouses and the construction of new buildings in that idiom.

Management of the industrial heritage as a cultural resource, however important, must not blind us to the fact that it is only one aspect of industrial archaeology. It is all too easy to become obsessed with the statutory processes of scheduling and listing and to forget that the main purpose of industrial archaeology is the study, not the conservation, of physical evidence. Research in the last decade has often been prompted, and indeed made possible, by the demolition of buildings such as textile mills or the decontamination of former mining landscapes. As a result, we have a much better understanding of the use of cast iron in the construction of buildings and of the typological development of many classes of building. Within the landscape, greater attention has been paid to the relationship of buildings both to each other and to the production process, transport networks and patterns of settlement. Above all, industrial archaeology has moved away from a concentration on the concept of the monument to a broader study of the material culture of the industrial period. The full range of evidence, when the physical remains are considered alongside documentary sources, reveals a very different picture from that indicated by the latter alone. Industrialisation was a very gradual process, in which innovation in one aspect of production did not automatically transform the remainder. The physical evidence, in fact, indicates how desperately the workforce clung on to the illusion of independence by continuing out-work on a domestic basis. But it also reveals the growing power of the entrepreneur, even though his workforce was not factory-based. The nail-maker in his back-yard workshop in the Black Country or the weaver in his loomshop high in the Pennines were as much a part of a controlled process of production as the child piecer or female spinner in a cotton mill. The study of industrial archaeology therefore has a vital role to play in revealing the whole cultural context of the process of industrialisation.

# Bibliography

In addition to works referred to in the text, this bibliography includes a number of books and articles that are of general background interest.

Agricola, Georgius (1556) *De Re Metallica*, trans. H. and L. Hoover, London: *Mining Magazine*, 1912; reprinted New York: Dover Publications, 1950.

Alderton, David and Booker, John (1980) *The Batsford Guide to the Industrial Archaeology of East Anglia*, London: Batsford.

Alfrey, Judith and Clark, Catherine (1993) *The Landscape of Industry: Patterns of Change in the Ironbridge Gorge*, London: Routledge.

Alfrey, Judith and Putnam, Tim (1992) *The Industrial Heritage: Managing Resources and Uses*, London: Routledge.

Andrew, J.H. (1985) 'The Smethwick Engine', *IAR*, VIII, 1: 7–27.

—— (1995) 'The canal at Smethwick – under, over and finally through the high ground', *IAR*, XVII, 2: 171–92.

Andrews, David (1994) 'Written in rock and rust', *Federal Archeology*, 7, 2: 16–23.

Ashmore, Owen (1982) *The Industrial Archaeology of North-west England*, Manchester: Manchester University Press.

Association for Industrial Archaeology (1993) *Recording the Industrial Heritage*, Leicester: SAS.

Atkinson, Frank (1974) *Industrial Archaeology of North-East England*, Vols 1 and 2, Newton Abbot: David and Charles.

Atterbury, Janet (1995) 'Saving industrial records, is there progress?', in Palmer, Marilyn and Neaverson, Peter (eds) *Managing the Industrial Heritage*, Leicester: SAS: 9–14.

Austen, B., Cox, D. and Upton, J. (eds) (1985) *Sussex Industrial Archaeology: A Field Guide*, Chichester: Phillimore.

Baker, D. (1991) *Potworks: the Industrial Architecture of the Staffordshire Potteries*, London: RCHME.

Balchin, W. G. V. (1983) *The Cornish Landscape*, London: Hodder and Stoughton; revised edn of his *Cornwall: an Illustrated Essay on the History of the Landscape* (1972).

Barton, D. B. (1965) *The Cornish Beam Engine*, Truro: D. Bradford Barton.

—— (1967) *A History of Tin Mining and Smelting in Cornwall*, Truro: D. Bradford Barton.

Battye, Kay, Doncaster, Richard, Mitchell, Ian and Newing, Don (1991) 'Summerley Colliery coke ovens', *IAR*, XIII, 2: 152–61.

Baxter, Bertram (1966) *Stone Blocks and Iron Rails (Tramroads)*, Newton Abbot: David & Charles.

Beamon, Sylvia P. and Roaf, Susan (1990) *The Ice Houses of Britain*, London: Routledge.

Belhoste, J.-F. (1988) *Les Ardoisières en pays de la Loire*, Nantes: IG.

—— (1991) *Fonte Fer Acier, Rhone-Alpes, XVe–début XXe siècle*, Lyon: IG.

Belhoste, J.-F., Bertrand, P. and Gayot, G. (1984) *La Manufacture de Dijonval et la draperie sedanaise 1650–1850*, Paris: IG.

Belhoste, J.-F., Claerr-Roussel, C., Lassus, F., Philippe, M. and Vion-Delphin, F. (1994) *La métallurgie comtoise, XVe–XIXe siècles: Etude du val de Saône*, Besançon: IG.

Bennett, John (ed.) (1995) *Minera: Lead Mines and Quarries*, Wrexham: Wrexham Maelor Borough Council.

Bennett, John and Vernon, Robert W. (1993) *Mines of the Gwydyr Forest, Part 5: Coed Mawr Pool, Cyffty and Other Mines in South West Gwydyr*, Cuddington: Gwydyr Mines Publications.

Bettess, F. (1984) *Surveying for Archaeologists*, Durham: University of Durham: 40–53, 69–77.

Bick, D.E. (1989) 'The beam-engine house in Wales', *IAR*, XII, 1: 84–93.

Biddle, Gordon and Nock, O. S. (1983) *The Railway Heritage of Britain*, London: Michael Joseph.

Binney, M., Fitzgerald, R., Langenbach, R. and Powell, K. (1979) *Satanic Mills: Industrial Architecture in the Pennines*, London: SAVE Britain's Heritage.

Binney, M., Machin, F., and Powell, K. (1990) *Bright Future; the Re-Use of Industrial Buildings*, London: SAVE Britain's Heritage.

Boast, R. and Chapman, D. (1991) 'SQL and hypertext generation of stratigraphic matrices', in Lockyear, K. and Rahtz, S. (eds) *Computer Applications and Quantitative Methods in Archaeology, 1990*, Oxford: Tempus Reparatum: 43–50.

Boland, Pete (1995) 'The identification and preservation of the industrial archaeology of the Black Country', in Palmer, Marilyn and Neaverson, Peter (eds) *Managing the Industrial Heritage*, Leicester: SAS: 91–6.

Booker, Frank (1967) *Industrial Archaeology of the Tamar Valley*, Newton Abbot: David & Charles.

Bourne, J. C. (1839) *Bourne's London and Birmingham Railway*, reprinted 1972, Newton Abbot: David & Charles.

Branch Johnson, W. (1970) *Industrial Archaeology of Hertfordshire*, Newton Abbot: David & Charles.

Briggs, C. Stephen (ed.) (1992) *Welsh Industrial Heritage: a Review*, CBA Research Report No. 79, York: CBA.

Brook, Fred (1977) *The Industrial Archaeology of the British Isles: 1 The West Midlands*, London: Batsford.

Brown, Anthony (1987) *Fieldwork for Archaeologists and Local Historians*, London: Batsford.

Brown, Jonathan (1983) *Steeped in Tradition: The Malting Industry in England since the Railway Age*, Reading: University of Reading.

Buchanan, C. A. and Buchanan, R. A. (1980) *The Batsford Guide to the Industrial Archaeology of Southern England*, London: Batsford.

Buchanan, R. A. (1980 [1972]) *Industrial Archaeology in Britain*, Harmondsworth: Penguin Books.

Buchanan, R. A. and Watkins, George (1976) *The Industrial Archaeology of the Stationary Steam Engine*, London: Allen Lane.

Buchanan, Terry (1983) *Photographing Historic Buildings*, London: HMSO.

Buck, Colin and Smith, John R. (1995) *Hayle Town Survey and Historic Audit*, Truro: Cornwall County Council.

Burns, John A. (ed.) (1989) *Recording Historic Structures*, Washington: the American Institute of Architects Press.

Burritt, Elihu (1868) *Walks in the Black Country and its Green Border-Land*, London: Sampson Low.

Burt, Roger and Waite, Peter (1988) *Bibliography of the History of British Metal Mining*, Exeter: University of Exeter.

Butt, John (1967) *The Industrial Archaeology of Scotland*, Newton Abbot: David & Charles.

Butt, John and Donnachie, Ian (1979) *Industrial Archaeology in the British Isles*, London: Paul Elek.

Calladine, Anthony (1993) 'Lombe's Mill: an exercise in reconstruction', *IAR*, XVI, 1: 82–99.

Calladine, Anthony and Fricker, Jean (1993) *East Cheshire Textile Mills*, London: RCHME.

Camp, A. J. (1963) *Wills and their Wherabouts*, Chichester: Phillimore.

Campion, G. (1996) 'People, process and the poverty-pew: a functional analysis of mundane buildings in the Nottinghamshire framework-knitting industry', *Antiquity*, 70: 847–60.

Cattell, John and Falconer, Keith (1995) *Swindon: the Legacy of a Railway Town*, London: HMSO.

Cerdà, Manuel (1991) 'Industrial archaeology and the working class', in Cerdà, Manuel and Torro, Josep (eds) *Arquelogia Industrial*, València: Diputació de València.

Chaloner, W. H. and Musson, A. E. (1963) *Industry and Technology*, London: Vista Books.

Chapman, S. D. (1981) 'The Arkwright mills – Colquhoun's census of 1788 and archaeological evidence', *IAR*, VI, 1: 5–27.

Cherry, Martin (1995) 'Selection criteria for listing industrial buildings', in Palmer, Marilyn and Neaverson, Peter (eds) *Managing the Industrial Heritage*, Leicester: SAS: 119–24.

Clarke, Richard J. (1987) 'The Closeburn limeworks scheme: a Dumfriesshire waterpower complex', *IAR*, X, 1: 5–22.

Cleere, Henry and Crossley, David (1985) *The Iron Industry of the Weald*, Leicester: Leicester University Press.

Clough, Robert Taylor (1980 [1962]), *The Lead Smelting Mills of the Yorkshire Dales and Northern Pennines*, Keighley: Author.

Coad, Jonathan G. (1989) *The Royal Dockyards, 1690–1850*, London: RCHME and Scolar Press.

Collins, P. and Stratton, M. (1993) *British Car Factories from 1896: A Complete Historical, Geographical, Architectural and Technological Survey*, Godmanstone: Veloce Publishing.

Cornish Engine Preservation Society (1943) *Cornish Pumping Engines and Rotative Beam Engines*, Truro: the Trevithick Society.

Cossons, Neil (1975, 1983, 1993) *The BP Book of Industrial Archaeology*, Newton Abbot: David & Charles.

Cranstone, David (ed.) (1985) *The Moira Furnace*, Coalville: North West Leicestershire District Council.

—— (1989) 'The archaeology of washing floors: problems, potentials and priorities', *IAR*, XII, 1: 40–9.

—— (1992) 'Excavation: the role of archaeology', *IAR*, XIV, 2: 119–25.

Crossley, David (ed.) (1989) *Water Power on Sheffield Rivers*, Sheffield: Sheffield Trades Historical Society and University of Sheffield.

—— (1990) *Post-medieval Archaeology in Britain*, Leicester: Leicester University Press.

—— (1994) 'The Wealden glass industry revisited', *IAR*, XVII, 1: 64–74.

Dallas, Ross (1980a) 'Surveying with a camera: photogrammetry', *The Architect's Journal*, 171, 5 (30 January): 249–55.

—— (1980b) 'Surveying with a camera: rectified photography', *The Architect's Journal*, 171, 8 (20 February): 395–9.

Daumas, M. (1980) *L'Archéologie industrielle en France*, Paris: PUF.

Davies, M. (1993) 'The application of the Harris Matrix in the recording of standing structures', in E. C. Harris *et al.* (eds) *Practices of Archaeological Stratigraphy*, London and San Diego: Academic Press: 167–80.

Davies-Shiel, Mike (1978) *Watermills of Cumbria*, Lancaster: Dalesman.

Day, Joan (1973) *Bristol Brass: The History of the Industry*, Newton Abbot: David & Charles.

—— (1991) 'Copper, zinc and brass production', in Day, Joan and Tylecote, R. F. (eds) *The Industrial Revolution in Metals*, London: the Institute of Metals: 131–99.

Deetz, J. (1977) *In Small Things Forgotten: The Archaeology of Early American Life*, New York: Anchor.

Defoe, Daniel (1724–6) *A Tour Through the Whole Island of Great Britain*, reprinted London: J. M. Dent, 1927: 144–6.

Dobson, S. (1994) 'Computer Aided Design in Buildings Archaeology', unpublished MSc thesis, University of Leicester.

Dolan, J. E., and Oglethorpe, M. (1996) *Explosives in the Service of Man: Ardeer and the Nobel Heritage*, Edinburgh: Royal Commission on the Ancient and Historical Monuments of Scotland.

Dolman, Peter (1986) *Lincolnshire Windmills: a Contemporary Survey*, Lincoln: Lincolnshire County Council.

Donnachie, Ian (1971) *Industrial Archaeology of Galloway*, Newton Abbot: David & Charles.

—— (1981), 'Industrial archaeology in Australia', *IAR*, V, 2: 96–113.

Douglas, G. J., Hume, J. R., Moir, L. and Oglethorpe, M. K. (1985) *A Survey of Scottish Brickmarks*, Glasgow: the Scottish Industrial Archaeology Survey.

Drummond, Diane K. (1994) *Crewe: Railway Town, Company and People 1840–1914*, Aldershot: Scolar Press.

Earl, Bryan (1991) 'Tin preparation and smelting', in Day, Joan and Tylecote, R. F. (eds) *The Industrial Revolution in Metals*, London: the Institute of Metals: 71–5.

Ellis, Monica (1978) *Water and Wind Mills in Hampshire and the Isle of Wight*, Southampton: Southampton University Industrial Archaeology Group.

English Heritage (1995a) *Manchester Mills: Understanding Listing*, London: English Heritage.

—— (1995b) *Industrial Archaeology: a Policy Statement*, London: English Heritage.

Falconer, Keith (1980) *Guide to England's Industrial Heritage*, London: Batsford.

Farey, John (1811–13) *General View of Agriculture and Minerals of Derbyshire*, two volumes, London.

Ferris, I. M. (1989) 'The archaeological investigation of standing buildings', *Vernacular Architecture*, 20: 12–17.

Fitzgerald, R. S. (1980) *Liverpool Road Station, Manchester*, Manchester: Manchester University Press.

—— (1988) 'Albion Mill, Manchester', *IAR*, X, 2: 204–30.

Fletcher, Mark (1994) 'Excavation and survey at Higher Woodhill Mill, Bury', *IAR*, XVII, 1: 44–63.

Ford, P. and Ford, G. (1972) *A Guide to Parliamentary Papers*, 3rd edn, Shannon: Irish University Press.

Foster, Janet and Sheppard, Julia (1995) *A Guide to Archive Sources in the United Kingdom*, 3rd edn, Basingstoke: Macmillan.

Fowkes, D. (ed.) (1992) *Pre-1650 manuscript maps held by county record offices in England and Wales*, Microform Academic Publishers (eight fiches).

Gale, W. K. V. (1969) *Iron and Steel*, London: Longman.

Garrad, L. S. with Bawden, T. A., Qualtrough, J. K. and Scatchard, W. J. (1972) *The Industrial Archaeology of the Isle of Man*, Newton Abbot: David & Charles.

Gibson, Jeremy and Peskett, Pamela (1988) *Record Offices: How to Find Them*, 4th edn, Birmingham: Federation of Family History Societies.

Giles, C. (1993) 'Housing the loom, 1790–1850: a study of industrial building and mechanisation in a transitional period', *IAR*, XVI, 1: 27–37.

Giles, C. and Goodall, I. (1992) *Yorkshire Textile Mills 1770–1930*, London: HMSO: 132–3.

Glassie, H. (1975) *Folk Housing in Middle Virginia: A Structural Analysis of Historical Artifacts*, Knoxville: University of Tennessee Press.

Gordon, Robert B. and Malone, Patrick M. (1994) *The Texture of Industry: An Archaeological View of the Industrialization of North America*, Oxford and New York: Oxford University Press.

Gould, Shane and Ayris, Ian (1995) *Colliery Landscapes: An Aerial Survey of the Deep-mined Coal Industry in England*, London: English Heritage.

Grant, E. G. (1987) 'Industry: landscape and location', in Wagstaff, J. M. (ed.) *Landscape and Culture*, Oxford: Blackwell: 96–117.

Grant, Cathy and Ballantyne, James (1985) (eds) *Discovery and Invention: A Review of Films and Videos on the History of Science and Technology*, London: British Universities Film and Video Council.

Greater Manchester Council and West Yorkshire County Council (1984) *Mills in the 80s: a Study of the Re-use of Old Industrial Buildings in Greater Manchester and West Yorkshire*, report jointly commissioned and published.

Greatrex, Nan (1986–7) 'The Robinson enterprises in Papplewick, Nottinghamshire, parts one and two', *IAR*, IX, 1 and 2: 37–56, 119–39.

Greenwood, John (1985) *The Industrial Archaeology and Industrial History of Northern England: A Bibliography*, Cranfield: Kewdale Press.

—— (1987) *The Industrial Archaeology and Industrial History of the English Midlands: A Bibliography*, Cranfield: Kewdale Press.

—— (1990) *The Industrial Archaeology and Industrial History of South-Eastern England: A Bibliography*, Cranfield: Kewdale Press.

Greeves, T. A. P. (1981) 'The archaeological potential of the Devon tin industry', in *Medieval Industry*, CBA Research Report 40, London: CBA.

—— (1994) 'Summary report on the third season of excavation at Upper Merrivale tin blowing and stamping mill', *The Newsletter of the Dartmoor Tinworking Research Group*, 6 (January): 8–11.

Greeves, T. A. P. and Newman, P. (1994) 'Tin-working and land use in the Walkham Valley: a preliminary analysis', *Devon Archaeological Society Proceedings*, 52: 199–219.

Grenter, Stephen (1992) 'Bersham Ironworks excavations: interim report', *IAR*, XIV, 2: 177–92.

Griffin, A. R. (1971) *Coalmining*, London: Longman.

Hadfield, C. (1955–6) 'Sources for the history of British canals', *Journal of Transport History*, 2: 80–9.

Hair, T. H. (1844) *Views of the Collieries in the Counties of Northumberland and Durham*, reprinted Newcastle upon Tyne: Davis Books, 1987.

Hamond, Fred (1991) *Industrial Heritage: Antrim Coast and Glens*, Belfast: HMSO.

Harley, J. B. (1972) *Maps for the Local Historian*, London: the Standing Conference on Local History.

Harley, J. B. and Phillips, C. W. (1964) *The Historian's Guide to Ordnance Survey Maps*, London: the Standing Conference on Local History.

Harris, E. C. (1979) *Principles of Archaeological Stratigraphy*, 2nd edition, London and San Diego: Academic Press.

Harris, Helen (1968) *Industrial Archaeology of Dartmoor*, Newton Abbot: David & Charles.

—— (1971) *Industrial Archaeology of the Peak District*, Newton Abbot: David & Charles.

Harris, J. R. (1985) 'Industrial espionage in the eighteenth century', *IAR*, VII, 2: 127–38.

Harris, T. R. (1974) *Dolcoath: Queen of Cornish Mines*, Camborne: the Trevithick Society.

Hay, Geoffrey D. and Stell, Geoffrey P. (1986) *Monuments of Industry: an Illustrated Historical Record*, London: HMSO.

Hayman, Richard (1986) 'Aberdulais Falls', *IAR*, VIII, 2: 147–65.

—— (1987) 'Artists' impressions of Aberdulais Mill', *IAR*, IX, 2: 155–66.

—— (1997) 'The archaeologist as witness: Matthew Harvey's Glebeland Works, Walsall', *IAR*, XIX: 61–74.

Henderson, W. O. (1954) *Britain and Industrial Europe 1750–1870: Studies in British Influence*, Leicester: Leicester University Press.

Herring, P. (ed.) (1988–90) *Kit Hill Archaeological Survey*, Vols 1 and 2, Truro: Cornwall County Council.

Hewison, Robert (1987) *The Heritage Industry*, London: Methuen.

Higgins, David (1989) 'Perceiving the pipe', *AIA Bulletin* 16/4, Telford: Association for Industrial Archaeology: 1–2.

Hills, Richard L. (1967) *Machines, Mills and Uncountable Costly Necessities*, Norwich: Goose.

—— (1989) *Power from Steam: a History of the Stationary Steam Engine*, Cambridge: Cambridge University Press.

—— (1994) *Power from Wind: A History of Windmill Technology*, Cambridge: Cambridge University Press.

Hodder, Ian (1982) *Symbols in Action*, Cambridge: Cambridge University Press.

—— (1986) *Reading the Past, Current Approaches to Interpretation in Archaeology*, Cambridge: Cambridge University Press.

Holt, Richard (1988) *The Mills of Medieval England*, Oxford: Blackwell.

Hudson, Kenneth (1972) *Building Materials*, London: Longman.

—— (1983) *The Archaeology of the Consumer Society: the Second Industrial Revolution in Britain*, London: Heinemann.

—— (1984) *Industrial History from the Air*, Cambridge: Cambridge University Press.

Hughes, S. (1979) 'The Swansea Canal: navigation and power supplier', *IAR*, IV, 1: 51–69.

—— (1988) *The Archaeology of the Montgomeryshire Canal*, revised edn, Aberystwyth: RCAHMW.

—— (1990) *The Brecon Forest Tramroads: the Archaeology of an Early Railway System*, Aberystwyth: RCAHMW.

Hughes, Stephen, Malaws, Brian, Parry, Medwyn and Wakelin, Peter (n.d.) *Collieries of Wales: Engineering and Architecture*, Aberystwyth: RCAHMW.

Hume, John (1976–7) *The Industrial Archaeology of Scotland*, Vol. 1, *The Lowlands and Borders*, Vol. 2, *The Highlands and Islands*, London: Batsford.

Hutton, Barbara (1986) *Recording Standing Buildings*, Sheffield: University of Sheffield.

*Industrial Archaeology Review* (1979) special issue, III, 2.

James, N. W. (1992) 'The Historical Manuscripts Commission and the history of British business and industry', *IAR*, XIV, 2: 193–6.

Johnson, L. C. (1953–4) 'Historical records of the British Transport Commission', *Journal of Transport History*, 1: 82–96.

Johnson, M. (1993) *Housing Culture*, London: UCL Press.

—— (1996) *The Archaeology of Capitalism*, Oxford: Blackwell.

Jones, E. (1985) *Industrial Architecture in Britain, 1750–1939*, London: Batsford.

Jones, O.T. (1922) *Special Reports on the Mineral Resources of Great Britain*, Vol. XX, *Lead and Zinc. The Mining District of North Cardiganshire and Montgomeryshire*, London; reprinted Sheffield: Mining Facsimiles, 1986.

Jones, William (1996) *Dictionary of Industrial Archaeology*, Stroud: Sutton Publishing.

Jones, Gwen and Bell, John (1992) *Oasthouses in Sussex and Kent*, Chichester: Phillimore.

Kealey, Edward J. (1987) *Harvesting the Air: Windmill Pioneers in Twelfth-Century England*, Woodbridge: Boydell Press.

Klingender, Francis D. (1947) *Art and the Industrial Revolution*, London: Paladin; revised edn 1968.

Leach, Peter (1988) *The Surveying of Archaeological Sites*, London: Institute of Archaeology.

Lewis, M. J. T. (1970) *Early Wooden Railways*, London: Routledge & Kegan Paul.

Lewis, M. J. T. and Denton, J. H. (1974) *Rhosydd Slate Quarry*, Cottage Press; reprinted Mold: Adit Publications, 1994.

Lipe, William D. (1984) 'Value and meaning in cultural resources', in Cleere, Henry (ed.) *Approaches to the Archaeological Heritage*, Cambridge: Cambridge University Press: 1–11.

Lowe, Jeremy (1977) *Welsh Industrial Workers' Housing, 1775–1875*, Cardiff: National Museum of Wales.

McCutcheon, W. A. (1980) *The Industrial Archaeology of Northern Ireland*, Belfast: HMSO.

McNeil, Ian (1972) *Hydraulic Power*, London: Longman.

Major, J. Kenneth (1975) *Fieldwork in Industrial Archaeology*, London: Batsford.

—— (1978) *Animal-powered Engines*, London: Batsford.

Malaws, Brian (1997) 'Process recording on industrial sites', *IAR*, XIX: 75–98.

Markus, Thomas A. (1993) *Buildings and Power*, London: Routledge.

Marshall, Gary (1995) 'Redressing the balance – an archaeological assessment of North Yorkshire's coastal alum industry', *IAR*, XVIII, 1: 39–62.

Marshall, Gary, Palmer, Marilyn and Neaverson, Peter (1992) 'The history and archaeology of the Calke Abbey limeyards', *IAR*, XIV, 2: 145–76.

Marshall, J. D. and Davies-Shiel, Michael (1969, 1977) *The Industrial Archaeology of the Lake Counties*, Beckermet: Michael Moon.

Menuge, Adam (1993) 'The cotton mills of the Derbyshire Derwent and its tributaries', *IAR*, XVI, 1: 38–61.

Miles, Mary (1989) 'Halse Maltings, Somerset', *IAR*, XI, 2: 136–40.

Miller, M. G. and Fletcher, S. (1984) *The Melton Mowbray Navigation*, Oakham: Railway & Canal Historical Society.

Moir, Esther (1964) *The Discovery of Britain*, London: Routledge & Kegan Paul.

Morgan, Bryan (1971) *Civil Engineering: Railways*, London: Longman.

Morrison, T. A. (1980) *Cornwall's Central Mines: The Northern District, 1810–1895*, Penzance: Alison Hodge.

—— (1983) *Cornwall's Central Mines: The Southern District, 1810–1895*, Penzance: Alison Hodge.

Munby, L. M. (n.d.) *Short Guides to Records*, by topic, London: Historical Association.

Musson, Chris (n.d. [1996]) *Wales from the Air: Patterns of Past and Present*, Aberystwyth: RCAHMW.

Muter, W. Grant (1979) *The Buildings of an Industrial Community: Coalbrookdale and Ironbridge*, London and Chichester: Phillimore.

Newell, Dianne and Greenhill, Ralph (1989) *Survivals: Aspects of Industrial Archaeology in Ontario*, Ontario: Boston Mills Press.

Newman, Philip (1993) 'Week Ford tin mills, Dartmoor', *Devon Archaeological Society Proceedings*, 51: 185–97.

Nijhof, Peter (1991) 'Industrial archaeology in the Netherlands', *IAR*, XIII, 2: 103–13.

Nixon, Frank (1969) *Industrial Archaeology of Derbyshire*, Newton Abbot: David and Charles.

Noall, Cyril (1970) *Levant: the Mine beneath the Sea*, Truro: D. Bradford Barton.

—— (1972) *Botallack*, Truro: D. Bradford Barton.

—— (1973) *The St. Just Mining District*, Truro: D. Bradford Barton.

Norton, Jane E. (1984) *Guide to the National and Provincial Directories of England and Wales*, London: Royal Historical Society.

Oliver, Richard (ed.) (1991) *Ordnance Survey of Great Britain. England and Wales. Indexes to the 1/2500 and 6-inch scale maps*, Newtown: David Archer, reprint of work published London *circa* 1905.

—— (1993) *Ordnance Survey Maps: a Concise Guide for Historians*, London: the Charles Close Society.

Ordish, H. G. (1967) *Cornish Engine Houses, A Pictorial Survey*, Truro: D. Bradford Barton.

—— (1968) *Cornish Engine Houses: A Second Pictorial Survey*, Truro: D. Bradford Barton.

Palmer, Marilyn (1983) *The Richest in All Wales*, British Mining 22, Sheffield: Northern Mine Research Society.

—— (1991) 'Industrial archaeology: working for the future', *IAR*, XIV, 1: 17–32.

—— (1994a) 'Industrial archaeology: continuity and change', *IAR*, XVI, 2: 135–56.

—— (1994b) 'Mining landscapes and the problems of contaminated land', in Swain, Hedley (ed.) *Rescuing the Historic Environment*, Hertford: Rescue: 45–50.

Palmer, Marilyn and Neaverson, Peter (1987) *The Basset Mines: their History and Industrial Archaeology*, British Mining 32, Sheffield: Northern Mine Research Society.

—— (1989) 'The comparative archaeology of tin and lead dressing in Britain during the nineteenth century', in *Bulletin of the Peak District Mines Historical Society*, 10, 6: 316–53.

—— (1990) 'The steam engines at Glyn Pits Colliery, Pontypool: an archaeological investigation', *IAR*, XIII, 1: 7–34.

—— (1990–1) 'Carlton Hayes Model Farm', *Leicestershire Industrial History Society Bulletin*, 13: 30–48.

—— (1992) *Industrial Landscapes of the East Midlands*, Chichester: Phillimore.

—— (1994) *Industry in the Landscape, 1700–1900*, London: Routledge.

Pitt, W. (1809) *A General View of Agriculture in the County of Leicester*, London.

Porter, Stephen (1990) *Exploring Urban History: Sources for Local Historians*, London: Batsford.

PPG 15 (1994) *Planning Policy Guidance 15: Planning and the Historic Environment*, London: DOE/DNH.

Prest, John (1960) *The Industrial Revolution in Coventry*, Oxford: Oxford University Press: 96–135.

Pye, Andrew and Weddell, Peter (1992) 'A survey of the Gawton Mine arsenic works, Tavistock Hamlets, West Devon', *IAR*, XV, 1: 62–95.

Rahtz, Philip (1981) 'Medieval milling', in Crossley, David (ed.) *Medieval Industry*, CBA Research Report 40, London: CBA: 1–15.

Raistrick, Arthur (1970) *West Riding of Yorkshire*, London: Paladin.

—— (1972) *Industrial Archaeology: an Historical Survey*, London: Hodder & Stoughton.

RCHME (1985) *Industry and the Camera*, London: HMSO.

—— (1991) *Report on the Historic Buildings in the Area of the Black Country Development Corporation*, London: RCHME.

—— (1994a) *The Royal Gunpowder Factory, Waltham Abbey, Essex*, London: RCHME.

—— (1994b) *Poplar, Blackwall and the Isle of Dogs*, Volumes XLIII and XLIV of the *Survey of London*, London: Athlone Press/RCHME.

—— (1996) *Recording Historic Buildings: a Descriptive Specification*, 3rd edn, Swindon: RCHME.

RCHME and English Heritage (1995) *Thesaurus of Monument Types: A Standard for Use in Archaeological and Architectural Recording*, Swindon: RCHME.

Reedman, K. And Sissons, M. (1985) 'Unstone coke ovens', *IAR*, VIII, 1: 78–85.

Rees, D. Morgan (1975) *The Industrial Archaeology of Wales*, Newton Abbot: David & Charles.

Renfrew, K. and Bahn, P. (1991) *Archaeology: Theories, Methods and Practice*, London: Thames & Hudson.

Riden, P. (1987) *Record Sources for Local History*, London: Batsford.

—— (1993) *A Gazetteer of Charcoal-fired Blast Furnaces in Great Britain in Use since 1660*, Cardiff: Merton Priory Press.

Ritchie-Noakes, Nancy (1984) *Liverpool's Historic Waterfront: The World's First Mercantile Dock System*, London: HMSO.

Rix, Michael (1955) 'Industrial archaeology', *The Amateur Historian*, 2, 8: 225–9.

Ross, Michael (1991) *Planning and the Heritage: Policy and Procedures*, London: Spon.

Rowlands, Marie B. (1987) *The West Midlands from AD 1000*, London: Longman.

Rowley, Gwyn (1984) *British Fire Insurance Plans*, Old Hatfield: Chas E. Goad.

Royal Commission on Historical Manuscripts (1990) *Records of British Business and Industry, 1760–1914: Textiles and Leather*, London: HMSO.

—— (1992) *Record Repositories in Great Britain: a Geographical Directory*, 9th edn, London: HMSO.

—— (1994) *Records of British Business and Industry, 1760–1914: Metal Processing and Engineering*, London: HMSO.

Sande, Theodore Anton (1976) *Industrial Archeology: A New Look at the American Heritage*, Brattleboro: the Stephen Greene Press.

Shanks, Michael and Tilley, Christopher (1987) *Social Theory and Archaeology*, Cambridge: Cambridge University Press.

Sharpe, Adam (1995) 'Developments under derelict land grants: the potential, the problems', in Palmer, Marilyn and Neaverson, Peter (eds) *Managing the Industrial Heritage*, Leicester: SAS: 133–6.

Sharpe, Adam *et al.* (1991) *Engine House Assessment: The Mineral Tramways Project*, Truro: Cornwall County Council.

Sherlock, Robert (1976) *Industrial Archaeology of Staffordshire*, Newton Abbot: David & Charles.

Simmons, J. (1953–4), 'Railway history in English local records', *Journal of Transport History*, 1: 155–69.

—— (1957–8) 'Scottish records of the British Transport Commission', *Journal of Transport History*, 3: 158–67.

—— (1961) *The Railways of Britain*, London: Macmillan.

Smith, D. (1965) *Industrial Archaeology of the East Midlands*, Dawlish: David & Charles.

—— (1971) *Industrial Location: An Economic Geographical Analysis*, 2nd edn, New York: John Wiley.

Smith, David (1990) 'The representation of industry on large-scale county maps of England and Wales 1700–c.1840', *IAR*, XII, 3: 153–77.

Snell, J. B. (1971) *Mechanical Engineering: Railways*, London: Longman.

Stanier, P. H. (1993) 'Dorset limekilns: a first survey', *Proceedings of the Dorset Natural History and Archaeological Society*, 115: 33–49.

Stocker, David (1995) 'Industrial archaeology and the Monuments Protection Programme in England', in Palmer, Marilyn and Neaverson, Peter (eds) *Managing the Industrial Heritage*, Leicester: SAS: 105–10.

Stratton, M. and Trinder, B. (1988) 'Stanley Mill, Gloucestershire', *P-MA*, 22: 143–80.

—— (1997) *Industrial England*, London: Batsford/English Heritage.

Swallow, Peter, Watt, David and Ashton, Robert (1993) *Measuring and Recording of Historic Buildings*, London: Donhead Publishing.

Tangye, Michael (1984) *Tehidy and the Bassets*, Redruth: Truran.

Tann, Jennifer (1967) *Gloucestershire Woollen Mills*, Newton Abbot: David & Charles.

Thackray, David (1995) 'The industrial archaeology of agriculture, rural life collections and the National Trust', *IAR*, XVIII, 1: 117–31.

Thompson, K. M. (ed.) (1994) *Short Guides to Records*, by topic, London: Historical Association.

Thompson, W. J. (n.d.) *Industrial Archaeology of North Staffordshire*, Buxton: Moorland Publishing.

Thornes, R. C. N. (1981) *West Yorkshire: 'A Noble Scene of Industry'*, no place: West Yorkshire Metropolitan County Council: 9–14, 35, 38.

—— (1994) *Images of Coal*, London: RCHME.

Timmins, J. G. (1977) *Handloom Weavers' Cottages in Central Lancashire*, Lancaster: Centre for North-West Regional Studies.

Todd, A. C. and Laws, Peter (1972) *Industrial Archaeology of Cornwall*, Newton Abbot: David & Charles.

Trinder, Barrie (1982) *The Making of the Industrial Landscape*, London: Dent.

—— (ed.) (1992) *The Blackwell Encyclopaedia of Industrial Archaeology*, Oxford: Blackwell.

—— (1996) *The Industrial Archaeology of Shropshire*, Chichester: Phillimore.

Trinder, Barrie and Cox, Jeff (1980) *Yeomen and Colliers in Telford*, Chichester: Phillimore.

Trounson, John H. (1968) *Historic Cornish Mining Scenes at Surface*, Truro: D. Bradford Barton.

—— (1980–1) *Mining in Cornwall, 1850–1960*, Volumes One and Two, Ashbourne: Moorland Publishing.

Trueman, Michael R. G. (1992) 'The Langcliffe quarry and limeworks', *IAR*, XIV, 2: 126–44.

Tucker, Gordon (1991) *Some Watermills of South-West Shropshire*, Birmingham: Midland Wind and Water Mill Group.

Unwin, Robert (1986) 'An industrial dimension to land tax studies: the Barnsley coalfield 1690–1830' in Turner, Michael and Mills, Dennis (eds) *Land and Property: the English Land Tax 1692–1832*, Gloucester: Alan Sutton: 136–57.

Viaene, P. (1986) *Industriële Archeologie in België*, Gent: Stichting Mens en Kultur.

Wailes, Rex (1954) *The English Windmill*, London: Routledge & Kegan Paul.

Wales Tourist Board (1978) *A Glimpse of the Past*, Cardiff: WTB.

Ward, J. T. and Wilson, R. G. (eds) (1971) *Land and Industry*, Newton Abbot: David & Charles.

Watson, Mark (1990) *Jute and Flax Mills in Dundee*, Tayport: Hutton Press.

Watt, David and Swallow, Peter (1996) *Surveying Historic Buildings*, Shaftesbury: Donhead Publishing.

Weatherill, L. (1988) *Consumer Behaviour and Material Culture in Britain*, London; 2nd edn, London: Routledge, 1996.

Welding, J. D. (ed.) (1984) *Leicestershire in 1777*, Leicester: Leicestershire Libraries and Information Service.

West, J. (1982) *Town Records*, Chichester: Phillimore.

White, Robert (1991) 'Arresting decay: archaeology in the Yorkshire Dales', in *Archaeology in the National Parks*, Leyburn: Yorkshire Dales National Park: 55–64.

Williams, Mike (1993) 'Havelock Mill, Manchester: a case-study in the emergency recording of a large urban mill complex', *IAR*, XVI, 1: 100–10.

Williams, Mike with Farnie, D. A. (1992) *Cotton Mills of Greater Manchester*, Preston: Carnegie Publishing.

Willies, Lynn (1989) 'The industrial landscape of Rio Tinto, Huelva, Spain', *IAR*, XII, 1: 67–76.

—— (1991) 'Lead: ore preparation and smelting', in Day, Joan and Tylecote, R. F. (eds) *The Industrial Revolution in Metals*, London: the Institute of Metals: 102–19.

Willies, Lynn and Cranstone, David (eds) (1992) *Boles and Smeltmills*, Matlock Bath: Historical Metallurgy Society.

Wilson, Anne (1988) 'The excavation of Clydach Ironworks', *IAR*, XI, 1: 16–36.

Wood, J. (ed.) (1994) *Buildings Archaeology: Applications in Practice*, Oxford: Oxbow Monograph 43.

Wrathmell, S. (1990) 'Why the archaeologist cannot be a camera', *Scottish Archaeological Review*, 7: 37–40.

York, Robert and Warburton, Stuart (1991) 'Digging deep in mining history', *AIA Bulletin*, 18, 4: 1–2.

Young, Arthur (1771) *A Six Months Tour through the North of England*, Vol. I, reprinted New York: Augustus Kelley, 1967: 49.

# Index